Concealments in Hemingway's Works

Concealments
in Hemingway's Works

GERRY BRENNER

Ohio State University Press : Columbus

Quotations from the following books by Ernest Hemingway are used by permission of Charles Scribner's Sons, 597 Fifth Avenue, New York, New York 10017; Jonathan Cape Ltd., 30 Bedford Square, London WC1, England; and the Executors of the Ernest Hemingway Estate:

The Sun Also Rises. Copyright 1926, Charles Scribner's Son;
  copyright renewed 1954 Ernest Hemingway.
  (Published in England as *Fiesta*.)

A Farewell to Arms. Copyright 1929 Charles Scribner's Sons;
  copyright renewed 1957 Ernest Hemingway.

Death in the Afternoon. Copyright 1932 Charles Scribner's Sons;
  copyright renewed 1960 Ernest Hemingway.

Green Hills of Africa. Copyright 1935, Charles Scribner's Sons;
  copyright renewed 1963 Mary Hemingway.

To Have and Have Not. Copyright 1937 Ernest Hemingway;
  copyright renewed 1965 Mary Hemingway.

The Short Stories of Ernest Hemingway. Copyright 1938 Ernest Hemingway;
  copyright renewed 1966 Mary Hemingway.
  (The stories quoted were published in England in *The First Forty-nine Stories*.)

For Whom the Bell Tolls. Copyright 1940 Ernest Hemingway;
  copyright renewed 1968 Mary Hemingway.

Across the River and into the Trees. Copyright 1950 Ernest Hemingway;
  copyright renewed 1978 Mary Hemingway.

The Old Man and the Sea. Copyright 1952 Ernest Hemingway;
  copyright renewed 1980 Mary Hemingway.

A Moveable Feast. Copyright © 1964 Ernest Hemingway Ltd.

Quotations from the following books by Ernest Hemingway are used by permission of Charles Scribner's Sons, 597 Fifth Avenue, New York, New York 10017, and William Collins Sons and Company Ltd., 14 St. James's Place, London SW1A 1PS, England:

By-Line: Ernest Hemingway. Copyright © 1967 Mary Hemingway.

Islands in the Stream. Copyright © 1970 Mary Hemingway.

Quotations from *Ernest Hemingway, Selected Letters: 1917–1961* are used by permission of Charles Scribner's Sons, 597 Fifth Avenue, New York, New York 10017, and Granada Publishing Ltd., Frogmore, St. Albans, Hertfordshire AL2 2NF, England. Copyright© 1981 The Ernest Hemingway Foundation, Inc., Copyright© 1981 Carlos Baker.

Quotations from Parts 1, 2, and 3 of "The Dangerous Summer," by Ernest Hemingway, published in the September 5, 12, and 19, 1960, issues of *Life*, are used by special permission of Mary Hemingway.

(*Continued on page vi*)

for Terry and our three sons

Pat, Kyle, and John

(*Continued from page iv*)

The chapter entitled "A 'Vulgar' Ethic: *The Sun Also Rises*" in Part 1, "The Thesis Phase," has been revised from "Hemingway's 'Vulgar' Ethic: Revaluating *The Sun Also Rises*," originally published in the *Arizona Quarterly*, 33 (Summer, 1977). Used by permission of the publisher.

The chapter entitled "A Classical Epic: *For Whom the Bell Tolls*" in Part 3, "The Aristotelean Phase," has been revised from "Epic Machinery in Hemingway's *For Whom the Bell Tolls*," originally published in *Modern Fiction Studies*, 16 (Winter, 1970–71), © 1971 by Purdue Research Foundation, West Lafayette, Indiana 47907, U.S.A. Used by permission of the publisher.

The chapter entitled "A Dantesque 'Imitation': *Across the River and into the Trees*" in Part 4, "The Imitative Phase," has been revised from "An 'Imitation' of Dante's *Divine Comedy*: Hemingway's *Across the River and into the Trees*," originally published in the 1976 volume of the *Fitzgerald/Hemingway Annual*. Used by permission of the publisher.

The chapter entitled "A Classical Tragedy: *To Have and Have Not*" in Part 3, "The Aristotelean Phase," has been revised from "*To Have and Have Not* as Classical Tragedy: Reconsidering Hemingway's Neglected Novel," originally published in *Hemingway: In Our Time*, edited by Richard Astro and Jackson J. Benson (Corvallis, Oregon: Oregon State University Press, 1974). Used by permission of the publisher.

Library of Congress Cataloguing in Publication Data:

Brenner, Gerry, 1937—
Concealments in Hemingway's works.

Bibliography: p.
Includes index
1. Hemingway, Ernest, 1899–1961—Criticism and interpretation. I. Title.
PS3515.E37Z5826   1983   813'.52   83–6283
ISBN 0–8142–0338–8

Contents

Acknowledgments

Grateful acknowledgment for permission to quote from his works is made to Ernest Hemingway's publishers.

I am also grateful for permission to reprint, in revised form, studies of mine that have appeared in earlier forms: "Hemingway's 'Vulgar' Ethic: Revaluating *The Sun Also Rises*," *Arizona Quarterly*, Summer 1977; "*To Have and Have Not* as Classical Tragedy: Reconsidering Hemingway's Neglected Novel," Richard Astro and Jackson J. Benson, eds., *Hemingway: In Our Time* (Oregon State University Press, 1974); "An 'Imitation' of Dante's *Divine Comedy:* Hemingway's *Across the River and into the Trees*," *Fitzgerald/Hemingway Annual 1976*; "Epic Machinery in Hemingway's *For Whom the Bell Tolls*," *Modern Fiction Studies*, Winter 1970–71.

For several Summer Research grants that freed me from teaching and enabled me to write portions of this work, I gratefully thank the University of Montana Foundation and those colleagues who saw fit to award me those grants.

For many classes with many good Hemingway students here at the University of Montana, I am also thankful. The vitality and inquisitiveness and skepticism and intelligence they brought to the classroom and to my version of Hemingway made for some memorable sessions and stimulated my thinking again and again.

For challenging me with, and encouraging my study of, Freud, and for carefully reading a large portion of an earlier draft, I owe a special debt to my colleague Doug Purl.

For her scrupulous copy-editing and his cheerful assistance in the various stages of publishing this book, I am grateful to the Ohio State University Press's Carol S. Sykes, book editor, and Weldon A. Kefauver, director.

For their help typing various versions of the manuscript, I thank Lucille Smith, Jan Schultz, Pat Meeker, and Ilona Hruska.

For her patience, support, and excellent editing, no acknowledgment can adequately express my gratitude to my wife, Terry.

Author's Note

I cite page references to quotations from Hemingway's works in the body of my text. Where the source of a quotation is clear, I cite only page references; where the source is unclear, I adopt the short titles below. In both cases all citations are from the following editions published by Charles Scribner's Sons, of New York:

Sun Rises	*The Sun Also Rises*, 1926 and 1954, Student's Edition
Farewell	*A Farewell to Arms*, 1929 and 1957, Scribner Library
Afternoon	*Death in the Afternoon*, 1932 and 1960, Scribner Library
Green Hills	*Green Hills of Africa*, 1935, Scribner Library
Have Not	*To Have and Have Not*, 1937 and 1965, Scribner Library
Bell Tolls	*For Whom the Bell Tolls*, 1940, Scribner Library
Across the River	*Across the River and into the Trees*, 1950
Old Man	*The Old Man and the Sea*, 1952, Scribner Library
Stories	*The Short Stories of Ernest Hemingway*, 1953, Modern Standard Authors
Feast	*A Moveable Feast*, 1964, Scribner Library
By-Line	*By-Line: Ernest Hemingway: Selected*

*Articles and Dispatches of Four
Decades*, ed. William White, 1967

Islands   *Islands in the Stream*, 1970
Letters   *Ernest Hemingway: Selected Letters,
                1917–1961*, ed. Carlos Baker, 1981

Concealments in Hemingway's Works

Introduction: Three Theses

There are two sorts of guide books; those that are read before [you see a bullfight] and those that are to be read after[,] and the ones that are to be read after the fact are bound to be incomprehensible to a certain extent before. . . . So from now on it is inferred that you have been to the bullfight. [*Afternoon*, 63]

There is no dispute over Hemingway's early work. It was experimental and imitative. His early fiction imitated and parodied Ring Lardner, Sherwood Anderson, and Gertrude Stein; his poetry, Stephen Crane, Ezra Pound, and the imagists.[1] But self-discipline, stints as journalist and correspondent, his own experimental urgings, and the creative ambiance of postwar Paris—all helped Hemingway cultivate his own prose style. Once realized, that style presumably changed little, let Hemingway coast through the rest of his career without further imitations or experiments: "He learned early in life," declared Faulkner, "a method by which he could do his work, he has never varied from that method, it suited him well, he handled it well."[2] My first thesis not only disputes Faulkner's widespread conclusion—that Hemingway is an example of "arrested" literary development; it also tilts with its relatives, conclusions that monocularly stare at Hemingway's one theme, his one technique, his one style, his one kind of hero, and the like.[3] I argue that until the fifties Hemingway's books were continuously experimental. Having exorcised his novice phase with *The Torrents of Spring*, he proceeded to write books that I group in four phases of experimentation—thesis, esthetic, Aristotelean, and imitative—before he wrote the more conventional books of what I call his antithetical phase. A sentence or two about the works I put into each phase should give some notion of the content in specific chapters, should let a reader decide quickly whether my revisionary readings see Hemingway terrain afresh.

Into Hemingway's thesis phase I put *A Farewell to Arms* and *The Sun Also Rises*. Didactic novels with untrustworthy narrators, they subtly express Hemingway's vision of the world he finds himself inhabiting. To demonstrate in *Farewell* his conviction that existence is thoroughly irrational, he creates a disoriented narrator whose therapeutic or testamentary story recounts the bizzare events that have led to the recent death of the marginally neurotic woman he loves. *Sun* tells how to live in that irrational world. Marry discriminating hedonism, it says, to vivifying traditions. The novel says this, but not its narrator, who fails to see that his most significant immoral act, pimping, contributes to achieving—if only symbolically—that ethical ideal.

Too limited and diffident to risk Faulknerian flights, Hemingway was nevertheless too good an artist to replay either thesis with grace notes, too ambitious to rest upon the fame from two novels and a handful of superb stories, and too morally defensive to put up with either highbrow snootiness or convention-bound repugnance at his taste in subject matter. So he spent the next two decades camouflaging more highly experimental and derivative works. A pair of books on bullfighting and big-game hunting form his esthetic phase. In it he explores the relationship between beauty and that taboo topic, death. With perhaps a silent nod to Walton's *Compleat Angler*, Hemingway writes *Death in the Afternoon*, using aspects of the bullfight both to challenge "civilized" attitudes toward death and to endorse an integrated art whose esthetic of act, motion, and energy would repudiate the then-regnant, Aquinian esthetic of image, stasis, and quietude. The second work of this phase, *Green Hills of Africa*, is poetic, not venatic. In this openly avowed experiment, Hemingway covertly likens the trophy hunter's pursuit of exotically horned antelope to the artist's desire to arrest images of fleeting beauty.

In his Aristotelean phase Hemingway turns to traditional esthetic ideas. He puts to use the single most influential work "in the entire history of aesthetics and literary criticism," Aristotle's *Poetics*.[4] How Hemingway came by his knowledge of *Poetics* is uncertain. But it is demonstrable that he followed closely Aristotle's dicussion of tragedy and the epic, surreptitiously fashioning *To Have and Have Not* upon the formula of classical tragedy, *For Whom the Bell Tolls* upon the formula of the epic. In the former, Harry Morgan's dying words enunciate a tragic "recognition"

(" 'No matter how a man alone ain't got no bloody fucking chance' " [225]) brought on by hubris (his belief that alone and one-armed he is a match for four Cuban revolutionaries) and by hamartia (his mistaken assumption that he had slain his assailant). Divided and intelligent, Harry's acts are steeped in, but purified of, the moral repugnance demanded of heroes whose authors pursue Melpomene, the Muse of Tragedy. *For Whom the Bell Tolls* not only has such epic features as extended similes, catalogues, elevated language, and statement of theme. It also has a hero who regards a bridge in Spain's Guadarrama mountains to "be the point on which the future of the human race can turn" (43). That thought suddenly swells Robert Jordan's heroic stature. He becomes rival of both Leonidas, defending the mountain pass at Thermopylae, and Horatio, defending the bridge over the Tiber. Waiting to halt Lt. Berrendo's cavalry at the pass as his life ebbs, he even evokes Roland's rearguard martyrdom and so lets us watch Hemingway this time pursuing Calliope, the Muse of the Epic. (I wonder if, during his Aristotelean phase, Hemingway glanced back with consternation or self-amusement at this admonition eight years earlier: "Remember this too: all bad writers are in love with the epic" [*Afternoon*, 54].)

Less discernible are Hemingway's concealments during his "imitative" phase. But *Across the River and into the Trees* is a rendition of Dante's *Divine Comedy*. Like the poem the novel incorporates actual people and events, arcane allusions, private diatribes, encyclopedism, a double point of view, and much ado about hell and the salvation of a sinful warrior-pilgrim, Cantwell. The novel's Dantean quality is also evident in Hemingway's use of another feature of the poem—its merging of mimetic fiction, history, and dream fantasy. *Across the River* might not have stood alone in this phase had Hemingway completed what I guess was his Shakespearean "imitation," *The Garden of Eden*. Only a few scholars have seen the lengthy unfinished manuscript. But their summaries make it sound very much like one of the bard's mature comedies, complete with "the transfer of sexual identities."[5]

In the fifties Hemingway abandoned the experiments and derivative efforts of the previous three decades. The public had failed to appreciate what he referred to as his "calculus," *Across the River*. His artistic experiments were leading him into a cul-de-sac. Age and injuries were taking their toll. He could no longer repress an array of guilts. And his own three sons were either leaving him, failing to pursue occupations that reflected well upon him, or rejecting him.[6] These number among other factors that brought on the antithetical phase. In it Hemingway creates father figures whose behavior invites radically conflicting interpretations. Each father's exemplary benevolence and compulsive responsibility solicit admiration and approval. But at the same time each man's behavior is so excessive that subversive implications emerge, ones that create problematic effects, counterintended meanings that suggest unconscious influences at work.[7] Specifically, the "fathers" unconsciously aggrandize themselves and display hostility toward others, especially their "sons." Their lack of self-awareness generates scornful pity, an attitude Hemingway had not, I believe, sought. Such antithetical interpretations show an imbalance of affective currents in the four works of the fifties. They are, in brief, deeply flawed. But rather than depreciate them because they fail to meet that high standard of achieved literary art—unified constructs—I value them. After all, their counterintended meanings enrich the significance assignable to them, as I will later argue.

At the beginning of his last decade, then, Hemingway created in *The Old Man and the Sea* an aged fisherman whose exaggerated moral purity almost hides his self-aggrandizing motives and hostility. Anxious that he is losing influence over a surrogate son, Santiago performs libidinal and destructive feats that demand filial and fraternal adoration. The likelihood that excessive benevolence toward a substitute son hides some degree of hostility—particularly toward a real-life counterpart—is borne out in *Islands in the Stream*. Exemplary father though Thomas Hudson appears, his three sons' deaths, abundant grief, and Conradian pursuit of his double—the anonymous German submarine captain in "At Sea" who has slain or abandoned three young sailors—reveal his melancholia and strong filicidal wishes. In *The Dangerous Summer* Hemingway's avuncular regard for Antonio Ordóñez, a truly heroic surrogate son, seems to discount such filicidal tendencies. But Hemingway's obsessive protectiveness and his fascination with the *mano a mano* expose the tendency, for this form of bullfighting competition acts out a fratricidal contest between "brothers." The lethal undercurrents in these works surface again in *A Moveable Feast*. Superficially the work is a set of harmless reminiscences of fellow artists during the twenties in Paris and also a hymn to Hadley, the first Mrs. Hemingway. But the book harshly chastises her and fellow artists' self-indulgence and irresponsibility. It does so to single out the only hard-working, family-obligated, responsible artist in post-war Paris—Hemingway—and to justify himself to his father.

This overview and its revisionary readings will distress a conservative reader. And I must seem incapable of sustaining a single critical methodology, the benchmark of respected books of literary criticism. But pursuing the proof of Hemingway's literary experimentation and the trajectory of his career calls for differing critical lenses—with varying degrees of perception and imperception, I grant. In partial defense of my practice I cite Plotinus: "To every vision must be brought an eye adaptable to what is to be seen." To me that says that a single critical lens will be insufficient to see clearly the complex art of any major writer who seems to have a vision. My shifts from New Critical to generic to psychoanalytic methodologies, then, will only appear reckless.

I also own that my shifting focus from Hemingway's literary experiments and "imitations" of the thirties and forties to the psychobiographical concerns of his antithetical works of the fifties may seem to reveal a schizophrenic critical perspective in me or a radical change in Hemingway. Neither thought, at least to my consciousness, is correct. In 1935 he wrote that "the only people for a serious writer to compete with are the dead that he knows are good" (*By-Line*, 219). Naturally a writer cannot compete with literary precursors unless he enters their "event," unless he adapts, adopts, or imitates the modes, genres, or formulas they used. Otherwise there are no grounds for judging the competition. And an author who competes with precursors "he knows are good" displaces a more authentic desire: to compete against his father, real or surrogate. He does not compete unless he believes he is able to hold his own against, if not triumph over, his rival.[8] But neither does he compete unless he respects his rival as a worthy competitor, as someone he honors by the competition. For example, in the parodic *The Torrents of Spring* Hemingway simply disaffiliates himself from the paternal influence of Sherwood Anderson. But in the epical *For Whom the Bell Tolls* he competes against those who have written great war epics, predecessors he hopes to triumph over and pay oblique respect to. Both novels also show that Hemingway's antithetical phase marks no radical departure from his preoccupation with father-son relationships in his earlier work. Instead, it repeats that preoccupation, concentrating more nakedly and revealingly on his personal problems and so enriching and extending the earlier phases by illuminating their more subdued patterns. I repeat, then: to follow the protean shapes of Hemingway's preoccupation requires a shifting critical perspective.

One value in seeing Hemingway as a writer deeply committed to literary experimentation: it shows him in the mainstream of modern literature, aligns him—though on a much lesser scale—with his fellow artist-scholar-experimenters Eliot, Joyce, and Pound. Another value: it lets us better evaluate the creations Hemingway brought forth, for we can compare them against the literary wombs that may also have nurtured some of those experimental offspring. Yet a third value: it should contribute to any ultimate assessment of Hemingway's creative imagination. Was it original or finally derivative? And a last value: it should augment respect for Hemingway the man. Who, after all, credits him with the self-restraint to have kept his own counsel about such experiments? Isn't it more likely that he would have defended himself against his critics, abused them for having missed what he had been about? Could Hemingway have been so shrewd?

Hemingway's sustained literary experimentation has been relatively neglected. This is due partly to the long-standing critical attention given either his heroes as thinly veiled self-impersonations or the ethical preeminence of his alleged codes. It is due even more to his esthetic. It went beyond Oscar Wilde's epigram: "To reveal art and conceal the artist is art's aim." The aim of Hemingway's art, my second thesis, was to conceal both the artist and the art. Long acknowledged though Hemingway's complexity has been, its scope is greater than past estimates.[9] Even his earliest fiction finds him affecting artlessness and concealing implications so that readers would respond naively, oblivious to the complexity of his understatement, ambiguity, and irony. I have yet to understand, for instance, why otherwise perceptive critics dismiss "My Old Man" as "a mediocre story."[10] It would deserve scorn if it only imitated Sherwood Anderson. The story, written in 1923, does that, but it also does more. It scolds Anderson: *"This,* Sherwood, is how you should have treated a story of self-pity."

When motherless young Joe Butler narrates the story of his early life with his father, a steeplechase jockey, he does so just after his father's death and after discovering the true nature of his father. Butler quit racing in Milan and took Joe to Paris, where he rode less and less often. Inside information on a fixed race brought him big money. With it he bought and trained his own horse, but in his second race he died in a fall while trying to jump a hedge and water obstacle. As young Joe leaves the track with one of his father's friends, he overhears two men:

> "Well, Butler got his all right."
> "I don't give a good goddam if he did, the crook. He had it coming to him on the stuff he's pulled."
> "I'll say he had." [*Stories*, 205]

Joe is stunned by what he hears and concludes that his father had been a crook. And his story, we see, has focused on episodes that incriminate Butler and justify that conclusion.

Hemingway's story caters to our sentiments, Anderson-fashion. For it reveals a young boy's disillusionment, learning the truth about his father. And Hemingway nicely gains sympathy and sometimes tears for young Joe, not only orphaned but now burdened with the stigma that his father was a crook.

Hemingway's concealing art, though, gains more than that. Tucked inside the sentimental story is an ironic one of Joe's blindness. Although his story proves to him that his father was a crook, it better proves that Butler was an honest man. He not only raced during the war "in the south of France without any purses, or betting or crowd or anything just to keep the breed up" (*Stories*, 202). He also tried, single-handedly, to clean up the crooked world of fixed, rigged racing. The reason he had to leave Milan? Because he failed to lose the race he had been told to lose. The reason he had trouble on the Paris circuit getting horses to ride? Because owners knew he would not agree to throw races. The reason he bet heavily on an already rigged race? Because he had to buy his own horse to continue racing. That would be his only way of braking the rigged machinery of the races. After all, just one independent jockey, riding his own mount, restores to the racetrack unpredictability, genuine gambling, the world of chance. So when Joe overhears the two men at the end of the story call his dad a crook, Hemingway lets those who are more discerning than Joe realize that the two men are the crooks. And when crooks call a man a crook, naturally they testify to his honesty.[11] In this concealed story Hemingway gains genuine, not sentimental, sympathy for Joe, a gently satirized boy who mistakenly believes that his father was a crook and so is blind to his father's virtues.

Hemingway's habit of creating subtle concealments, cultivated in those early Paris years with sheer technique, warrants, I believe, digging for equally subtle concealments of potential sources, formulas, and precursors in the books of the thirties and forties. It warrants, further, the view that Hemingway's craft, apparently a compound of technical skill and talent, also has a sizable ingredient of craftiness, of sleight of hand, of cunning and duplicity that conceal him and his art.

An image, a statement, and a theory—all expressed by Hemingway—support such a view of his artistic deviousness. The image is an iceberg, the dignity of whose movement "is due to only one-eighth of it being above water" (*Afternoon*, 192). The statement is from Hemingway's acceptance speech for the Nobel Prize: "Things may not be immediately discernible in what a man writes, and in this sometimes he is fortunate, but eventually they are quite clear and by these and the degree of alchemy that he possesses will he endure or be forgotten."[12] The theory is Hemingway's "theory of omission."

The image of the iceberg interests me because of its immodesty and its challenge. Outdoing his American predecessor, Samuel L. Clemens, whose pen name rightly implied that his writing was two fathoms deep, "mark twain," Hemingway's image boasts that his is seven times deeper than its surface height. And it implies that his writing intentionally hides from ready view those other seven-eighths. It also notifies serious readers to bring special equipment or vision if they hope to see many of those eighths below the water line.

Referring to things not "immediately discernible in what a man writes" and so extending the iceberg image, Hemingway's Nobel Prize statement invites two conclusions, both curious. If a writer's permanence rests partly upon readers eventually seeing previously undiscerned "things" in his writing, then it should follow either that such things were unintended and thus unconsciously found their way into an author's text or else that they were consciously included but so disguised as to make them immediately undiscernible. If the former, then an author's permanence depends partly upon elements over which he has no conscious control—obsessions, drives, and anxieties he is unaware of. He can claim no credit for the effects of these elements, for they operate independently of his conscious artistry. If the things are, on the other hand, consciously included but disguised to prevent immediate detection, then their belated detection should augment an author's stature much as we applaud an adroit magician. Or to use Hemingway's image of the alchemist, surely we will applaud the craft that beguiles us to regard as brass those things that are truly gold.

I find these conclusions curious, because Hemingway's career-long concern had presumably been with the real, the true, the actual, and the honest: "I was trying to write then and I found the greatest difficulty, aside from knowing truly what you really felt . . . was to put down what really happened in action; what the actual things were which produced the emotion that you experienced" (*Afternoon*, 2). It is even more curious that a writer would feel sometimes fortunate in not having things discerned. Since undiscerning readers are likely to misunderstand his writing, to misjudge it and him, it seems more probable that a writer would feel unfortunate—with two exceptions. Spared the exposure of being shown unconscious drives he did not know existed in his works, a writer might feel fortunate that they were opaque. And a writer who did not wish his readers to discover things he had consciously concealed in his writing would also feel fortunate, perhaps even smug, that his surreptitious efforts had gone undetected: "I was learning very much about [Cézanne] but I was not articulate enough to explain it to anyone. Besides it was a secret" (*Feast*, 13).[13]

Hemingway's theory of omission was "that you could omit anything if you know that you omitted [it,] and the omitted part would strengthen the story and make people feel something more than they understood" (*Feast*, 75). Hemingway's gains by applying this theory are impressive and shrewd. The omission of Butler's honorable motives in "My Old Man" shows that theory in practice. Perhaps a few other examples will show just how well-rooted that theory is. "Big Two-Hearted River," for instance, is satisfying as an amply detailed fishing story. But Nick Adams's excessively methodical behavior and his peculiar reluctance to fish the strangely named "tragic" swamp hint that something has been omitted. When we learn the omission, that Nick is trying to recover from war-caused psychic wounds, then the story's shadows deepen and we read more closely as a psychological cripple carefully exercises his healing psyche.[14] Likewise, "Indian Camp" is properly admired for its economical treatment of Nick's initiations into birth and death processes, balanced as they are by two incisions, in a woman's abdomen and a man's neck. But the omission that Nick's Uncle George has fathered the child that Nick's father delivers makes for one of Hemingway's richest early applications of his theory.[15] In a less well known story, "The Mother of a Queen," Roger's dramatic monologue defames a homosexual bullfighter and former friend, Paco. Here the omission is that the self-righteous Roger is not only an unreliable narrator but also a jealous and thus vindictive "closet" homosexual. His peremptory dismissal of Paco's defensible values richly earns Hemingway's implied scorn.[16]

Hemingway sometimes uses his theory of omission in simple ways, or so it seems. He will omit, for instance, the single word that a story surrounds. This is the case in "The Sea Change," which omits the word *lesbian*, and in the better-known "Hills Like White Elephants" and its missing word, *abortion*. Still, both stories are not "solved" just because we reel to the shore their missing words. Indeed, Hemingway cunningly gulls us into thinking that once we have discovered the omitted words there is little left to the stories. The omitted words, however, prod a more thorough reading of those stories. Instead of expressing contempt for a perverse young lesbian in "The Sea Change," Hemingway generates admiration for her. She is considerate of Phil, the man she is leaving, and she is courageous to act upon the discovery of a new dimension of her sexual makeup. And rather than spurn for unreasonableness Jig, the pregnant girl in "Hills Like White Elephants," Hemingway mocks her nagging, selfish, infantile mate for being insensitive to her needs and unwilling to allow their relationship to develop beyond hotel-hopping. Hemingway also omits the end of the story: Jig's abortion and separation from her companion.

What these stories, and many of Hemingway's best fictions, have in common is doubleness. Ignorant of their omissions, we can, of course, appreciate them, analyze their techniques, and extract sustainable readings of character, theme, and affects. Attuned to their omissions, we usually come away with contrasting readings. Rather than nullify our "ignorant" readings, which may have felt "something more than [we] understood," they should enrich our pleasure by affording simultaneously antithetical or at least alternative readings. I give a more sustained defense of this idea in my revisionary readings of Hemingway's books in the chapters ahead. But Hemingway's own penchant for doubleness pervades his work and reveals him to be, as Theodore Roethke defines the type, "A poet: someone who is never satisfied with saying one thing at a time."[17]

Hemingway's penchant for doubleness may be difficult to accept, if even to tolerate. And my notion of his craftiness, his artistic duplicity, may appear misguided, perverse, or as proof of overexercised ingenuity. After all, Hemingway's most salient public trait was self-exposure. Far more than most artists he seemed addicted to sporting and military events that would give him high public visibility. And he was never loath to broadcast his tastes, opinions, and views, in interviews and in his many articles as war correspondent and journalist. As testimony to his lack of secretiveness, he openly declares in the foreword to *Green Hills of Africa* his intent: "to write an absolutely true book to see whether the shape of a country and the pattern of a month's action can, if truly presented, compete with a work of the imagination." Such candor surely denies any concealments, any double-dealing.

As Carlos Baker tells, however, Hemingway was a "man of many contradictions."[18] Beneath his masculine swagger lay puerile diffidence. An advocate of courage, he was fear-ridden. Given to exhibitionism, he highly prized the solitude of his morning hours, practicing his craft. Rigorously self-disciplined, he is better known for his self-indulgence. Seemingly profligate, he was actually a compulsive collector, as the innumerable papers and items in the John F. Kennedy Library's Hemingway Collection verify. As a child, " 'he shouts out *fraid a nothing* with great gusto' "; as an old man his paranoia finds him "fraid a plenty."[19] A personal library of over nine thousand books suggests "Ernest-the-bookworm," at odds with the popular image of "Papa Sportif."[20] And Professor Michael S. Reynolds's *Hemingway's First War: The Making of "A Farewell to Arms"* gives good reason to be suspicious of the kind of openness Hemingway presents in his foreword to *Green Hills*. Reynolds's excellent scholarship proves that Hemingway's early novel was not the product of mere autobiography and fiction. Rather it was also the product of considerable research and was deeply indebted to others' writings. For Hemingway had neither been present during, nor had he even visited the area that was the scene for, the central event that he chose to write about with such first-person authenticity: the retreat from Caporetto.[21]

Hemingway's attraction to concealments and doubleness is most visible in his one formal attempt as a playwright, *The Fifth Column*. Like many a failure, it is artistically and autobiographically revealing. Its main character, Philip Rawlings, is an espionage agent whose public image as a hedonistic roustabout hides his courageous cloak-and-dagger activities. When he falls in love, the usual melodramatic dilemma assails him. Should he give in to the rewards of a private life of pleasure by marrying the beautiful Dorothy Bridges? Or should he continue to serve the cause of humanity, reject pleasure for duty, fatal though it is sure to be? Hemingway fails to make credible or compelling his stereotyped hero, situation, or problem. He manages only to set up several antitheses: a hotel manager whose comic role collides with the disasters of a bomb-torn city, a stage set whose two rooms and connecting door symbolize Philip's double life, as do his two missions and the pair of romantic triangles that entwine him. Hemingway handles the problem of double identity awkwardly, even having a young idealist, mistaken for Philip, murdered. Nevertheless, Philip's reluctance to divulge his identity to the woman he presumably loves is significant. It expresses his and Hemingway's anxiety that detection of their secret identities will jeopardize their well-being.

This anxiety and its accompanying wish, for an undetectable second identity, recur throughout Hemingway's life and his writing. Naturally they were acquired early, many factors urging their development. His mother assigned Ernest's first double identity, frocking him out as his older sister's twin sister and continuing to have both children's hair Dutch-bobbed to make look-alikes of them through Ernest's sixth year.[22] The androgynous qualities of his parents must have confused his sense of their identity and, consequently, his own. Mother Grace, strongly promasculine and aggressive, spent more time giving voice lessons than in housewifery: her only culinary accomplishment was a teacake (89). It was she who took on the design and furnishing of the North Kenilworth Avenue home, a telling instance of her dominance in running the lives of the Hemingways.[23] It was to father Clarence that such normally female, domestic duties fell: marketing, cooking, and canning. Moreover, this dignified, fastidious, suburban obstetrician and general practitioner in Illinois would transform himself during summers in Michigan into a woodsman with patched trousers, stained hat, and old flannel shirt. "It was," Hemingway's older sister Marcelline concludes, "as though he lived two lives" (45). It must have been perplexing to have a father whose forceps delivered new life one day and whose shotgun dispatched it the next. Certainly it perplexed his children to witness or be victim of his rapidly shifting moods, as Marcelline noted:

> My father's dimpled cheeks and charming smile could change in an instant to the stern taut mouth and piercing look which was his disciplinary self. Sometimes the change from being gay to being stern was so abrupt that we were not prepared for the shock that came, when one minute Daddy would have his arm around one of us or we would be sitting on his lap, laughing and talking, and a minute or so later— because of something we had said or done, or some neglected duty of ours he suddenly thought about—we would be ordered to our rooms and perhaps made to go without supper. [31]

The different inflexibilities of Dr. and Mrs. Hemingway unwittingly encouraged duplicity. Marcelline recalls secretly slipping a sheet of ragtime piano music to her younger sister, Sunny. Surreptitiously she learned to play the forbidden item, a musical obscenity to their mother, who had thrown over a promising career in opera by marrying Dr. Hemingway (124). Marcelline also confesses that several times she snooped on young Ernest, presumably practicing his cello in the family music room. He would be bowing away on open strings with his right hand. But in his left hand would be not the cello's fingerboard but a book he would be reading (124). Moral absolutist though Dr. Hemingway was, Marcelline even tattles on him, smuggling fish from Michigan into Illinois one time, poaching birds out of season another (42, 82). Small wonder that a son might practice comparable deceptions in matters marital or literary.

By the time Hemingway was only two or three he was already engaging in one form of double identity that he never outgrew, adopting nicknames. Then he was "Bobby-the-squirrel" or "Carlo-gleaming-fiery-eyes-coming-through-the-dark," after real or toy animals (11). Later he was Eoinbones, the Old Brute, Wemedge, Stein, Heminstein, and, of course, Papa.[24] An innocuous practice? Perhaps. But when combined with his antipathy to his own Christian name and his deletion of the family-inherited middle name, Miller, it indicates a strong wish to hide his real identity, to be different from either the person he actually was or the person others thought him. And though fiction writing was clearly an adult way of trying to fulfill this wish, as a child Hemingway's practice of adopting nicknames was a normal part of the process of formulating what personality theorists call a child's idealized self, what Freud called ego ideals. Based on parental values, and therefore incorporations of role models, ego ideals answer "to everything that is expected of the higher nature of man."[25] Their creation not only instills religion, morality, and a social sense. It also helps one to avoid or to cope with the anxiety caused by feelings of parental disapproval or rejection and, in many cases, anxiety exacerbated by the parents' own conflicts.

A number of details about Hemingway's early domestic situation must have complicated his formulation of ego ideals and contributed to at least some contradictions, fluctuations, or instabilities in them.[26] Along with the already noted characteristics of Dr. and Mrs. Hemingway, the house that Hemingway spent his first six years in must have been a perplexing place, for it was also home to widowed grandfather Ernest Hall and to Grandfather

Hall's bachelor brother-in-law, "Uncle" Tyley Hancock. Which among this trio of father figures was his real father, a child might ask? And after which of them should he formulate his ego ideals? This question would be complicated by grandfather "Abba" (i.e., "Father") Hall's pronounced patriarchal ways and strong affection for the grandson named after him (5–6, 11), by "Uncle" Tyley's unflagging gaiety and affection for his grandnieces and grandnephew (9–10), by Grace Hemingway's doting on both father and uncle (15), and by her domineering role in the home. Such a cluster of "fathers" would surely complicate one's ego ideals.

Still other factors during those early years might explain the inclusion of secretiveness in the ego ideals Hemingway formulated. During his early mental development Grandfather Hall annually wintered in California (13) and Uncle Tyley traveled as a salesman "all over the Middle West" (9). Young Ernest might have construed their disappearances and returns as proof of his "fathers'" omnipotence, their possession of some magical powers. This illusion might have been encouraged by Uncle Tyley, whose "sleight-of-hand demonstrations endeared him to all of us at one age or another."[27] A father with remarkable eyesight and secret powers to heal the sick—as a young child would regard a doctor-father—might also encourage the illusion. So too could the doctor's obstetrical ability to deal with that monumental childhood mystery, where babies come from. Hemingway's parents' command of esoteric languages—music and medicine—might have further added to formulating ego ideals that would issue in at least a double self, one that would prize not only aggressive masculinity but also the passive pleasures of writing quietly, one that could be common and esoteric, public and private, tough and tender, visible and inscrutable.

Perhaps I labor biographical and fictional particulars. If so, I do it not only to help see consciously intended concealments that enrich Hemingway's art, but to examine as well its repressed, unintended, but nevertheless potentially discoverable patterns. For such repressed patterns also enrich a work's and a writer's significance, even when they cause problematic effects and reveal counterintentions that clash directly with intended meanings. To be sure, repressed meanings and patterns can overpower a work's artistically intended effects. But as Hemingway himself said, the eventual discernment of "things . . . not . . . immediately discernible" contributes to evaluating whether a writer will "endure or be forgotten."

Hemingway's esthetic of concealment serves well the affective and esthetic aims of his writing. But ultimately it also answered his psychological needs, which brings me to my last thesis. As reflected in his life, his esthetic, and his work, Hemingway was fixated upon his father, the chief emotional object of his life. In several works—clearly some Nick Adams stories and *For Whom the Bell Tolls*—Hemingway consciously fictionalized his relationship with his father. But more often Hemingway seems unconscious of how extensively father-son dynamics empowered his writing.[28]

As I have mentioned, Hemingway must have had complications in formulating his ego ideals. But his father's character and values most sharply affected that process. As a young boy Hemingway idolized his father's professional abilities, his interest in the out-of-doors, and his self-discipline. These constellated much of Hemingway's ego ideals. But his father's selflessness puzzled him, especially as it came out in submissiveness to a domineering wife. Clarence Hemingway's lack of assertiveness in the husband-wife relationship must have signaled to his son a sizable fear of woman. And it must have disturbed the stability that the formation of ego ideals tried to establish. An arresting episode in "Now I Lay Me," based upon an actual event in Hemingway's childhood, suggests the shock of witnessing a father's submissiveness.[29] Suffering insomnia because of a battle injury, Nick Adams gets through the dark hours by remembering. One of his earliest memories is of his father's return home from a hunting trip to find that his wife has burned his collection of Indian artifacts—in the interests of " 'cleaning out the basement, dear' " (*Stories*, 366). Hemingway does not have Nick register shock at his father's failure to scold, to protest, or to retaliate against his wife—this story's significant omission. But the scene is traumatic for Nick, for it influences his refusal to see marriage as a solution to any problems, indeed, influences his deep fear of women. Even more, Nick's recent trauma of being blown up at night and feeling his soul leave his body has activated his repressed infantile conflicts, ones that came to a head in the artifacts-burning episode. Nick's insomnia, then, mirrors at a distance those nocturnal fears and puzzlements that he had had after he witnessed his father's submission, an equally explosive event in his psychic life.

Like "Now I Lay Me" and "My Old Man," other stories record disappointment in a father whose treachery or betrayal—intended or not—undermines his virtues. "The Doctor and the Doctor's Wife" studies Nick's weak father, who backs down before a taunting Indian and, worse, before an invalid wife. Nick does not enter the story until it is almost over. But his delayed entrance artfully shows that Hemingway focuses upon him, inviting us to imagine the inevitable scars a weak father will leave on Nick's psyche. Even "Ten Indians" turns upon betrayal, not so much a girl's as a father's. Hemingway laces the story's first scene with sexual innuendoes between the Garners, who are bringing Nick home from celebrating Independence Day in town. Those innuendoes carry over into the second scene, in which Dr. Adams tells Nick that he found Nick's girl, Prudie, "threshing around" with another man. Yet why had Dr. Adams chosen not to spend the holiday with his son? Had he dishonorable reasons? Had he gone off to the Indian camp to find Nick's girl for himself rather than to find her as he says he did? Nick's adolescent heartbreak screens Hemingway's omission here, Dr. Adams's intended sexual treachery.

The Nick-on-the-road stories fit the "family romance" pattern that Freud found common to fairy tales, heroic myths, fiction, and most children's development: the search for the "true" father. But they also verify Hemingway's fixation on, and disillusionment with, his own father. After all, the stories ask us to see that even Nick's surrogate fathers fail to measure up to the ideal father he seeks. In "The Battler" the "friendly" brakeman punches Nick, boyish Ad Francis turns vicious on him, and gentlemanly Bugs shows his gentleness by sapping Ad with a blackjack. The surly bartender, the homosexual cook, and Steve Ketchel—over whose love two whores bizarrely debate in "Light of the World"—again represent men who opaquely justify Nick's filial distrust. The strongest record of Nick's shock at paternal betrayal is "The Killers." Organized around a motif of mistaken identities, the story climaxes in Nick's stunned discovery that an aging professional fighter, a boxer, refuses to fight for his life, fails to be what he is supposed to be.

In still other stories Hemingway projects upon men the disillusionment and hurt that his own father's defects caused him. In "Fifty Grand" Jerry Doyle tells about an unheroic surrogate father, Jack Brennan, who boxes simply to make a living and whose main anxiety is economic, a disappointment that Jerry tries hard to conceal. In "A Simple Enquiry" Pinin discovers that his "father," the company major, has homosexual designs upon him. And in "In Another Country" Nick's surrogate father, the major, lacks the stoicism he preaches.

Hemingway's fixation upon his father is also evident in the many stories that are partly propelled by his wish to compensate for weak fathers. Admired men, who show their capability to do better or more than one could have expected from them, include the Jesus of "Today Is Friday," Manuel of "The Undefeated," Cayetano of "The Gambler, the Nun, and the Radio," and the old men of "A Clean Well-Lighted Place" and "Old Man at the Bridge."

Hemingway's fixation on, and ambivalence toward, father figures obliges me to draw the necessary inference, that Hemingway was latently homoerotic.[30] Many things urge this. Mrs. Hemingway's unchallenged efforts to transform Ernest and Marcelline into look-alikes might well have made him feel at an early age that both mother and father preferred girls to boys, instilling in him a need to adopt some "feminine" tendencies. The successive arrival of siblings into the Hemingway household and young Ernest's disappointment at the failure of any of them to be boys would also have persuaded him that girls were a preferred commodity.[31] If they were not, then surely his father would have exercised what a very young Ernest would have believed was in his father's power, the ability to choose the sex of his own children. Clearly Ernest's "fraid a nothing" motto asserted pride in his own maleness. But his delight in sewing " 'something for Papa to wear [,] . . . in mending Daddy's pants' " would early note his desire to win his father's love through "feminine" means.[32] So too might have been his pleasure in sharing his father's love of the outdoors, one highlight of his childhood being his fourth-year birthday present, "an all-day fishing trip with his father."[33]

The recurrent domestic quarrels, conflicts, and tension between the doctor and the singer would have compelled Ernest to choose between them. Rather than develop a normal ambivalence of tender and hostile feelings toward both parents, he clearly distributed the larger share of hostility to his mother, tenderness to his father. And his hatred of his mother, offset though it was by his secret admiration of her Pilar-like dominance, was augmented by his view of her as the disruptive rival in his love for his father, thus fitting the classic outline of a homoerotic, "negative" Oedipal complex.[34] Identification with, but disappointment in, his father partly explains Hemingway's lifelong ambition to prove himself superior to his father. It also partly explains his overdeveloped masculinity, the customary symptom of reaction formation, by which a man represses the wish to be the object of his father's or father-surrogates' love. To compete against mother and sisters for his father's affection meant, then, that Hemingway had to adopt "passive," "feminine" traits.[35] One sign that he did could be his lifelong career as a writer, expressing as it may an outward renunciation of masculinity and of active sexual rivalry with his father. A surer sign is the gallery of men his imagination and psychic needs created. The heroes in his fiction are more passive than active, feminine than masculine, either naive adolescents, "men without women," winners who "take nothing," or altruistic, maimed, or innocuous males.[36] Hemingway's latent homoeroticism is categorically confirmed by the paranoia that afflicted him during his last years, paranoia invariably linked to homoerotic wishes.[37]

To be sure, Hemingway's latent homoeroticism does not prove him abnormal. Without a doubt he led a relatively normal heterosexual life, facilitated as it was by the several sisters who enabled him to transfer original erotic desires from his mother to women outside the immediate family, proof that a "positive" Oedipal complex accompanied his "negative" one. And certainly Hemingway's feelings toward his father were not exclusively "passive," "feminine" ones. His masculine aggression found many chances to vent hostility toward his father: parricidal motifs in his fiction repeatedly vouch for that. Nevertheless, because his father was the chief emotional object of his life, it is not surprising that his father's weakness not only shocked and distressed him but also ignited an accompanying wish to come to his father's aid. And that wish, to rescue the father, customarily contains homoerotic as well as parricidal wishes.

Proof of Hemingway's latent homoeroticism is best borne out by the number of short stories that deal with it. It is latent in the relationships between Nick Adams and a chum in "The End of Something," "Three-Day Blow," and "Cross-Country Snow." It is overt in "The Battler," "Mr. and Mrs. Elliot," "A Simple Enquiry," "The Sea Change," and "The Mother of a Queen." Moreover, any scanning of the short fiction I have not yet pointed at will find Hemingway most often writing about two men engaging in some activity together: Robert Wilson and Francis Macomber, Guy and the narrator of "Che Ti Dice La Patria," John and the narrator of "An Alpine Idyll," the anonymous pair in "Wine of Wyoming." I interpret this pattern as Hemingway's projected wish for fraternal experiences that would gratify his more deeply rooted wish for the approval and affection and relationship he earlier sought from his father. Surely Hemingway's lifelong pref-

erence for masculine activities and for comradeship with men—
Ezra Pound early, General Charles Trueman (Buck) Lanham
later—acts out his wish to ingratiate himself with his father. And
by displacing virility from bedrooms to battlefields, by showing
allegiance to father-approved goals, he would also, of course, deny
his father any reason to perform on him that act every man, consciously or not, dreads—castration.[38]

Finally, Hemingway's father fixation and homoeroticism show
up in the dominant wish in his fiction—affiliation. Common
though it has become to see Hemingway competing for power or
achievement, those wishes are less significant to him than his
overriding need for association with others, even when such relationships subordinate him. Psychologists declare, for instance,
that we can discover people's basic wishes—even their unconscious ones—by observing the recurrent concerns that emerge
when people talk or write about their daydreams. If they daydream about improving or accomplishing things, then they wish
for achievement. If they daydream about who is boss and how
they can keep authority or wrest it from another person, then they
wish for mastery, power. If they daydream about family, friends,
and associates, then they wish for affiliation.[39] (Although these
same psychologists prefer to ignore the model from which their
formulation derives, Freud's Oedipal triangle looms large. Crudely put, normally the child pursues achievement [to woo a parent of
the opposite sex and to challenge the parent of the same sex], the
father seeks power [to intimidate a son, master a wife, and woo a
daughter], and the mother strives for affiliation [to nurture for
herself the nonsexual affection of her family's males].)

Hemingway's fiction certainly allows scope to all three wishes.
And in it I hear loudly the wish to achieve, even though its aim
may be homoerotic, to woo his father. But I hear even more loudly
the wish for affiliation, due, I believe, to his homoerotic aim to
nurture for himself the nonerotic affection of his father. Consider
briefly, for instance, the 1927 collection of stories *Men without
Women*. Its unity depends not upon thematic issues or literary
techniques. Rather its stories deal with affiliative situations, ones
that ultimately sublimate homoerotic aims. "The Undefeated"
comes closest to demonstrating a wish for power: Manuel's come-
back attempt seems driven by his need to show that he is still a
great matador, "boss." Yet this wish is complicated by his wish to
achieve: recognition as a great matador will come by proving his
ability in the plaza de toros. But success with the bulls will do

more than demonstrate achievement or mastery. It will gain him spectators' approval, aficionados' esteem, and, most of all, the paternal regard of Zurito, the father figure whose benediction will symbolize affiliation. (Little wonder that Manuel reacts strongly to Zurito's ambiguous, castrative gesture of cutting off his coleta.) Projected onto Manuel, then, is Hemingway's affiliative wish: to obtain his father's nonerotic affection and approval.

"A Simple Enquiry" and "A Pursuit Race" openly display homoerotic situations and the accompanying affiliative wish. Other stories in the volume do so too, but less openly. The unwillingness to marry, a motif dominant in "In Another Country" and "Now I Lay Me," responds less to the fears and complications of heterosexual entanglements than to the repressed aim of homoerotic relationships. After all, both stories reject confident, assertive men—the "hawks" in the former, the orderly, John, in the latter. They favor sympathetic, "feminine" men—the young man whose face was blown up and the diminutive major who breaks down in "In Another Country," the sensitive listener to whom Nick is telling "Now I Lay Me." By writing about Jack Brennan in "Fifty Grand," Jerry Doyle acknowledges his preference for a man whose domestic concerns—family and genuine relationships—are more important than retaining his title (achievement) or showing crooked fight-fixers who is boss (power). "Che Ti Dice" criticizes fascism, a manifestly political but latently personal story. It rejects, that is, the tyranny of powerful males and the fatherland, prefers democracy's fraternal governance. In "Today Is Friday" Jesus wins one Roman soldier's admiration for being " 'pretty good in there today' " (*Stories*, 358). His behavior neither achieves anything nor demonstrates power, but it creates an affiliative bond. And in "Banal Story" the collective mourning for Maera (a cortege of 147 bullfighters accompanies his coffin) measures considerable affiliative regard.

Aware that I may overwork the evidence that the affiliative wish in Hemingway's fiction subordinates to it the wishes for achievement and power, let me end my case by simply pointing to the title of that 1927 volume *Men without Women*. Almost blatantly it declares the affiliative wish and homoerotic aim. And impelling both wish and aim, I believe, is Hemingway's fixation upon his father.

Hemingway's fixation, aim, and wish oftentimes lead to irreconcilable interpretations of his fiction. Intended meanings and artistic effects will be at odds with unconscious drives and subversive implications. A conscious concealment will be contradicted or compromised by a repressed obsession. I hear, for instance, Hemingway's intent to portray Robert Jordan as an epic hero who commendably sacrifices his life to shield Pablo's fleeing band; to protect the life of his true love, Maria; and to serve magnanimously a country and a cause he loves. But I also hear the subversive desires of Jordan's repressed wishes: to commit suicide now that he has redeemed that degraded father, Pablo; to punish Maria by abandoning her, thus driving her mad again, loathsome woman that she truly is to him; to have the chance to slay at least one more "brother" before dying.

These views of Jordan are irreconcilable, of course. But I think it is unnecessary to be drawn into the position of deciding whether this or another work's unconscious implications and problematic effects either complement and enrich its intended meanings or damage and detract from them. I find no compelling reason to force literary criticism into such weary either-or alternatives. A work's unconscious counterintentions, to put the matter plainly, always enrich it, for they insist on adopting an attitude of both-and. Surely our modern critical heritage has taught us to hallow ambiguity (and, alas, to ignore Freud's richer term, "condensation," from which ambiguity sprang). And ambiguities demand a both-and response. Esthetic purists and formalists who insist upon beholding an objet d'art in isolation, immune from the artist's inartistic, undesigning unconscious, will quibble, at the least. But their either-or modes of esthetic mentation dehumanize the very art upon which they practice their priestly craft.[40]

I expect to hear many conservative students and scholars of Hemingway scoffing at my three theses and the revisionary readings and afterwords that follow. I too scoffed when, fifteen years ago, I stumbled upon epic machinery in *For Whom the Bell Tolls*, a bit of pure happenstance that came of teaching Milton's epic and Hemingway's novel at the same time. And I scoffed again at the prospect that Hemingway could have attempted a tragedy; but I rooted away, pig after a second truffle, and found it. I scoffed even more at the notion that Hemingway was artistically deceptive, crafty, for I too had suckled on the belief that his autobiographical fictions were a clean, well-lighted place. I scoffed most at a colleague's challenge that out-of-date Freudian theory could help me over the obstacles of why Hemingway concealed his experiments, of what was truly going on in his fiction. More scoffs will be nothing new to my ears.

But I write not to exercise scoffers. Much less do I write to convince Hemingway students and scholars that my perceptions and conclusions are correct, theirs flawed. For as with every book of literary criticism, this one too must settle for trying to be heuristic. Nevertheless, I intend it to probe some dimensions of Hemingway and his work that will let stand before us a more elusive Hemingway than we have yet looked at.

THE THESIS PHASE

1

A Hospitalized World: *A Farewell to Arms*

Like *The Scarlet Letter's* scaffold, *Anna Karenina's* railroad tracks, *Bleak House's* court of chancery, *A Passage to India's* caves, *As I Lay Dying's* coffin, *Confidence Man's* riverboat, *Huckleberry Finn's* raft, and *The Old Man and the Sea's* skiff, *A Farewell to Arms'* hospitals are central to many of its events. And whether in an ambulance, aid station, or hospital, Hemingway's hero and heroine are never far from the flag that waves above their actions—the Red Cross. Admittedly Hemingway's World War I experiences partly determine hospitals as the novel's chief stage property. But were the novel truly dictated by personal experience, then Frederic Henry would not have been wounded as an officer of an ambulance unit but rather as Hemingway had been, as a *cantinier*, doling out sweets, tobacco, and postcards to Italian troops.[1]

Esthetic considerations must have been among Hemingway's reasons for altering the facts of his own experiences. The medical duties of an ambulance officer and a nurse lend greater plausibility to Frederic's love story than had Frederic been a *cantinier*. And his medical status makes inconspicuous the hospitals, which unify the plot's action: Frederic and Catherine meet in the hospital in Gorizia, reunite and consummate their romance in the Milan hospital, and separate in the Lausanne hospital. And the alteration from *cantinier* to ambulance officer allows the ubiquitous image of the Red Cross to unify the novel's settings and to urge the inevitability of its conclusion: from Frederic's compatriot's hernia to Catherine's fatal hemorrhage the novel's steady tattoo of injury and ailment prepares for calamity. That Red Cross banner even invites the ironic view that Frederic and Catherine's Swiss idyll is less pastoral romance than medical reciprocity. That is, since the Swiss flag inverts the colors of the Red Cross flag, it could be argued that as Catherine nursed Frederic through his convalescence in Milan, he inverted their relationship in Switzerland, nursing her through pregnancy—almost.

As a stage property, hospitals generate more than esthetic felicities. They indicate that Hemingway's principal subject is not war and love but wounds. Whether caused by war, family, or accident, and whether physical, emotional, spiritual, or psychological, wounds define the world of this novel: injury ridden. The traditional "physician" for such wounds, the priest, can poorly administer to the needs of such a world. Yet equally ineffective are the surgeons, medics, and nurses who work in the novel's hospitals and care for injured bodies. Their anesthetics, operations, dressings, and therapy cannot prevent that most normal of human functions—the cycle of reproduction—from going terribly awry. Neither can they cure the wounds that accompany Frederic when he walks away from the hospital at the novel's end. Symbol of the clean, well-lighted place to which modern man turns in the hope of being made whole, Hemingway's hospitals seem small improvement over the institutions they historically replace, churches.

Unlike Sinclair Lewis's hospitals, which expose the abuses of the medical profession in *Arrowsmith*, or Thomas Mann's sanatorium, which completes the education of his hero in *Magic Mountain*, Hemingway's hospitals cannot heal the deeper injuries common to the human condition. But their failure is symptomatic of the failure of any system that offers or allows the illusion that it can give humankind health, order, meaning, or significance. In short, the thesis of *A Farewell to Arms* is that no institution, belief, system, value, or commitment can arm one against life's utter irrationality.[2] Recognizing this thesis clarifies the novel's structure, my first concern. It also explains why and when Frederic narrates his story, the characters of both Frederic and Catherine, and the aptness of their fantasy-driven romance, my second set of concerns. And it explains some reasons why Hemingway wrote the novel, one of the concerns of my afterword.

The sequence of Frederic Henry's major decisions reveals both his awareness of life's irrationality and the novel's underlying structure. His decision that family and country offered him no meaningful value is borne out by his disparaging references to the former and by his expatriation from the latter. His decision to stop studying architecture in Italy indicates that it obviously failed to satisfy his needs too. But that pursuit, however brief it may have been, also indicates that initially he decided to study a profession concerned with design, formal order, and tangible structures. Frederic is offhanded about his joining the Italian army and getting assigned to an ambulance unit. Yet except for medicine, no profession theoretically requires more discipline, regimentation, and obedience to orders than the military. That fact may underlie Frederic's decision to enlist, for it shows his continued search for order.

The opening chapters of the novel indicate that Frederic has served for more than a year, so he has been in the army long enough to know the gap between the military's theoretical order and reality. Futility, then, not irony, propels his remark that medicine stops the cholera epidemic only after seven thousand men die. And Catherine sees that the Italians occupy a " 'silly front' " (20), dismantling any elevated notion of military rationality. Frederic notes early how ridiculous it was to carry a pistol that so sharply jumped upon firing that one could hit nothing (29). During the retreat later he sarcastically thinks that it is only as disorderly as an advance (188). Although Frederic falls in love with Catherine during his Milan convalescence, it is not until his next major decision, to desert the army at the Tagliamento, that he also decides to commit himself to her, seeking order and meaning now in their intimate relationship. Her death, of course, insists that nothing can immunize her against irrational forces. Neither science and Rinaldi's medical skill, nor faith and the priest's prayers, nor love and Frederic's care—none of these can keep her alive. Hemingway's borrowing the novel's title from that of George Peele's poem, then, is ironic, for he rejects the poem's conviction that "duty, faith, love are roots, and ever green"—that they offer meaningful value.[3]

While deciding at the Tagliamento to commit himself to Catherine, Frederic makes two other decisions: to eschew thought and the processes of reasoning, and to seek order through his senses and the processes of nature. He tells himself that he was made not to think but to eat, to drink, and to sleep with Catherine (233).

Frederic's justification for the former decision rests upon more than the travesty of rationality he hears the battle police at the bridge declaim. After all, the military landscape abounds in irrationality. Pleasure palaces on the front lines? An offensive campaign in the mountains? Gas masks that fail to work? An ambulance unit of anarchists? Bridges not blown to slow the German offensive? Medals of honor for victims of accidents? No less irrational is the social landscape Frederic portrays. Were it not for the pain in his legs, his arrival at the Milan hospital would be Chaplinesque: an unkempt nurse, unprepared rooms, unmade beds, unanswered bellcords, and an absent doctor. Puzzled and angry he asks how there can be a hospital with no doctor (87). Just as the fixed horse races violate one activity over which chance and unpredictability should rule, so too do Frederic and Catherine violate the idea of a hospital: their romance transforms a ward for physical suffering into a haven of sensual gratification. The "comic opera" of their interrogation by the Swiss police at Locarno further justifies Frederic's derision of reason, aped as reason is by absurd civil formalities. His refrain throughout the last third of the novel, then, that he does not want to think, does not reflect a wish to escape or delay responsibility. It expresses his belief that thinking is a poor remedy for human problems.

Frederic's decision to embrace sensory experience and nature's processes is just as poor a remedy. Nature is no more orderly, controllable, or predictable than reason. Frederic's shrapnel-filled legs fail to raise his temperature. But Miss Gage patronizingly tells him that foreign bodies in his legs would inflame and give him a fever (85). Contrary to Miss Van Campen's belief, he cannot keep from contracting jaundice. Neither can Catherine prevent conception, assuring Frederic that she did everything she could, but that nothing she took made any difference (138). More to the point, Catherine's narrow hips thwart nature's reproductive cycle. And the umbilical cord, rather than nourishing fetal life, becomes a hangman's noose. At the novel's end neither spring nor rain will bring their normal regeneration.

The British major at the club in Milan tells Frederic how to respond to their world: "He said we were all cooked but we were all right as long as we did not know it. We were all cooked. The thing was not to recognize it" (133–34). Stripped as Frederic has been of virtually everything that would give him reason to continue living, when Catherine dies he cannot avoid seeing that he too is "cooked." And that prompts his next-to-last decision, to tell his story.

Frederic's motive for telling his story is elusive. If his motive is altruism, then as an ex-ambulance officer he may believe that to cure such a "cooked" world first requires diagnosing its condition and that telling his story will do that. If his motive is vindictiveness, then he may sadistically want to force others to see that they too are "cooked." If it is self-pity, then he may hope that telling his story will console himself and justify his apparent callousness. If his motive is self-aggrandizement, then he may feel that telling it will gain our admiration. If it is objectivity, then he may simply be telling it "the way it was." His motive, however, is revealed by his narrative manner, which leads me to three conclusions that I take up in reverse order. His manner reveals that he is disoriented by what has happened to him and so is an untrustworthy narrator; that he tells his story soon after Catherine's death; and that if he can discover in his story meanings that will nurture a desire to continue living, then his motive has been therapeutic. If not, then his motive has been testamentary: his story will explain his last decision—to commit suicide.

Farewell presumably conforms to the tradition of the *Bildungsroman*. Charting Frederic's development, the novel teaches that he grows by learning something: neither to "say 'farewell to arms' " nor to "sign a separate peace" but to "live with life," to "tolerate it"; "to become eventually quite strong" by being broken; to become "humanely alive" by caring for Catherine and saying "farewell to 'not-caring-ness' "; to reject eros for agape; to value life by discovering death and the "step-by-step reduction of the objects" he had found meaningful.[4] These statements about Frederic's "growth" assume that at the time he writes his story Frederic-the-narrator understands the significance of what has happened to him. Moreover, they assume that he has been chastened by experience and so will be a better person morally than he was at the beginning of his story. Most importantly, they assume that Frederic goes on living after he has told his story. And so they imply that Frederic's motive has been therapeutic.

Slightly modifying the end of Frederic's most anguished internal monologue, I ask, " 'But what if he should die? Hey, what about that? What if he should die?' " (321). The well-known "original" ending to the novel finds Frederic alive "and going on with the rest of my life—which has gone on and seems likely to go on for a long time."[5] But that staccato of negatives—nos, nothings, and nots—in Hemingway's splendid revision courts a different conclusion. Frederic's decisions have shown him turning to—but finding no life-sustaining meaning in—family, country, profession, religion, duty, reason, nature, or love. Having found only life's irrationality, Frederic would more likely decide now to commit suicide than to go on living an utterly hollow life. He is likely to tell himself the same thing he tells the dog sniffing the garbage cans, that there is nothing (315).

Whether Frederic goes on living or commits suicide is, of course, unknowable. But that fact cautions against predicting moral conduct from him now that Catherine is dead. Indeed, to confirm any of the statements about what Frederic learns and how he will now behave requires knowing what he does after he returned in the rain to the hotel (332). Clearly, he tells his story. But what does he do after he has told it? No Marlow, David Copperfield, Nick Carraway, or Jack Burden, Frederic gives no epilogue and scarcely any glimmer of where or to whom he tells his story. But Frederic does indicate when he tells it. He tells it shortly after Catherine's death.

We have long been schooled to conclude the opposite: as narrator, Frederic "speaks from a position several years remote from the occurrence of the action he describes"; and "the entire warm and loving story that constitutes the novel [is] a story told years after its occurence."[6] To be sure, Frederic gives the impression that some years have elapsed by referring to "the late summer of that year" or by remarking, "We had a lovely time that summer." And his essayettes, like those on abstract words or on how the world breaks everyone, reveal an eye steadied by time. Even his recall of Catherine seems to indicate narrative distance when, in a two-paragraph sequence, he recounts how he took down her hair as she sat quietly on his bed, dipping down suddenly to kiss him as he took out each hairpin and lay it on the sheet, dropping her head to let her hair cascade over him when he removed the last two pins, then, later, twisting it up and letting the light from the doorway draw out its shining luster (114). The second paragraph of this representative and lyrical reminiscence has the summarizing quality of a memory recounted several years after the events of the novel. But the first paragraph's detailed immediacy is not a summary, does not generalize, is not brief. So recently had Frederic and Catherine gone through this ritual that he can reconstruct it, hairpin at a time. The paragraph's evocative recall has the quality of wish to it: to conjure the scene fully may dispel the reality of Catherine's death. And to savor the erotic pleasure he found in taking down her hair confesses the pain of no longer being able to repeat it, a pain that time would have lessened.

And Frederic's essayettes: do they reveal an eye steadied by time, "slacken somewhat the objective tautness, the firm gaze upon outward reality, which is so characteristic of [*The Sun Also*

Rises]?"[7] That is not their effect on me. They obtrusively, but fittingly, break the "illusion of continuous action" because Frederic is unable to reflect calmly or maturely upon his experiences. His essayettes self-pityingly complain against the world that breaks everyone (249) and the "they" who throw one into a game, tell the rules and then kill the first time they catch one off base (327). But the essayettes are justifiable. Having just suffered physical, emotional, and psychological injuries, Frederic lacks the composure to control or suppress his feelings with the objective tautness or firmness of Jake Barnes, whose injury considerably antedates his story.

Let us briefly compare Frederic with the first-person narrator of "Now I Lay Me," allegedly Nick Adams, to see better that Frederic narrates his story shortly after it happens. Nick does two things that measure the distance between himself as he tells his story and himself as he was when an insomniac. First, he carefully differentiates between then and now, gives a time frame. The opening paragraph says, "So while *now* I am fairly sure that [my soul] would not really have gone out [of my body], yet *then, that summer*, I was unwilling to make the experiment" (*Stories*, 363; italics added). The last paragraph also acknowledges that "he [John, my orderly] came to the hospital in Milan to see me *several months after* and was very disappointed that I had not yet married; and I know he would feel very badly if he knew that, *so far, I have* never married" (371; italics added). Second, Nick records, outline-fashion, the "different ways of occupying myself while I lay awake" (363). He refishes streams, recites prayers "for all the people I had ever known," and remembers "everything that had ever happened to me" (365) or "all the animals in the world by name" (367). Or he just listens. Both the time frame and the outline that shape Nick's recitation of the sequence of his nocturnal ritual are absent in Frederic's story. But rightly so, for until time gives Frederic some perspective upon his experiences, his narrative will tend to lose its thread, as it does in this sentence:

> That night in the mess after the spaghetti course, which every one ate very quickly and seriously, lifting the spaghetti on the fork until the loose strands hung clear then lowering it into the mouth, or else using a continuous lift and sucking into the mouth, helping ourselves to wine from the grass-covered gallon flask; it swung in a metal cradle and you pulled the neck of the flask down with the forefinger and the wine, clear red, tannic and lovely, poured out into the glass held with the same hand; after this course, the captain commenced picking on the priest. [6–7]

The more orderly narrators of "Now I Lay Me" or "In Another Country"—both of whom resemble Frederic—would not digress as Frederic does. They would delete the irrelevancies of how everyone ate and drank, and attend instead to the point: "That night in the mess the captain commenced picking on the priest." They might allow the phrase "after the spaghetti course," or at most the clause "which everyone ate very quickly and seriously," but no more.[8]

I exercise this issue of when Frederic tells his story because the novel hangs together best when heard on the heels of Catherine's death. To believe that considerable time has elapsed before he tells it invites the corollary conclusion: that the style of Frederic's story is "tough." Hemingway may be "a hard man who has been around in a violent world, and who partially conceals his strong feelings behind a curt manner."[9] But can the same be accurately said of Frederic? Does he refuse, as Walker Gibson argues, to be concrete about such details as *the* year, *the* river, *the* plain, and *the* mountain in his opening sentence to insinuate an intimacy between himself and his reader? Does he imply that we, fellow insiders, know what he speaks of without requiring him to elaborate upon it? Does he fail to subordinate his ideas and to define causal relationships because he knows that we know that he knows that we know? Does he, for example, say, "There was fighting in the mountains and at night we could see the flashes from the artillery" (3), confident that we know that what he means to say is, "We knew there was fighting in the mountains, for at night we could see the flashes from the artillery"?[10] To support my nays to these questions the terms of one of *Farewell*'s most spirited detractors are excellent—although I adopt them for altogether opposite reasons. According to John Edward Hardy, in Frederic's "anonymous and crippled sensibility . . . Hemingway produces what seems to me a radically maimed prose, a style that does not simply reflect but is the victim of the spiritual malady that afflicts his characters."[11]

Both the "tough" and "maimed" labels judge Frederic's style upon the basis of the perennial illusion that Hemingway, a crippled tough, a sentimentalist masquerading behind he-man brusqueness, wants his reader to endorse Frederic's values, to emulate his conduct, and to imitate his style. Setting this issue aside for now, I turn instead to the descriptive accuracy of the label "maimed." It is because Frederic is maimed, defensive, and still feeling vulnerable—not because he is hardened—that he tells his story in a "curt," " laconic," "close-lipped" style: the secure can afford to be expansive. It is because Frederic is crippled that he tries to retaliate with ironic indignation, not sophistication, with understated emotion, not wit, as when he tells that the only result of his contracting jaundice was that he was denied his leave (145). It is because Frederic's recent experiences make him skeptical of reason and causality that he avoids subordinating his ideas. And it is because he is preoccupied with his feelings and experience, rather than with our understanding, that Frederic is an inconsiderate, and ultimately an untrustworthy, narrator.

Frederic is inconsiderate of the audience who hears his story because he is mentally disoriented, so preoccupied with his recent injuries that he is unaware that his listener is unfamiliar with the details of his life. Frederic ignores the amenities of formally introducing himself—"Call me Ishmael"—not to presume quickly upon the reader as insider, but because when he begins his story he is unsure of who he is. When his fictional predecessor, Jake Barnes, began his story, he already knew who his scapegoat was; even the deleted first chapters of his novel had similarly announced, "This is a novel about a lady."[12] But Frederic cannot begin by focusing on the person most important in his story. Sorely wounded, he avoids touching directly its most tender spot, Catherine. He keeps her offstage until his narrative is into its fourth chapter, enough time for its anesthetic, as it were, to take effect. Guilt, severe emotional stress, and paranoid tendencies also explain Frederic's reluctance to identify himself. Ferguson and Catherine call him "Mr. Henry" once each in chapters 5 and 6. But whether Henry is his surname or his Christian name is unclear. Nor is it clarified when his name gets joked about during the second mess scene, whether his name is Frederico Enrico or Enrico Frederico (40). Rinaldi only once calls him Frederico (76), on the eve of his departure to Milan. Not until Miss Gage asks him in book 2 what his name is does he divulge it: " 'Henry. Frederic Henry' " (84).

Many things demonstrate that Frederic is a disoriented and, ultimately, untrustworthy narrator. For all of its poetry, the much-praised opening paragraph to *Farewell* is confusing—as any reader new to Hemingway and the novel will affirm.[13] The first sentence alone generates no fewer than seven unanswered questions. And the following paragraphs fail to answer the questions of who the narrator is, where he is, why and what he is doing there, and when these events are taking place. So ambiguous is

Frederic's narration that we can even mistakenly think that he sees his friend the priest while sitting with a fellow officer rather than with a whore.[14] The mess table riddles, allusions, jokes, and shadow games certainly convey the impression that this must have been the way it really was. And they advance the novel's irrationality. But they also convey Frederic's trouble with selecting, organizing, and discriminating between significant and insignificant details. So do his occasionally lengthy recordings of, say, the inebriated dialogue of Rinaldi and the major from the mess in the last chapter of book 1. More revealing of his disordered sensibility are soberly written sentences that need considerable rereading before sense emerges. Telling of Gorizia, for example, Frederic drones on in a 164-word sentence about its brothels, railway bridge, the destroyed tunnel, trees around the town square, tree-lined avenues, house interiors, street rubble, and visits by the small, long-necked, gray-bearded king in his automobile (5–6).

Most persuasive of Frederic's disoriented sensibility is his confession that he cannot analyze or define his experience. In his only unequivocal reference to the time he is writing his story, he admits, "I tried to tell [the priest] about the night and the difference between the night and the day and how the night was better unless the day was very clean and cold and I could not tell it; *as I cannot tell it now*" (13; italics added). During revision Hemingway struck from the manuscript one of Frederic's monologues with the same confessional thrust. As the third paragraph of chapter 12, Frederic comments,

> I do not like to remember the trip back to Milan. If you have never travelled in a hospital train there is no use making a picture of it. This is not a picture of war, nor really about war. It is only a story. That is why, sometimes, it may seem there are not many people in it, nor enough noises, nor enough smells. There were always people and noises unless it was quiet and always smells but *in trying to tell the story I cannot get them all in always but have a hard time keeping to the story* alone and sometimes it seems as though it were all quiet. But it wasn't quiet. If you try and put in everything you would never get a single day done. *Also when you are wounded or a little out of your head or in love with someone* the surroundings are sometimes removed and they only come in at certain times. But I will try to keep the places in and tell what happened. It does not seem to have gotten anywhere and it is not much of a love story so far but it has to go the way it was although I skip everything I can.[15]

Given his theory of omission, it seems reasonable that Hemingway deleted this confession because he was confident that Frederic's narrative manner had already exposed his psychologically crippled sensibility, that the explicit confession of his condition was inartistic.[16]

Admittedly Frederic has long stretches of narrative—like the retreat—that exhibit little, if any, disorientation. But I do not contend that he is totally disoriented. After all, once he gets into his narrative its chronology coheres, his characters gather consistency, and even his use of details loses ambiguity, as a comparison of the first chapters of books 1 and 3 shows. No "diary of a madman," Frederic's story holds firmly enough to external reality to compel empathy. He is "one of us," not a clinical case. His disorientation, his being "a little out of [his] head," then, waxes and wanes, just as his regard for the priest seesaws against his affection for Rinaldi.

Not to see Frederic disoriented at all mandates the conclusion that Hemingway lacks esthetic distance from his narrator: Frederic's self-pity is Hemingway's. This view ignores Hemingway's early exposure to, and the influence of, writers who calculatedly created untrustworthy narrators to achieve esthetic distance. To discount the facts that Hemingway worked with and read writers like Ford, Stein, and Joyce and that one of his favorites was Conrad is to imply that Hemingway was an authorial naif. To deny his detachment from his characters also ignores Hemingway's early achievements in characterization. Surely one of his earliest discoveries was the importance of limited characters in fiction, characters perceptive enough about their experiences to engage readers emotionally, but just imperceptive enough to detach them simultaneously. Hemingway's justly acclaimed Nick Adams stories astutely maintain that tension between a youth's discerning intelligence and his obtuseness. Just think of "Three-Day Blow." Hemingway undercuts Nick's adolescent swagger and savvy by having him naively think he can resume his relationship with Marge and that it will be the same as before. To Nick's confident, "There was not anything that was irrevocable" (*Stories*, 124), I hear the retort, " 'Isn't it pretty to think so?' "

It is Hemingway's variation on this tension that makes Frederic an untrustworthy narrator. Perceptive enough to recount the decisions and events that have led him into a cul-de-sac, he is too disoriented, because he is emotionally unstrung, to confront and answer the many questions he generates. What was it, Frederic, that the priest had always known that you did not know and that, when you learned it, you were always able to forget (14)? And what happened, Frederic, between you and your family that caused your rift? And what are you going to do, Frederic, after

you've finished telling your story? And most of all, Frederic, was
Catherine crazy? Or was she sane?

To see that Frederic is a "little out of his head" gives us a better
view of both Catherine and the nature of their love. She is a poorly
characterized heroine, as readers have long complained. More accurately, she is poorly characterized only if Hemingway's intent
was to create a "round," richly complex human being. But I find
little to support the idea that such an intent was among Hemingway's considerations.[17] Some readers may wish to elevate Catherine to sainthood.[18] But her fragile grasp of reality persuades me
that Frederic loves a marginally neurotic woman who is more
than a little out of her head.[19]

I find it impossible to gainsay Catherine's addiction to fantasy.
Her romantic dream of marrying her childhood sweetheart was
interrupted by the war. But still she envisioned him arriving at
the hospital at which she was stationed, cut by a sabre and sporting a head bandage or else shot in the shoulder: " 'Something pic-
turesque' " (20). By calling this a " 'silly idea,' " she implies that
when she found out that he had been blown to bits, her schoolgirl
fantasies also disintegrated. Yet her responses to Frederic's romantic advances border on neurosis. During their second meeting
she one moment scolds him for talking nonsense (26) and the next
pleads that he be good to her, telling him that their life together
will be strange (27). And their third meeting flips from " 'Oh, dar-
ling, you have come back, haven't you' " (30) to " 'You don't have
to pretend you love me. That's over for the evening' " (31).

By the time Frederic sees Catherine in Milan he realizes, "I was
crazy about her" (92). And so it is understandable that he resists
the truth of his initial conclusion—that "she was probably a little
crazy" (30)—by not contesting her later assertion that she is no
longer crazy: " 'When I met you I was nearly crazy. Perhaps I was
crazy' " (116). Yet her desire to dwell amid fantasies does not
abate. When he denies having slept with other women, she ironically tells him to keep lying to her, that she wants him to lie to her
(105). But her avowals to obey his wishes, lacking that irony, are
fantasy-driven, declaring that she will say and do and want what
he wishes her to say and do and want, for " 'there isn't any me any
more' " (105–6). Frederic admits that they pretended that they
were married, and when he presses the issue and tells her that he
wants to marry her for her sake, the urgency with which she must
cling to fantasy is unmistakable in her insistent—if not imper-

ious—reproach: " 'There isn't any me. I'm you. Don't make up a separate me' " (115).

Symptoms of her flight from reality are strewn throughout the novel. She concels her pregnancy and denies that it worries her; but her insistence that Frederic not worry edges toward hysteria, confirming his impression that "she seemed upset and taut" (137). Possessive, she gets "furious" if anyone else touches Frederic. And she wants to be completely alone with him, rejoicing that they know only one person in Montreux, that they see nobody (303). Her wish to merge her identity into his, telling him that she desires him so much that she even wants to be him, exhibits psychological dependency, not selflessness. Paranoid, she initiates the two-against-the-others view that Frederic adopts later in the novel; when he assures her they won't fight between themselves, she insists that they must not, for if anything were to come between them, then they would have no chance against the rest of the world (133). Her indefatigable cheerfulness is admirable. But it too signals a defensive reaction. When Frederic wants to discuss problems, she blithely disregards them just as she blithely tells her hairdresser in Montreux that she is pregnant with her fifth child or her obstetrician that she has been married for four years. Her final words are poignant. But they are completely in character, one last bit of fantasy, promising that she will come to spend the nights with him (331).

Frederic cannot ignore the fact that he loves a psychologically maimed woman. To her irrational fear of the rain he asks her to stop, adding that he does not want her to be " 'Scotch and crazy tonight' " (126). His last word here, "tonight," rejects her wish to believe that she no longer has "crazy" moments. During the farewell scene in the Milan hotel before Frederic returns to the front, he records this exchange:

> "I'm a very simple girl," Catherine said.
> "I didn't think so at first. I thought you were a crazy girl."
> "I was a little crazy. But I wasn't crazy in any complicated manner. I didn't confuse you did I, darling?"
> "Wine is a grand thing," I said. "It makes you forget all the bad." [154].

Frederic's failure to answer her question, denying her what she wants to hear, recurs during their Switzerland "idyll." He wakes one moonlit night to find Catherine also awake. She asks if he remembers how she was "nearly crazy" when they first met. He comforts her by admitting that she was " 'just a little crazy.' " She then asserts that she is no longer that way, that she is " 'not crazy now' " (300). Frederic's response, " 'Go on to sleep,' " can be tender, loving. But it does refuse to confirm her assertion, allowing us to conclude that perhaps she protesteth too much. And after she falls asleep, Frederic notes that he lay awake for a long time, thinking things over and watching the moonlight on Catherine's sleeping face (301). This suggests to me that it is a strain on Frederic to maintain the illusion of her sanity. Yet again, in response to Catherine's cheery jabber about cutting her hair and getting thin again and being "a new and different girl" and going together to get it cut or going alone and surprising him, Frederic registers that he "did not say anything" (304). Rather than implying masculine superiority to such concerns, his silence again implies weariness at having to support continuously Catherine's need for their "grand" romance.

Reluctant though Frederic is at times to nurse Catherine's delusion of sanity, he fears her mental relapse and tries to shield her. Just as he gives her the gas she needs during labor, he faithfully administers the medicine she needs to keep from cracking up. In one overdose of ardor he assures her that she is his " 'good girl,' " a " 'lovely girl,' " a " 'grand girl!' " a " 'fine simple girl,' " and a " 'lovely girl' " (153–54). And the banality of their love talk in Switzerland seems partly calculated by Frederic to give Catherine the narcotic she needs, the assurance that his love is unflagging, that he is content to be alone with only her, that their togetherness does not bore him, that " 'we're the same one' " (299).

Though Frederic shoulders the psychological burden that Catherine's fragile mental condition imposes upon him, he should not get uncritical applause. After all, he too is psychologically dependent, needs her as much as she needs him. He tells her that he has a " 'fine life' " (298). And he tells us that they had a "fine life" and were "very happy" (306), that not once did they have a "bad time" (311). But what prompts these statements is Frederic's need to convince himself of his happiness, just as his assurances to Catherine had been calculated to make her feel secure in his love. Hemingway deleted from the novel other passages of Frederic stepping out of his self-mesmerizing account of the sequence of events to reflect upon the nature of his relationship with Catherine.[20] But he does keep one of Frederic's reflections: "Often a man wishes to be alone and a girl wishes to be alone too and if they love each other they are jealous of that in each other, but *I can truly say* we never felt that" (249; italics added). Jake Barnes's sarcastic

" 'Isn't it pretty to think so' " again tempts me. But that would miss the point of Frederic's boast. Crediting it as fact and not wish, I think it measures the extent to which a crippled couple has retreated from even the reality of their own psychic individuality. Indeed their isolationism, their illusion of self-sufficiency, and their wish to make the convulsions of their erotic love the center of everything add up to a regressive withdrawal from reality. Frederic does not hide this fact, admitting that when reunited at Stresa they felt that they had returned home to be together and to waken in the night and find one another there, not absent: *"all other things were unreal"* (249; italics added). Summed up in Frederic's " 'Let's get back to bed. I feel fine in bed' " (251), their escapist fantasy amply proves that the object of their romantic love is to fend off reality, replete as it is with suffering and irrationality. "The weak side of this technique of living," as Freud so cogently and poignantly noted, "is that we are never so defenceless against suffering as when we love [because we make ourselves dependent upon one other person], never so helplessly unhappy as when we have lost our loved object or its love."[21] The unhappy survivor of this defense against reality, a man neither innately strong nor confident nor supported by any traditional values, Frederic would have little reason to continue living once he has told his story, written his testament.

A "Vulgar" Ethic: *The Sun Also Rises*

Any recital of the many interpretations given *The Sun Also Rises* affirms its richness: a document of the "lost generation," a variant of Eliot's *Waste Land,* an anatomy of the death of love, a satire of sentimentality, an analogue of the bullfight's *corrida,* or a definition of the wounded hero.[1] My interpretation also affirms its richness, hoping to clarify its esthetic quality and ethical pertinence. A thesis novel, *The Sun Also Rises* answers Jake Barnes's moral concern: "I did not care what [the world] was all about. All I wanted to know was how to live in it" (148). To know "how to live," the novel says, requires yoking the ethical principles in a discriminating hedonism and in vivifying traditions. Egoistic but selected sensuous gratification must wed selfless deference to selected social customs.

By not insisting upon this thesis, Hemingway achieves much of the novel's esthetic quality. He dismisses the option of letting Jake exemplify the thesis. And so Jake's impotence points not only at his sexual inadequacy, defective intelligence, and narrative unreliability but also at his inability to synthesize in his own actions the opposing ethical principles, even though he seems to sense the need to do so. Hemingway's deadpan narrative style is another indication that he resists telling us to hear the thesis. Two sentences, representative of the disinterest in Jake's narrating voice, do not even ask us to differentiate among facts: "The bull who killed Vincente Girones was named Bocanegra, was number 118 of the bull-breeding establishment of Sanches Taberno, and was killed by Pedro Romero as the third bull of that same afternoon. His ear was cut by popular acclamation and given to Pedro Romero, who, in turn, gave it to Brett, who wrapped it in a handkerchief belonging to myself, and left both ear and handkerchief, along with a number of Muratti cigarette stubs, shoved far back in the drawer of the bed table that stood beside her bed in the Hotel Montoya, in Pamplona" (199). The second sentence is long and complex, but the style of both sentences is the same. The difference between the facts in each sentence, however, is as great as the significance of the ear—a memento to Romero and the Spanish, a bit of refuse to Brett. The facts of the first sentence are insignificant because they are "historical": the bull's name, number, and breeder have value only as realistic details. But the facts of the second sentence are important because they are ethical: they concern values inferable from human actions and relationships. Yet Jake's narrative voice underplays their importance, allows us to be lulled by the irrelevance of the historical facts that precede them. Confident, then, that other means are communicating the novel's thesis, Hemingway refuses to italicize it stylistically.[2]

Hemingway also disperses the novel's thesis among analogues. Although there is little dialogue or comment about ethical considerations per se, a good deal of it is about money, payment, and the characters' financial situation.[3] Attitudes about money are, of course, as symbolic of ethical priorities as are the analogues of the bullfight and the Tour de France, of Pamplona and Paris, as I will explain later.

One of Hemingway's nicer touches is his concealment of the thesis in the novel's apparently random narrative structure. The novel's immediate effect on many readers is that of a loose amalgam of events. Some of them might well have been deleted: Jake's chat with Harvey Stone, his and Bill Gorton's encounter on the train with the pilgrimaging priests, their later meeting with the old Basque who had been in the States " 'forty years ago,' " the goring of Vincente Girones during the *encierro*. The cluttered gallery of minor characters adds to the impression that the novel has no principle of selection. What have these snapshot characters to do with the novel: the Montana couple and their son, Hubert; Edna, "a friend of Bill's from Biarritz"; Robert Prentiss, "a rising new novelist"; the waiter who finds disgusting the "fun" of the *encierro*; Harris, the Englishman whom Jake and Bill befriend in Burguete? There is also the problem of the novel's double plot. The episodic adventures of the expatriates confuse the Aristotelean story of Robert Cohn's love and loss.[4] Or so it seems until we see the plots as metaphors of hedonism and traditionalism. Unlike the straightforwardness and limited casts of most thesis novels, then, this one's digressions, cluster of characters, and double plot mask its thesis.

Throughout the novel Hemingway subordinates his thesis to

the illusion of reality, achieving something no other novel of his does, the sustained verisimilitude that an authentic "imitation of an action" must have. This novel is superior to *A Farewell to Arms*, his other thesis novel, for *Farewell's* thesis depends heavily upon an event that courts improbability, Catherine's death. In contrast, the anticlimactic and ambiguous ending of *The Sun Also Rises* nicely obscures this novel's thesis.

Book 1 does not depict a "lost generation" whose lives have been cut adrift from traditional values by the disillusioning experience of World War I. Instead it depicts characters who find value in hedonism. The book's characters seek, for one thing, sensual gratification. Georgette prostitutes herself in exchange for dinner. The Braddocks drink, dine, and dance their time away. Brett cavorts with faggots and parties with counts who indulge in cigars that " 'really draw.' " Even Jake seeks sensual pleasure in the tennis and sparring that sustain his friendship with Robert Cohn. Most of Jake's acquaintances also give little thought to the past or the future, living for the moment. This seize-the-day ethic is aptly caught both in the book's quickly shifting scenes, which objectify the characters' impulsiveness, and in Frances Clyne's complaint, " 'No one keeps theirs [appointments], nowadays' " (46). And the book's hedonists determine values egoistically, indifferent to others' feelings or values. Drunken Harvey Stone enjoys baiting Cohn, the homosexuals tease Georgette, and Brett rudely bursts in on Jake in the middle of the night. Finally, these hedonists shun rational effort. The larger portion of book 1's dialogue records sensory concerns, its verbal unintellectuality best heard in the "nigger" drummer's incoherence at Zelli's: " ' . . .' the drummer chanted" (64).

Hemingway gives point to the hedonism in book 1 by including expatriates who are not hedonists. This is the purpose, I assume, for such family- and job-obligated expatriates as Jake's fellow correspondents, Woolsey and Krum. Better, this accounts for Cohn, anathema to hedonism. Only he is anxious about the future and given to philosophic moralizings: " 'Don't you ever get the feeling that all your life is going by and you're not taking advantage of it? Do you realize you've lived nearly half the time you have to live already?' " (11). He is also atypically plagued by a sense of responsibility: " 'I can't [tell Frances to go to Hell]. I've got certain obligations to her' " (38). Though financially well off, he lacks the independence to follow his impulses, urging Jake to accompany him into the South America of Hudson's *Purple Land*. Yet Cohn's San Sebastian affair with Brett, which crowns the book's hedonistic activities, indicates that hedonism might redeem him from his stodgy ways. At least it rescues him from his three-year mistress, Frances, "the lady who had him."

Hemingway's endorsement of hedonism emerges partly from his negative attitude toward Cohn. Yet his endorsement is not wholesale, for book 1 contrasts two models of hedonism, Brett and Count Mippipopolous. Initially the two seem indistinguishable, Brett's comment to Jake, " 'I told you he was one of us,' " aligning them. Yet the two significantly differ. Whereas a mindless self-indulgence motivates Brett, the count is selective about his pleasures. For example, remembering nothing from one night to the next, Brett forgets both her appointment with Jake at the Hotel Crillon and her visit with the count to Jake's apartment. She makes no distinctions among her "friends," herding unselectively with "faggots," counts, Jake and Cohn. She guzzles the count's fine champagne as though it were table wine. By going off with Cohn she seems concerned only with immediate consequences: " 'I rather thought it would be good for him' " (83). In contrast the count is a connoisseur. He appreciates Brett's beauty and "class," enjoys hearing her talk and watching her dance, and he desires her—but as an esthete, not a sensualist. He likes maximum pleasure from individual sensations, chastizing Brett's whim to drink a toast: " 'You don't want to mix emotions up with a wine like that. You lose the taste' " (59). A pure hedonist, he is never ruffled because, unlike Brett's recurring hope that she and Jake might yet be happy together, he has no romantic longings for future permanence. Being " 'always in love,' " he is ever resilient. Although, for example, he prefers to stay at a quiet restaurant to drink an after-dinner brandy—another devotee of Hemingway's clean, well-lighted places—he is not annoyed by Brett's wish to go to crowded, noisy Zelli's.[5]

When Bill Gorton enters the novel in book 2 Hemingway keeps the focus on hedonism, for he invests both kinds in Bill. Onto the self-indulgent Bill-on-a-binge of the beginning of book 2, Hemingway superimposes the discerning Bill-on-the-fishing-idyll. And Bill's bantering irony and satiric wit continually intensify his sensory pleasures.

More importantly, Hemingway "utilizes" Bill for the transition from hedonistic values to traditional ones. Unlike most of the egoistic hedonists, Bill is socially responsible. Not only does he frat-

ernize with Jake, with Jake's crowd, and with the Spanish pea-
sants on the trip to Burguete, but as his first conversation with
Jake indicates, he is also brotherly to people in need of help, like
the "noble-looking nigger" boxer in Vienna. Rather than pursue
experiences meaningful only to himself, Bill seeks shared experiences and fellow feeling, as the fishing trip with Jake indicates.
(The hazard in fellow feeling is that it can become sentimental.
The Englishman Harris, whom Jake and Bill befriend during
their fishing retreat, illustrates that hazard: " 'I say. You don't
know what it's meant to me to have you chaps up here. . . . I say.
Really you don't know how much it means. I've not had much fun
since the war. . . . I say, Barnes. You don't know what this all
means to me' " [129]. In short, Bill's behavior adumbrates the several features of Spanish traditions that await the vacationing
expatriates.

Whereas individuals determine simple hedonistic values, traditional values are collective products. Hemingway nudges us to see
that difference by echoing scenes from book 1 in book 2. He sets
the Braddocks' sarcastic drinking party and Harvey Stone's or
Jake's solitary drinking against the Burguete bus trip's communal
wine-drinking and the Pamplona wineshop camaraderie, everyone eating and drinking from the same bowl and wineskin. And
whereas hedonists' pleasures are ephemeral because they live for
one day at a time, traditionalists gain more durable pleasures because each new pleasure links to those of the past and is part of a
larger ceremony. Since A.D. 1126 the annual six-day festival of
San Fermin conforms to a predictable pattern of street dances,
religious processions, *encierros*, fireworks, boys dancing around
well-slain good bulls.[6] Hemingway nicely records the meaningful
formalization of Spanish experience in the collective response to
the death of Vincente Girones, the farmer gored during the *encierro*: "The coffin was carried to the railway-station by members
of the dancing and drinking society of Tafalla. The drums
marched ahead, and there was music on the fifes, and behind the
men who carried the coffin walked the wife and two children.
. . . Behind them marched all the members of the dancing and
drinking societies of Pamplona, Estella, Tafalla and Sanguesa"
(198). Hedonists explore and express private emotions and sensations, but traditionalists sublimate both needs either through the
religious activities of the festival, through the vicarious ceremony
of the bullfight, or through *aficion* for bullfighting. Finally,
though the hedonists are also empiricists, the rituals of piety and

pleasure acknowledge, for Spanish traditionalists, a spiritual dimension to life.[7]

The cultural differences between France and Spain have received critical analysis aplenty.[8] But in my reading they function to underscore the antithesis of hedonism and traditionalism. Friendship, for instance, is a commodity in France. Jake's concierge speaks rapturously of Brett—after Brett has tipped her well. When Jake returns to France he tips heavily to ensure future hospitality: "Everything is on such a clear financial basis in France. It is the simplest country to live in. No one makes things complicated by becoming your friend for any obscure reason. If you want people to like you, you only have to spend a little money" (233). In Spain friendship is either gratuitous or granted to the morally deserving. Soon after Jake arrives in Pamplona, a porter thoughtfully brushes the road dust from his shoulders; Jake offers no money and the porter asks for none. When the bus to Burguete stops along the way and Jake buys drinks, a serving-woman returns his tip, "thinking I had misunderstood the price" (106). Just as Jake's *aficion* earns Montoya's respect, pandering Brett to Romero loses it. Hemingway also uses the cultural differences in the national sports, bicycling and bullfighting, to emphasize antithetical values. Though the bike race is a group activity, individuals compete to win. But the bullfight requires teamwork among the toreros and is ultimately a representative ceremony, the matador reenacting every man's attempt to subdue the brute forces of nature. The Tour de France asks for strength, endurance, and scant mental attention. The bullfight demands skill, grace, concentration, and courage. The tour's competitors, riding the same direction, obviously risk little compared to the bullfight's antagonists, who meet head on, risking death.

Presented with such opposite value systems, ethic-questing Jake neither chooses between them nor synthesizes them in himself. Instead he weds the two by pandering Brett to Romero, the novel's central event, out of which come the thesis, the moral complexities, and the major ironies of the novel.

Jake's pandering is primarily significant because it begets the affair that yokes the novel's exemplars of hedonism and traditionalism, the event necessary to dramatize its thesis of "how to live." That the affair is "immoral," brief, and sparely treated is intentional: it brilliantly soft-pedals the thesis. Jake's pandering is also significant for its revelation of Romero. More than the exemplar of traditionalism or the code hero with "grace under pressure," he is also part hedonist. Desirous of sensory gratification he declares, " 'I always smoke cigars' " (185), recalling the novel's only other cigar smoker, Count Mippipopolous. Certainly Romero is aware of the behavior his fellow Spaniards expect: " 'It would be very bad, a torero who speaks English' " (186). Yet his affair with Brett shows him defying convention to mix hedonistic pleasure with his traditional role, a mixing whose importance I will argue shortly.

Jake's pandering also highlights the novel's moral complexity. His act seems simply of a piece with his friends' moral irresponsibility. But the novel disabuses us of that notion. At the beginning of chapter 16, for instance, Jake advises Montoya not to give Romero the American ambassador's invitation to evening coffee. Jake is as aware as Montoya that partying and hobnobbing with influential people will corrupt Romero's considerable talents. To further deny any thought of seeing Jake's pandering as the act of an irresponsible inebriate, Hemingway carefully records Jake's sobriety throughout the entire chapter. He is "uncomfortable" at being "so far behind" the drinking "gang" and embarrassed at Mike's vulgarities to Romero. He sees that Montoya does not nod his customary greeting when he sees Romero with Jake's friends. And Jake diverts Mike from brawling with Cohn. He also censures both Cohn's "childish, drunken heroics" and Brett's desire for Romero: " 'You oughtn't to do it' " (183). Most of all Jake is conscious of "the hard-eyed people at the bull-fighter table" who watch him leave Brett with Romero: "It was not pleasant" (187). Jake's moral awareness incriminates his pandering.

It is possible that Jake's act is an inconsistency in his character, a flaw in the novel. But that act pinpoints the novel's specific ethical dilemma. Jake's commitment to hedonism and his love for Brett tell him to help gratify her desire, to sympathize with her plea: " 'I've got to do something. I've got to do something I really want to do. I've lost my self-respect' " (183). Simultaneously his *aficion* for the bullfight tells him to be loyal to its values, to acknowledge the social obligation of keeping Romero uncontaminated for the sake of tradition. He shares Montoya's worry: " 'People take a boy like that. They don't know what he's worth. They don't know what he means. Any foreigner can flatter him. They start this Grand Hotel business, and in one year [he's] through' " (172). Jake's dilemma necessitates betraying one of the two imperatives. And his pandering, of course, betrays traditionalism.

But Hemingway exonerates Jake's act since, though strictly un-
ethical, it serves the ethical ideal of joining the novel's antithetical principles, if only symbolically. To me this seems the primary
irony of the novel.

The novel's secondary irony, which also displays its moral
complexity, is Jake's Nick Adams–like obtuseness. Like his fictional predecessor, Jake too suffers from limited vision.[9] Intelligent though he is, he fails to see or to sense that his pandering
achieves the ethical ideal he seeks. His disapproval of Brett's desire for Romero and his reluctance as go-between initially mark
his failure. His depression at the end of the fiesta also marks it, as
does his inability to discern between Brett's affairs with Cohn and
Romero: "That was it. Send a girl off with one man. Introduce her
to another to go off with him. Now go and bring her back. And
sign the wire with love. That was it all right" (239). Like the difference between Brett and Count Mippipopolous, the parallel here
asks Jake to discern the inferiority of Cohn's sterile to Romero's
virile traditionalism. But Jake neither says nor does anything to
show that he sees, much less takes joy in, the ethical synthesis of
Brett's second affair. Finally, Jake's attitude toward Brett in
Madrid confirms his obtuseness. For if he saw any value in Brett's
affair, he would treat her with greater, not less, regard.

The episode in Madrid needs extended comment because it
shows still another degree of Hemingway's craft. During the
episode Jake's conduct is as much at odds with his normal
manner as Brett's rectitude is with hers. To be sure, in the Hotel
Montana he consoles Brett, sincerely calling her " 'Dear Brett' "
(243) as she cries in his arms. Yet his compassion is short-lived.
Something about her behavior sours him. In the Palace Hotel bar
he begins to mouth moral inanities: " 'It's funny what a wonderful gentility you get in the bar of a big hotel. . . . No matter how
vulgar a hotel is, the bar is always nice. . . . Bartenders have
always been fine' " (244). And to her remark that Jake "think of"
the fact that Romero was born while she was still in school in
Paris, he sarcastically replies, " 'Anything you want me to think
about it?' " (244). Lunching with her at Botin's he gorges on "roast
young suckling pig" and drinks several bottles of *rioja alta*, a
strange burst of hedonism. Finally, his retort to Brett's notion
that they " 'could have had such a damned good time together' "
is sardonic, even malicious: " 'Isn't it pretty to think so?' "

Jake's behavior here reveals three different interpretations. It
may reveal a bitter man who resigns himself to the futility of his

ethical search, but not before he abusively takes out his frustrations on a scapegoat, Brett. This interpretation would add to the ways Hemingway mutes the novel's thesis, for Jake's behavior would deny that the novel offers any answer to his wish to find out how to live. Or Jake's behavior may reveal his acumen as a moral realist. Even though he has not yet found out how to live, his behavior would indicate that he knows a victim of self-deception when he sees one. Brett obviously regards her break with Romero as an act of self-denial: " 'You know I'd have lived with him if I hadn't seen it was bad for him' " (243). Added to her tears, to her preoccupation with the effect Romero has had upon her, and to her solicitousness that Jake not "get drunk," her behavior shows genuine moral growth. But Jake's behavior repudiates it. His dialogue conveys disgust at her moral rationalizations. And his burst of hedonism dramatizes his judgment that by sending Romero away she merely arrested her appetite before it became glutted. This interpretation also contributes to the novel's thesis by rebuking a facile synthesis of hedonism and traditionalism: a fraudulent model for the novel's ethic, Brett would justify Jake's conduct.

Finally, Jake's behavior may reveal defensiveness. Given his ethical concern and his presumed love for Brett, Jake could respect and reinforce any sign of moral development in her, as when she tells him, " 'You know it makes one feel rather good deciding not to be a bitch' " (245). But Jake expresses no approval, for he may be unwilling to accept what he recognizes: that she has acquired the self-esteem his pandering lost him, that she threatens to be his moral equal if not his superior, that she needs neither his pity nor his help. Like his sarcasm, his indulgence at Botin's would be self-protective. Both actions refuse to consider that Brett has outdistanced him in his search for discovering how to live. So his novel-ending, sardonic remark, " 'Isn't it pretty to think so?' " although true, would expose a moral pettiness and resentment that show his immaturity. This interpretation of Jake's conduct would also be appropriate to the novel's thesis. Surely it would be fine irony that ethic-questing Jake actually did not want to know how to live. Intolerant, envious, and defensive, his behavior would scorn the possibility that Brett might achieve the ethical ideal he professed to be seeking. I favor this third way of interpreting Jake's behavior, for it is consistent with his limited vision in the rest of his narrative. And it shows Jake doing at the novel's end precisely what he was doing at its beginning—bad-mouthing a friend, Hemingway's first clue that Jake was not a trustworthy narrator. This interpretation, though, can coexist with the other two—and more—thanks to Hemingway's dexterity.

Although enriching complexities account for much of the stature of *The Sun Also Rises*, they also account for the long-held misunderstanding of the universality of Hemingway's ethic. The late Delmore Schwartz best put the case against his ethic over thirty years ago. Observing Hemingway's "extraordinary interest" both in sensuousness and in conduct, Schwartz found no "clear link" between the two. And then he charged Hemingway's ethic with irrelevance: "The morality cannot be directed to other kinds of situations and other ways of life without a thoroughgoing translation. It is a morality, to repeat, for wartime, for sport, for drinking, and for expatriates; and there are, after all, a good many other levels of existence, and on those levels the activities in question fall into place and become rather minor. Consider, for example, how irrelevant the morality would be when the subject matter was family life."[10]

Schwartz's first oversight is visible by looking again at the bullfight. Its elaborate ceremony makes it seem a pure example of codified conduct. But Hemingway uses it as he does Romero, to fuse hedonism and traditionalism, to "link" sensuality and conduct. As I earlier noted, Romero's linking is outwardly visible in the separate activities of a public bullfight and a private affair. But he also links the two in the single activity of the bullfight itself. Mentally obedient to prescribed rules, the matador simultaneously must respond to and discriminate among the sensory stimuli of each moment. And though his performance serves tradition, he also does "it all for himself inside" (216). A conformist to ritual, Romero is resilient too. On the last day of the fiesta he draws by chance a bull with impaired vision: "He worked accordingly. It was not brilliant bull-fighting. It was only perfect bull-fighting" (217). Finding in the bullfight a synecdoche of life and its paradoxes, Hemingway would have us see that its total experience is individual and collective, physical and cerebral, ephemeral and permanent. A dynamic sporting event and a structured work of art, it is concerned both with senses and with conduct.

Hemingway's answer to Jake's concern with "how to live" also applies to Schwartz's charge of "irrelevance." After all, the basic "oughts" of its ethic are like the antithetical imperatives in most moral systems. It seems obvious to me that respect for traditionalism acknowledges communal values, and respect for hedonism simultaneously acknowledges personal values. Such an ethic is "irrelevant" only if we ask Hemingway to "translate" it and codify in detail how we must apply it to specific situations. Hemingway credits us with the intelligence to deduce the codes applicable to our varied situations. Be they military or political, legal or commercial, athletic or domestic, academic or civic—all experiences have their analogue in the opportunities and obligations of the bullfight. In every social situation mature and moral individuals attempt, like the matador, to balance self-effacement and self-assertion, duty and pleasure. Hemingway says, then, that to draw fullness from any experience requires weighing action against thought, spontaneity against discipline, sense against intellect, rights against rules, the past against the present and the future. Though different in degree but not in kind, the same synthesizing process confronts matador or hostess, fisherman or farmer, boxer or businessman, hunter or teacher, soldier or spouse.

Hemingway's most brilliant achievement in this novel is ultimately its paradoxical vulgarity. Etymologically speaking, it expresses sophisticated ideas in the language of, and through the experience of, common people. I refer not just to Hemingway's vernacular style, although that contributes to the novel's achievement. I refer more to his domestication of such abstract considerations as esthetics and ethics. He renders them accessible to the general public, for he implies that beauty can be found, as Count Mippipopolous finds it, in such immediate things as cigars, food, wine, and women. By urging emulation of such a connoisseur of the commonplace, Hemingway democratizes esthetics, reclaiming it from the cultured few for the ordinary many. Similarly Hemingway implies that one can find, as Romero does, a system of right conduct as well as beauty in such an event as the spectacle of a bullfight. By democratizing ethics, usually the preserve of religion and philosophy, Hemingway demonstrates that socially affirmative ethical systems can even be derived from debauchery and athletics. Though he "coarsens" esthetics and ethics, I think he does so to offer an answer to that question common to the lives of all people. Two immoral and vulgar acts, Jake's pandering and Brett and Romero's affair, paradoxically contain Hemingway's subtle answer of how to live.

Afterword

Hemingway dealt neither Jake Barnes nor Frederic Henry a pleasant fate. And I have certainly not dealt them a better one, regarding them less favorably than most Hemingway critics. They mistakenly applaud Jake, impressed by his ability to cope with his sexual impairment, by his superiority to most of his friends, and by his putdown of Lady Brett. They also mistake Frederic. But that is understandable. After all, he, too, is confused—having been christened with two first names befuddles one's self-concept. Even more, people in his story are confused about his identity. The aid-station surgeon who treats his injuries acknowledges the confusion that echoes in both the novel and criticism on it: " 'I've known him before. I always thought he was French' " (60). Any thoughtful reading of Hemingway's fiction, I think, should see how central to it is this motif of confusion, this use of confused and confusing characters. Be they old men in clean, well-lighted places or at bridges; young boys who think that temperatures are calculated only in centigrade or that lustful feelings can be voided by cutting off one's penis; men unable to deal maturely with "unreasonable" or lesbian women; immigrants perplexed by Prohibition laws; or mentally unstable young soldiers—these characters all testify to a dominant pattern in Hemingway's works. Not only does it provide the foundation for *The Sun Also Rises* and *A Farewell to Arms*, but it also reveals the major "figure in the carpet" of *Men without Women* and *Winner Take Nothing*. Indeed, "The Light of the World" is the purest example of the pattern, one that traces back to its origin in young Ernest's confusion about his confusing father.

Pattern or not, perhaps I have only assigned Jake and Frederic one more mistaken identity. But in my discussion of *Farewell* I have tried especially to respond fully to Hemingway's fictive illusion: I take Frederic exclusively at his word. For one thing, I am less confident than some readers of hearing when Frederic's voice leaves off and Hemingway's begins.[1] For another thing, by listening to Frederic's story as it emerged from his consciousness, I think I can now separate Frederic's reasons for telling his story from some speculations I want to advance for Hemingway's writing it. The question I turn to, then, is why Hemingway dealt Frederic and Jake such unpleasant fates.

Assuming that *The Sun Also Rises* defines an ethic of how to live, I assume further that in his "second" novel, *A Farewell to Arms*, Hemingway attempts to answer the question that the formulated ethic of his first novel generates: Why must he find a way to live that differs from his predecessors'? His answer, naturally enough, is that he views the world differently than they. For them it was orderly and predictable. For him it is irrational. For them institutions, beliefs, and commitments were emblematic of some cosmic orderliness and offered humans the means to attune themselves to such order. For him they are self-deceptions. Frederic's inability to find meaning in family, country, profession, religion, duty, reason, nature, and love is due to no flaw in him. The flaw is rather in the irrational nature of things.

One thing clear about *Farewell* is that Hemingway insists upon his thesis, as I earlier indicated. In *The Sun Also Rises* he seems above caring whether anyone, even Jake Barnes, realizes that Romero's yoking of hedonism and traditionalism answers the question of how to live. But in *Farewell* Hemingway stoops, albeit slightly. He does not have Frederic tell his story years after its events. That would have required making Frederic sound as though he had age, experience, knowledge, and perspective—as though he were some wise, mature Count Greffi whose pronouncement of the novel's thesis would be in order, whose whining complaints against the universe would not. Nor does Hemingway have Catherine blurt out the thesis while regaining consciousness from one of her hemorrhages.[2] But he does have Catherine die in childbirth rather than as the victim of some bizarre accident. And he has the fetus strangled in its umbilical cord. Both details force his thesis that even nature is irrational, suggesting that there must be especially compelling reasons for writing *Farewell*. Let me come at them in a roundabout way.

Thesis novels all grind an ax. Artistic or inartistic, they present arguments that emerge from authors' personal needs more than from some dispassionate wish to communicate an idea. Like fables (stories written to prove a point), they seem to differ from fictions (stories written to convey an experience) and fantasies (stories written to gratify a wish and externalize an anxiety). Thesis novels, then, like fables, seem to express relatively conscious personal needs, in contrast to fictions and fantasies, which seem to express less conscious, if not altogether unconscious, personal needs.

So what personal needs, besides Hemingway's ambition and desire for fame, do *Sun Also Rises* and *Farewell* express? They express the intellectual need to explain to both his own and the preceding generation just why he and others cast off the values handed down by those predecessors, as I noted a few paragraphs back. But I would assign an even stronger personal need. Marcelline Hemingway tells us that the Hemingway children were required to keep account books of how they spent their weekly allowance, books that father Clarence examined weekly.[3] This early habit, which Hemingway's letters and other records prove to have been a compulsive, lifelong trait, suggests that both thesis novels are variants of those account books. *The Sun Also Rises* expresses Hemingway's personal need to account to his parents for his behavioral ideal. It was wrong, he found, to repress his senses and to strap himself to a set of outdated traditions. But it was also wrong for him to abandon himself to sensual anarchy. The bullfight, he saw, integrated vital traditions and heightened sensations. Similarly, *Farewell* would account to his parents that such an ethic was made necessary by his insight and conviction that he dwelt in an irrational universe, an alien concept to them.

But thesis novels, like fables, are also defensive. They argue ideas and advocate views that benefit their moralistic authors. By dramatizing his arguments of an ethical ideal and the world's irrationality, Hemingway, that is, rationalizes his own misconduct.

Compounded as *The Sun Also Rises* is of travelogue, tauromachy, historically inspired events, thinly veiled acquaintances, and gossip, its complexity conceals many of the personal needs that writing the novel sought to gratify. Yet among the various conscious needs had to be Hemingway's wish to deal with misconduct he felt susceptible to, namely, the allure of the temptress. As Baker suggests, Lady Duff Twysden tantalized Hemingway, before, during, and after the 1925 Pamplona *feria* that inspired *The Sun Also Rises*.[4] So on the one hand, Hemingway wishes directly to abuse her for sexual profligacy and moral depravity and indirectly to abuse her prototype, Agnes von Kurowsky, who supposedly first lured and betrayed him. But on the other hand, Hemingway cannot deny that he desires her, even though he has marital obligations. He tries to assert his personal fidelity by characterizing the novel's men as sexually loyal to Lady Brett—as Jake, Count Mippi, Cohn, Campbell, and Romero all are. Yet their collective and admirable loyalty is insufficient to arrest Hemingway's sexual desires. Had it been, he would have written a less successful novel, for he would have ended the novel unambiguously. That is, he would have ended the novel by clearly betraying Brett, perhaps having her cast off Romero only after she was sexually glutted, perhaps having Jake morally censure her by refusing to respond to her telegram, perhaps having Jake maintain better self-control during the last episode in Madrid, subduing at least his immature sarcasm. Hemingway's ambiguous ending to the novel vouches for his ambivalent feelings toward Lady Duff Twysden and demonstrates the lure such a type holds for him.

Even more, Hemingway's adulterous relationship with Pauline Pfeiffer during the time he was revising *The Sun Also Rises* must have reinforced his ambivalence toward Brett and ambiguous treatment of her and Jake. For though Hemingway may have begun the novel with Lady Duff as Brett's model, by the time he was completing the novel he was in love with a women who had lured him from his marriage bed, a second model. To vilify the temptress was something he could not do without vilifying the man who succumbs to her. In effect, though Hemingway began *The Sun Also Rises* to deny his susceptibility and repudiate the wish to commit adultery, he completed it to rationalize the actual misconduct.[5]

The conspicuous misconduct that predated the writing of *Farewell* was of course the result of Hemingway's adultery, betrayal of Hadley. His divorce from her and marriage to Pauline also betrayed his family's values. It would benefit him to show his family that his conduct was consistent with the irrationalities of the world he inhabits. And by emphasizing as *Farewell* does that it is permissible to desert irrational commitments, Hemingway may have hoped to mollify his guilt for betraying Hadley.

The novel itself clarifies this point. During the retreat from Caporetto Frederic shoots at the two engineering sergeants who desert him when a vehicle gets stuck. The next day he himself deserts the Italian army, leaping into the Tagliamento River to avoid summary execution. It is usual to regard the first desertion as opprobrious and the second, though excusable, ironic in the light of the first.[6] But both acts are morally defensible. In the bridge episode Frederic is part of a massive evacuation, he is threatened harm along the road for being an officer, he sees the example of those summary executions, and he hears the fanaticism of the battle police. His leap into the river, then, repudiates the dangers and irrationalities compressed in the scene before him. By contrast the engineering sergeants have ridden along with Frederic's unit of three vehicles and have had the chance to get out when the unit leaves the main retreat column. The pair have even been forewarned that they will have to help if the vehicles get stuck, Frederic telling Bonello, in whose vehicle they are riding, " 'They'll be good to push' " (199). Since Frederic's retreat route has continually gotten them closer to Udine, nothing indicates that when Aymo's vehicle gets stuck their situation is hopeless. So when they desert Frederic's unit at the first sign of difficulty, Frederic shoots at them, not because he is obeying military regulations about how an officer must deal with insubordination, but because they are dishonoring a tacit personal commitment. Opportunists, the engineering sergeants let us see how their and Frederic's acts of desertion differ. Whereas they quickly abandon him and his men, Frederic stays with his men until either they are shot (Aymo), they desert him (Bonello), or they get lost in the crowd at the Tagliamento (Piani). And Frederic turns directly from this desertion to seek out the pregnant Catherine, faithful to his commitment to her.

Frederic's fidelity to her partly expresses and rationalizes Hemingway's need to believe that he too had been loyal to the Catherine of his actual experience, the Agnes von Kurowsky who allegedly jilted him. By portraying her as a marginal neurotic who imposes a psychological burden upon Frederic, Hemingway italicizes his own personal loyalty. But he even more directly rationalizes his conduct to Hadley. By reading Frederic's story as a veiled account of Hemingway's experience, she should understand that he too was part of the irrational fabric of the world he describes. She should also realize that irrational forces could erode a commitment to a person as well as to marriage vows, realize that, despite his self-assurance and take-charge manliness and glamour, he suffered from the feelings of inadequacy that

Frederic's noncommital blandness mirrors. She should further understand that their relationship could never be as deep as the one he wanted to think he and Agnes had. For example, declaring that he and Catherine never wished to be alone while they were with each other, Frederic says—in words perhaps aimed at Hadley's ears—"it has only happened to me once like that" (249). Finally, Hadley should understand that some of Catherine's neurotic tendencies are traced from her own. Not only had Hadley's father committed suicide when she was twelve, but her overprotective and domineering mother repressed her native impulsiveness and forced her to live a life of virtual seclusion for the last six years of Mrs. Richardson's life. Only with her mother's death in 1920 was Hadley able to emancipate herself. Gay and confident though her letters are during her courtship and engagement to Hemingway, their cheerfulness has a desperate note reminiscent of Catherine—the desperation one might expect in 1920 of a twenty-eight-year-old women dreading the prospect of spinsterhood.[7]

To venture a last step: thesis novels, like fictions and fantasies, ventilate unconscious anxieties and wishes, aggressions and guilts. The biographical circumstances during the composition of *The Sun Also Rises* were, as I have said, too unstable to assess Hemingway's unconscious drives with any certitude. But several tendencies do seem apparent. It is probable that Lady Brett evokes Hemingway's ambivalent Oedipal wishes for, and fears of, his own mother. If so, then Jake's craving for, and disgust with, a women who bestowed affection indiscriminately suggests why Jake suffers self-contempt: he is fixated upon a women he desires and detests. Stronger, I think, are Hemingway's aggressions and guilt feelings toward his father, cast as father Clarence is in Robert Cohn's old-fashioned sense of duty, honor, and obligation; and in Montoya's stern devotion to the noble traditions of bullfighting. Jake's rejection of Cohn, endorsed by Brett's own actions, would express Hemingway's hostility toward Cohn's prototype, Dr. Hemingway. But Hemingway could conceal that hostility by putting between himself and his father several mediators, ones whose competition for Lady Brett's charms would defy and deserve retaliation from the fatherlike Cohn. Insofar as Count Mippipopolous's values mock Cohn's asceticism, Bill Gorton's values mock Cohn's lack of genuine fellow feeling, Romero's values mock Cohn's romantic absolutism, and Mike Campbell's values mock Cohn's inability to be carefree—these four men become Hemingway's doubles, screens behind which he conceals both his incestuous wish and his accompanying hostility toward Dr. Hemingway.

As for the castration anxiety that always accompanies the Oedipal pattern, the novel has it too. In an act symbolic of castration, Cohn, the outraged father, beats up Romero, the taboo-violating son, in Brett's, the incestuous mother's, room. But in the same scene Romero vanquishes Cohn, just as he kills those other father surrogates, the bulls. For it is Romero's much-praised refusal to give up that drives Cohn off—an honorable analogue to parricide. More clearly, Hemingway deals with castration anxiety by making Jake sexually impaired. Declaring Jake's inability (and Hemingway's unwillingness) to penetrate the mutually sought-after woman, his impairment also denies the father the satisfaction of properly punishing the son's incestuous wishes, for Jake has already suffered the result of the punishment. The only punishment Hemingway allows Jake is the disapproval of the other outraged father, Montoya. But Montoya's unsmiling bow as he passes Jake on the stairs and his refusal to bid Jake goodbye are enough. Indeed, Jake's novel-ending depression and guilt feelings register less his grief over his irremediable physical situation and all that it entails than his grief over betraying Montoya, Hemingway's depression for betraying his father.[8]

Hemingway's feelings about Hadley's deficiencies, Pauline's treachery, Agnes's betrayal, and his mother's tyranny may account for the unconscious aggression in *Farewell*, resulting as it does in making Catherine die. But I am inclined to see his aggressions and guilt feelings more clearly directed at his father, for Hemingway's ambivalence toward him was heightened by the doctor's suicide during the time Hemingway was revising the novel. The aggressions first: not only was his father the stern moralist who inculcated into his son the antique illusions and beliefs that Hemingway has Frederic Henry reject, but Dr. Hemingway's profession had also nursed his son's illusion of invulnerability: "Well," Frederic thinks, "I knew I would not be killed. Not in this war. It did not have anything to do with me" (37). Hemingway's shelling at Fossalta shattered that illusion. And rejection by the wartime nurse, Agnes, was equally traumatic, as Marcelline remembers.[9] Both woulds could account for the hostility the novel directs against the medical profession and, thereby, Hemingway's father. After all, not only does Frederic never mention his actual father, but he also shows no filial regard for his stepfather. And in the novel Hemingway seems to find pleasure in unleashing his hostility toward those fictive replicas of his father, the ascetic house doctor in Milan and the repressive Miss Van Campen. (Though represented as a women, the dynamics of her relationship with Frederic resemble those of Dr. Hemingway's with his children.) But Hemingway manifests his hostility by having Catherine die in childbirth. Not a victim of narrow hips, she is instead a victim of the novel's unnamed, incompetent obstetrician, the ultimate fictive proxy of Hemingway's own father.

Hemingway's unconscious guilts are also present in the novel. To turn around the previous paragraph's conclusion, I think it is also evident why Hemingway insists on Catherine's death. He has her die so that he can be reconciled with his father. By indulging his incestuous wish in the novel, Hemingway would signal his unconscious that he had also betrayed his father. And to make amends to him Hemingway has Frederic show proper filial respect to another of Dr. Hemingway's stand-ins, wise old Count Greffi. More significantly, he punishes himself by depriving himself of the object who had encouraged his filial betrayal, Catherine. If that is not enough punishment, he also slays those other doubles of himself, Rinaldi and the engineering sergeant. Opportunists both, their self-seeking is incompatible with the filial respect due the father. Hence their disobedience is fittingly rewarded, Rinaldi punished with syphilis, the engineering sergeant shot down for desertion. The only double Hemingway lets survive intact is the priest, the chastened son whose passivity and obedience exemplify the behavior acceptable to a wronged father.

An abridgment of the plot of *A Farewell to Arms* would see a story of a young man's successive losses, ones that finally leave him entirely alone in a foreign country. One translation of that story would see it reflecting an Oedipal anxiety in which a vindictive father metes out a just punishment both to the women who has betrayed him—Catherine claimed that a bomb had blown him to bits—and to the son who has sought to replace him. A more basic translation of the story would see it reflecting the primary anxiety of separation. Frederic's story would be expressing Hemingway's deepest fear of being abandoned, of losing parental affection and attention, of being punished for defects he is incapable of correcting, of being deprived of his need for affiliation. Frederic and Catherine's love corroborates this anxiety since their relationship is its antithesis. They wish to retreat into mutual absorption, to be alone together, outside and above reality. That primary wish, of course, is the infantile dream of returning to a place of security and pleasure and gratification. Whether that place should be fetal or infantile—the womb or the bed of one's nursing mother—is immaterial. Hemingway evokes both images in the expanding girth of Catherine, in the beds in which the larger portion of Catherine and Frederic's relating occurs, and in that equally delusory sanctuary with its blanketing snow, Switzerland.

THE ESTHETIC PHASE

2

A Compleat Critique: *Death in the Afternoon*

Were we to search out a classic source for Hemingway's best piece of didactic exposition, *Death in the Afternoon*, we would find no more likely candidate than Izaac Walton's *The Compleat Angler*.[1] For one thing, each writer tries to change the low regard others have for his favorite pastime. Walton begins by politely disabusing a falconer and a hunter who disparage angling as "such a heavy, contemptible, dull recreation."[2] Hemingway begins by trying to disabuse bullfighting's detractors of their prejudices, particularly those who find disgusting and inhumane the harm done to picadors' horses. Walton structures his book upon a fictitious, five-day colloquy between himself, as Piscator, and Venator, a novice hunter whom Walton converts and uses as a sounding board for his monologues. Venator's latter-day counterpart? The ingenue of Hemingway's conversations, the Old Lady. Walton's exposition has no greater order than Hemingway's, marching from "observations of the Umber or Grayling, and directions how to fish for them" to subsequent "Observations and Directions" on salmon, pike, carp, bream, tench, pearch, eele, barbel, gudgion, roach, minnow, and so on. Hemingway's observations comment on no fewer than seventy-five matadors as well as on different kinds of spectators, picadors, banderillos, functionaries, breeders, hangers-on, and, of course, bulls. He too gives directions—on how to watch a bullfight and to appreciate the matadors' varying task of killing the bulls. Walton describes and evaluates "Several Rivers." For them Hemingway substitutes Spanish cities and their bullrings. Both writers thereby show their familiarity with a nation. In his closing chapters Hemingway writes of the torero's tools—cape, pic, banderilla, muleta, and sword (chaps. 15 through 19); this resembles Walton's penultimate chapter, "Directions for making of a Line and for the coloring of the rod and line."

Both writers' discourse on an outdoor pastime smells of the scholar's lamp. But both avoid pedantry, Walton by including poems on idyllic pleasures, Hemingway by including stories, anecdotes, and asides on death, decadence, and writing. With only slight alteration Hemingway could have prefaced his treatise with a paragraph from Walton's headnote, "To all Readers of this Discourse but especially to the HONEST ANGLER": "And I wish the *Reader* also to take notice, that in writing of [this discourse] I have made myself a *recreation* of a recreaton; and that it might prove so to him, and not read *dull* and *tediously*, I have in several places mixt (not any scurrility, but) some innocent, harmless mirth; of which, if thou be a severe sowre-complexion'd man, then I here disallow thee to be a competent judge: for *Divines* say, *There are offences given, and offences not given but taken*" (15). To "honest readers" who object to his digressions and interludes, Hemingway could also use Walton's self-defense: "And I am the willinger to justify the pleasant part of [my discourse] because, though it is known I can be serious at seasonable times, yet the whole Discourse is, or rather was, *a picture of my own disposition*" (15).

Walton is customarily praised for the simple humility of his disposition.[3] And he shares a friend's conviction that "you will find angling to be like the vertue of Humility" (49). Yet throughout *Angler* Walton says things better expected of Hemingway. He commends himself for "the pains I have taken to recover the lost credit of the poor despised Chub" (60). He assures Venator that "I both can and will tell you more than any common *Angler* yet knows" (58). He esteems himself as "a Master that knows as much both of the nature and breeding of fish as any man" (75). Hemingway's "disposition," especially in *Afternoon*, has been criticized for similar vauntings, even more for outrageously admitting that "killing cleanly and in a way which gives you aesthetic pleasure and pride has always been one of the greatest enjoyments of a part of the human race" (232). Surprisingly, Walton shares that pleasure. Rather than declare his pleasure only in hooking, playing, netting, and eating fish, he also readily admits, "I am not of a cruel nature, I love to kill nothing but fish" (56).

The resemblance between the two works also shows up in both writers' insistence that their pastime is complex. Hemingway went to Spain to study the bullfight, believing that its "violent death" would speed his development as a writer by helping him focus upon one of the most simple and most fundamental of all things, "violent death" (2). One page later he concludes that the bullfight was not simple, was, instead, very complicated. As the rest of *Afternoon* implies, there is even cause to question whether the bullfight's violent death excludes esthetic death. In Walton's opening chapter Venator similarly confesses his prejudice that anglers are "simple men." Walton's rejoinder defines much of the intent of his work: "If by simplicity you mean to express a general defect in those that profess and practice the excellent art of Angling, I hope in time to disabuse you, and make the contrary appear so evidently, that if you will but have patience to hear me, I shall remove all the Anticipations that discourse, or time, or prejudice have posses'd you with against the laudable and ancient art; for I know it is worthy the *knowledge* and *pratice* of a wise man" (30). Both Hemingway and Walton overwhelm a reader with the learning and lore of their respective pastimes, lead him through a labyrinth of discriminations on why, how, when, and where to appreciate best the complex activities of fishing and bullfighting.

Important though knowledge is to the angler or the aficionado, both writers subordinate it to art. The most repeated idea in *Angler*, expressed twice in the above quotation, is that "*Angling is an Art*" (13). And not, as Venator thinks, "an easie art." Piscator instructs him, for example, in the nature, breeding, kinds, and habits of trout as well as how to bait hook with worm, minnow, or artificial minnow when fishing for them. Yet Venator fails to catch one trout, even when he uses Piscator's own rod. Having caught "three brace of Trouts" during this interval, Piscator tells a brief allegory about a scholar who preached a borrowed sermon. Strongly commended when preached by its composer, "yet it was utterly disliked as it was preached by the borrower: which the sermon-borrower complained of to the lender of it, and was thus answered; I lent you indeed my *Fiddle*, but not my *Fiddlestick*; for you are to know, that every one cannot make musick with my words, which are fitted for my own mouth" (87). Hemingway similarly insists that if a bullfighter has skill, knowledge, bravery, and competence but lacks genius or inspiration; and if that bullfighter draws a brave, straight-charging, responsive, and noble bull but lacks magic wrists and an esthetic sensibility; then the result will not be sculpture but merely an undistinguished performance (13). Hemingway repeats his idea, writing that only if a matador's domination of a bull by knowledge and science is graceful will it also be beautiful to behold (21). The fundamental subject, then, for both Hemingway and Walton is the art of an angler's fishing and a matador's *suertes*, not how to catch fish and kill bulls.

Could I verify that Hemingway's work is consciously indebted to Walton's, I would still have to conclude that *Death in the Afternoon* is a critique rather than an imitation of Walton's study. Instead of discoursing on *The Contemplative Man's Recreation*, *Angler*'s subtitle, Hemingway discourses on The Active and Contemplative Man's Recreation, thereby faulting Walton's work. On stream and pond fishermen Walton rhapsodizes: "The hearts of such men by nature [are] fitted for contemplation and quietness; men of mild, and sweet, and peaceable spirits" (46). The men Hemingway writes of are of a different nature, matadors like Juan Belmonte whose "cold, passionate wolf-courage" has a "beautiful, unhealthy mystery" (212, 70); like Fortuna, who is "brave and stupid" but a "great killer of the butcher-boy type" (259); like Maera, who was "generous, humorous, proud, bitter, foul-mouthed and a great drinker" (82). But Hemingway sees in their activity a lofty subject that he contemplates to extract its esthetic and even spiritual burden, as I shall discuss shortly.

Both writers share the conviction that the art they endorse embodies a mode of conduct congruent with their view of the nature of existence. But again Hemingway's critique faults Walton. The latter believes in a providentially ordered existence and finds one of angling's basic values in its heritage. It descends, Walton claims, from Christ and the first four among His disciples—Peter, Andrew, James, and John—fisherman all (46). To emulate best the pacific virtues of a Christian life one should become an angler and learn its art, traditions, and science. And so Walton retreats to a stream, "a rest to his mind, a cheerer of his spirits, a diverter of sadnesse, a calmer of unquiet thoughts, a moderator of passions, a procurer of contentedness" (40). Hemingway faults such a retreat by buying a barrera seat at the *plaza de toros*. There he can observe at close hand the dangerous ritual that excites his mind and spirits, that guarantees sadness when it is over (4), that stirs up "unquiet thoughts," that intensifies passions, that procures stimulation. Seeing existence as dynamic and irrational, Hemingway finds one of the *corrida de toros*'s basic values in the matador's attempt to dominate esthetically the unpredictable and life-threatening energy that confronts man. To best emulate the matador's esthetic valor, Hemingway urges one to become an aficionado and to internalize the matador's conduct in one's private and public behavior.

If Hemingway wrote *Afternoon* as a twentieth-century critique of Walton's seventeenth-century discourse, he also faults its antique limitations. Though no longer the case, in Walton's time angling was an activity that only men of leisure could afford. The bullfight, in contrast, draws peasant and don, spectacle-seeker and esthete, tourist and aficionado. No isolationist activity like angling, it is a communal experience, shared vicariously to varying degrees by a public. Traditionally tied to a *feria* or religious festival, its claim to spiritual significance, however pagan, seems more tenable than Walton's claim of kinship to those "fishers of men," Jesus and four of his apostles. The angler can independently amble along, choosing his pastoral way, or find in his activity the therapy that Jake Barnes and Nick Adams of the war and postwar stories find in it. (I consciously ignore the hazardous fishing in *Old Man and the Sea* and *Islands in the Stream*; after all, Gulf Stream fishing is not "angling.") But the structure of the bullfight predetermines many of the matador's movements and demands interdependence among picador, banderillo, and matador. Walton's advocacy of withdrawing to purling streams and still ponds to practice the *"harmless* art" (41) reveals angling as a retreat from a world of conflict and the inevitable result of conflict, death. The bullfight insists upon confronting conflict, coping with hazards, fatal though they may be. Finally, Walton's assertions notwithstanding, angling requires skill, not art. Unwittingly he tells Venator, "You yet have not skill to know how to carry your hand and line, nor how to guide it to a right place: and this must be taught you (for you are to remember I told you, Angling is an Art) either by practice, or a long observation, or both" (88). Hemingway rightfully calls bullfighting a legitimate, though impermanent, art form, a performance judged by spectators: "A bullfighter can never see the work of art that he is making. He has no chance to correct it as a painter or writer has. He cannot hear it as a musician can. He can only feel it and hear the crowd's reaction to it."[4]

Although *Afternoon* may be a critique of *Angler*, Hemingway may have learned from *Angler* how a handbook can conceal a critique of one's era. Behind the 1653 publication of *Angler* was, to Walton, the senseless and evil war in which the loathsome Puritan cause triumphed. The secular monkishness of angling, Walton implies, is a way to retreat from a distasteful social and political scene. Angling is also an antidote to an era preoccupied with "businesse." And so Walton contrasts a frenzied episode of otter hunting against the sedentary peace of angling, and he pities lawyers "swallowed up with business," statesmen who must always be "preventing or contriving plots" (95), and landowners who have no "leisure to take the sweet content" (154) of their own fields. Virtually an anthology of pastoral poetry and song, *Angler* underscores Walton's critique of his era, more than two dozen poems shrewdly harking back nostalgically to an edenic Elizabethan age.

Hemingway's study is an undeclared critique of his era, too. One principal target is its attitude toward that "unescapable reality," death.

Rather than discourse upon the bullfight because he was personally obsessed with death and violence, Hemingway uses it as a momento mori, a healthy reminder of death and mortality. To this end he praises Spanish common sense, which he defines as "taking an intelligent interest in death" (266). An idiosyncratic definition, to be sure. But it challenges the term's conventional definition and the customary approval of it as "sound practical judgment." Inheritors of "Yankee ingenuity," Americans, Hemingway implies, are particularly commonsensical and adept problem-solvers, ingenious enough to "solve" the problem of death by exercising "sound practical judgment": classify it as a taboo topic. Anyone foolish or arrogant enough to violate that taboo, if Hemingway's case is symptomatic, deserves to be scoffed at or declared pathological.[5] Yet Hemingway studies that ritual death in the afternoon "to explain that spectacle both emotionally and practically" and, thereby, to write a critique of the "civilized" world's horror of death. What the twenties did to the taboo of sex Hemingway tries single-handedly to do to the taboo of death: to revolutionize our thinking about and attitudes toward it. Needless to say, he failed.

Hemingway summarizes Spanish values largely, it seems, to contrast the Spanish with the French and the English, both of whom, he maintains, live for life. Although the French respect the dead, more important to them is enjoying such things as family, security, position, and money. Likewise the English dislike considering, mentioning, seeking, or risking death except for sport, reward, or patriotism. Both the French and the English, he says, avoid death as an unsavory topic, something to moralize about but never to study (265).

These comments on Anglo-Gallic values apply also to American attitudes toward death; this is evidenced by noting the audience to whom Hemingway directs his critique. In the chapter "Some Reactions of a Few Individuals to the Integral Spanish Bull-fight," twelve of the seventeen "reactions" belong to Americans. Hemingway's remarks upon Galicia and Catalonia also show that he addresses an American audience. New Englanders should be affronted by his statement that in Galicia, a poor seaside country whose men either emigrate or take to the sea, Spaniards do not seek and meditate upon the mystery of death but avoid its daily peril, showing, thereby, their practicality, cunning, stupidity, and avariciousness (265). As well should a midwesterner feel the barb in Hemingway's analysis of the good farmers, businessmen, and salesmen of the rich country of Catalonia: life is much too practical for them to feel the "hardest kind of common sense" about death (266).

As these comments suggest, Hemingway links death and practicality to note that any culture unduly preoccupied with the latter will ignore or repress the former. Not only, of course, is America the birthplace of pragmatism, but it lacks the three Spanish traits he commends—common sense, impracticality, and, foremost, pride: "Because they have pride they do not mind killing, feeling that they are worthy to give this gift" (264).

Hemingway commends these Spanish traits to revitalize the atrophied emotions of Americans, sheltered from "an intelligent interest in death." To clarify I could do little better than cite Max Eastman, whose notorious review of *Afternoon*, despite Hemingway's reaction to it, was not, however, inspired by malice.[6] He sincerely faults Hemingway for not sharing the confession of those "poets and artists and sensitive young men" who witnessed "the insensate butchery of the World War." The confession was "that they were devastated and quite utterly shattered by that forced discipline in the art of wholesale killing[,] . . . the confession in language of blood and tears of the horror unendurable to vividly living nerves of the combination of civilized life with barbaric slaughter."[7] Eastman's attitude is characteristically American: Hemingway should regard any and all killing with horror, he should repress the many and ambivalent emotional responses that death makes acccessible, and he should, thereby, seal off an entire area of human experience. I do not rule out voyeurism in Hemingway's sustained study of bullring performances, in his having seen at least two hundred fifty bullfights before publishing *Afternoon*, each of which ends in at least six dead bulls and frequent gorings of picadors' horses and toreros.[8] But Eastman's repressively parental attitude is precisely what Hemingway addresses, for it shows atrophied emotions in need of exercise.

Hemingway knows that killing and death ignite more than a single or simple emotional response. Hunting with his father taught him early to find killing pleasurable because it conferred a feeling of power and intensified his senses. To deny that pleasure would be hypocritical, although sober Clarence Hemingway would have subdued it, shooting "for pot or sport."[9] And Hemingway's war experiences as ambulance driver, *cantinier*, and correspondent also taught him diverse emotional responses to killing and watching others being killed. For instance, one of the functions of many of the vignette interchapters in *In Our Time* is precisely to acquaint readers with such responses.[10] We may feel the *horror* Eastman asks for while reading of the retreat along the Karagatch road (chap. 2). We may also feel the sense of *shock* recorded by the narrator who tells of "potting" heavily equipped German soldiers as they climb over a garden wall at Mons (chap. 3). But Hemingway also gives us the *delight* of a British soldier who had set up an "absolutely topping" barricade for shooting Germans as they tried to cross a bridge (chap. 4), with the *fear* of a bombarded soldier in a trench (chap. 7), with the *callousness* of an Irish policeman mercilessly killing two Hungarian "wops" (chap. 8), with the *respect* an anonymous narrator has for a young matador who has to kill all six bulls during a bullfight (chap. 9), with the *ecstasy* of watching Villalta dominate and then kill, *ricibiendo*, a good bull (chap. 12), with the *dignity* of Maera's death (chap. 14), and with the *disgust* and *wonder* at Sam Cardinella's cowardice when hanged (chap. 15). To obey Eastman and respond with only horror to these vignettes betrays the reality of the situations with cruder labels than the ones my italics have assigned. As Hemingway declares at the outset of *Afternoon*, part of his difficulty as a young writer was "knowing truly what you really felt, rather than what you were supposed to feel, and had been taught to feel" (2). For him no experiences were more emotionally proscribed, no experiences more ripe for his critique, than death and killing.

In a finely sustained comparison to learning about bullfighting as an art, Hemingway notes that to appreciate wine takes an educated palate (10–12). In like fashion, it takes educated emotions to overcome a distaste for bullfights and an inclination to dismiss anything to do with death, pain, suffering, and violence. And so Hemingway's opening chapter cautions against the prejudices of humanitarians and animal lovers who feel that the goring of the horses is categorically cruel and disgusting. Hemingway shared these feelings before he saw a bullfight. But he implies that such feelings are sentimental because they are myopic and uninformed. An attitude toward horses from some earlier experience with them in one context, he says, should not preclude a different attitude towad individual horses in another context. He also points out that the parodic-looking gored horse, legs akimbo or galloping off in "a stiff old-maidish fashion," augments by incongruity the dignity of the bull, a noble animal. And the goring of the horses is a necessary, minor part of a larger, integral experience, not a gratuitous act of sadism. Since a severely gored horse feels no immediate pain, pity for its suffering is without cause. Tolerant of differences in taste, Hemingway admits that an informed spectator may still find the spectacle repugnant. He insists, however, that to reject bullfighting and so to suppress emotions that accompany its representative encounter with death should be responses based only on the criterion of taste. That subjective criterion is personally defensible. To base responses on moral grounds, in contrast, is an act of collective rationalization, disguised as objectivity and rationality.

Because Hemingway is concerned with exploring and sharing the range of emotions that bullfighting generates, he carefully discriminates between many opposing pairs: between humanitarians and "animalarians" (5–6); between the apprehension a picador and a matador feel (56–57); between bravery that is the temporary ability to ignore potential consequences and bravery that is the ability to despise potential consequences (58); between showing one's nervousness, which is not shameful, and admitting it, which is (20); between the cowardly, rule-violating Cagancho who lacks the integrity expected of a matador and the same Cagancho who is capable of doing things in a way that other bullfighters have never done before (13); between such bullfighters as Cagancho (13–14) and Hernandorena (17–20), Granero and Chaves (45–46), Belmonte and Joselito (e.g., 68–70, 161, 167), Nicanor Villalta and Niño de la Palma (85–90), and Zurito and Aguero (256–59); between Aranjuez's many streets, lined with brown-skinned girls selling strawberries and asparagus, and its street to the ring, "a dirty gauntlet between two rows of horrors. The town is Velasquez to the edge and then straight Goya to the bullring" (40); between Aranjuez and Ronda (40–43), Bilbao (38–39) and Valencia (44–46); between decadence and health (66–70); between wild and domestic (105–6), brave and cowardly (112–14), young and mature (126–29), bullfighter-bred and breeder-bred bulls (119–21); between natural and accidental *querencias* (150–53); between inflicting pain or weakening a bull and properly tiring him (189); between matadors (i.e., killers) and toreros ("highly developed, sensitive manipulators of cape and muleta") (178); between El Greco and other homosexuals (205); between killing *volapie* and *ricibiendo* (236–39); between architecture and interior decoration, characters and living people (191); between the feeling of immortality conveyed by the bullfight (213) and the godlike enjoyment of administering death (233).

That is an epic-sized catalogue, to be sure. But such discriminated comparisons, bulking so large and so fine in *Afternoon*, add to my conviction that just as, when still young, Hemingway sawed away on his cello's open strings with his right hand while he held a book to read in his left, [11] so too could he write with one hand a study of bullfighting while his other hand writes a critique of one more opposing pair: American and Spanish attitudes toward death.

Hemingway demonstrates his ability to do two things at once in the "story" he includes in *Afternoon*, his much-maligned "A Natural History of the Dead." [12] This story discomforts most readers, if not because it parodies a Christian naturalist in the essay portion, then because Hemingway joins that essay to a sketch. The sketch itself is vintage Hemingway. Its brief drama observes two men's humane concern for a dying soldier. A wounded artillery officer feels that his duty is to perform an act of euthanasia, declaring that he is a humane man (142). A doctor feels that his duty is to obey his humane oath, to care for, not to kill, a wounded man (142). Their clashing humanitarianism ironically ends in their being inhumane to each other.

Part of the value of the whole story is its union of essay and sketch, both dealing with perspectives toward dying and death. By implication Hemingway once again shows his studied disregard of narrative conventions. Here he rejects the Jamesian requirement of maintaining a single narrative perspective. The essay's parodic perspective glibly and ironically debunks Christian humanists and naturalists, presumably revealing Hemingway's perspective. But the sketch's omniscient perspective detaches Hemingway, for it objectively takes sides with neither the doctor's cynical humanism nor the officer's humanistic heroics. [13] This switch of perspectives facilitates what I think is Hemingway's point: it is stupid, when confronted with dying or dead human beings, to expect only one perspective, one feeling, one solution of how to respond humanely. The providential perspective of Mungo Park and Bishop Stanley may deserve Hemingway's narrator's mockery because it subordinates fact to faith and, thereby, evades the reality of death. And the romantic idealism of the humanists may deserve his mockery too because it sentimentally focuses on decorum, evading the indecorousness of many deaths. Yet Hemingway may mock the perspective of the mocker. The parodist's excessive contempt for men of faith and humanists, as well as his interest in sensationalizing grotesque deaths, reveals his immaturity. (A quick rereading of the opening of "A Way You'll Never Be" is enough to reassure me of Hemingway's intent to look askance at the parodist.) To these perspectives Hemingway adds, not only the doctor's and the wounded officer's but also the stretcher-bearers'. They are spooked by the breathing of a dying man who lies in the dark cave into which they have been carrying dead soldiers for two days. Their perspective is selfish. They want him moved to the area for the badly wounded, even though they know that moving him will surely kill him. Having presented these half-dozen perspectives, Hemingway dares us to choose only one as the correct one.

Hemingway refuses to give his story traditional form or conventional structure, hoping, I think, to prod readers tolerant of experiment to acknowledge the complicated feelings they truly have toward death. And the object upon whom the sketch focuses so much concern? He is a man whose head, broken like a flowerpot, was "held together by membranes and a skillfully applied bandage now soaked and hardened" (141). In this image Hemingway again nicely departs from convention. However damaged, the still pulsating head better transmits its message than the clichéd image of the bone-white skull: memento mori.

Hemingway's iceberg image, first used in this book, indicates that only one-eighth of a work's identity is readily visible. Unquestionably the identifiable tip of this iceberg, *Death in the Afternoon*, is, in Carlos Baker's felicitous phrase, a "Baedecker of the bullfight."[14] One of its not-submerged-enough eighths may be Hemingway's exhibitionism (even though I find him missing many chances to strut, mocking his own conduct in the arena and focusing carefully upon the many facets of bullfighting, not the facets of his personality).[15] Another eighth may testify to his conversion to Hispanic attitudes and values.[16] (Yet for a convert to censure so many aspects of bullfighting and to call the modern *corrida* "decadent" shows more blasphemy than worship.) Surely another eighth of the iceberg is a paean to matadors, embodying as they do prototypal Hemingway heroes.[17] (But Hemingway is highly critical of most of the matadors he writes of. The Old Lady remarks that he seems to criticize them " 'very meanly' " [171].)

Somewhere among *Afternoon*'s submerged seven-eights is Hemingway's critique of traditional spectator arts and so a case for bullfighting's preeminence as an art form.[18] Hemingway lets any who wish to save the world go on with their task (278). If he must save anything, it will perhaps be spectator arts. He will save them by pulling them from the Prado's gallery walls and setting them on the sand of Madrid's arena. He will move them from the acoustically designed and ornamented concert hall into the afternoon sun and air and sound of the plaza de toros. He will swap their plush theater seat for a plank at the bullfight ring. Pygmalion-like, he will seek to animate petrified form. Part of Hemingway's critique of traditional spectator arts, then, faults their preciousness, their artificial surrounding, their limited audiences, their effeteness.

A larger part of Hemingway's critique faults traditional spectator arts for splintering rather than integrating experience. Much of his concern in writing *Afternoon* is to write about the bullfight "*integrally*" (7), to convey its meaning as a "*whole* thing" (8), to emphasize minor aspects only in their relationship "to the *whole*" (9), to have a reader "see the *entire* spectacle" (15; my italics in these and the following quotations). Advising prospective spectators where to sit, he says that if the bullfight is not an "artistic spectacle," then "*for lack of a whole to appreciate*," a ringside seat will be best for seeing details, for learning whys and wherefores (31–32). Rather than save the world, he declares that he wants to "see it clear and as a *whole*. Then any part you make will represent the *whole* if it's made truly" (278). These remarks, particularly the synecdoche of the last one, obliquely inveigh against other art forms that, however permanent, civilized, and clean, do not represent a whole experience.

Part of the bullfight's wholeness, and so an element that in Hemingway's eyes lifts it above other art forms, is its inclusion of the arts of painting, sculpture, dance, and drama. And Hemingway superbly guides us among those coalesced arts. Sitting us down at the barrera, he analyzes a gallery of matadors, observing closely their artistic or inartistic *suertes*. He shows a scene in slow motion so that spectator-readers will not be so visually confused by the swarm of things they see that they cannot absorb them with their eyes (14). Hemingway's own eye fondles the precise image of a bull rising to anger, raising the solid-looking, wide horns of its head, swelling the hump of its neck and shoulder muscle, flaring its nostrils, and jerking the smooth points of its horns (30). Hemingway's attentiveness to the movements in the arena's *sol y sombre* also shows his appreciation of the chiaroscuro of the bullfight's choreography. And he lectures upon its theatrics to discern histrionic tricks from necessary capework, cowardly from courageous killing, spectacle from substance. As drama, the bullfight is analogous to classical tragedy, he would have us see. Its three phases constitute an entire action with a beginning, middle, and end; its majestic bull and prescribed ritual allow for the magnitude and order necessary to tragedy's beauty; its simple catastrophe is inevitable and emotionally purging. Hemingway's inclusion of photographs adds to the sense that he regards bullfighting as a whole art. Imitating its wholeness, he assembles a book complete with photographs, calendar, glossary, bibliographical note, sampler of reactions, and an estimate of America's matador from Brooklyn, Sidney Franklin.

A still larger part of Hemingway's critique of traditional spectator arts faults their Platonism. Had he been inclined to articulate his argument, it might have gone—in *Afternoon*'s style—something like this:

Now what is wrong with traditional spectator arts, I believe, is that they only imitate reality. Naturally the bullfight, like them, is artificial. It's an organized and manmade thing, not a spontaneous, natural event. Still it is real; the inevitable death of the bull and that ever-present danger which a brave bull's crescient intelligence increases and which the matador who is artist confronts, those two things make it, keep it, real. Now with the traditional spectator arts the element of death is missing, only imaginary, or attenuated (another bastard word) beyond immediate recognition; and they are without the dignity which death alone can give them. There is, after all, something which is common to all arts, as well as to life; and that something is conflict. All the arts commence in it, give expression to it, and work toward its resolution. But the conflicts may be abstract, as in music. Or they may be static, which is the case in painting and sculpture. And the conflicts in literature, and drama, and that new art, motion pictures, are imaginary; sometimes so much so that they disguise what that conflict is all about. For remember, all conflicts are just variations on the one big conflict: life against death. And this too remember: the more an art disguises that conflict, the more your awareness of the ultimate reality, death, will be diminished. Bullfighting is the one art that truly allows no escaping from reality; when you see death being given, avoided, refused and accepted six times in an afternoon for a nominal price of admission, you know that even if you have been artistically disappointed and emotionally defrauded, you are not going to have an easy time translating away your experience into some culturally elevating entertainment, into some pleasant experience that has no honest connection with your own existence. There is no pretending in the face of death. And it is that fact which makes bullfighting the only art that deals with truth.

Still another part of Hemingway's critique of traditional arts faults their overemphasis on technique. In this regard his definition of decadence as "the decay of a complete art through a magnification of certain of its aspects" (7) applies both to bullfighting and to other arts. He objects to decadent bullfighting because it emphasizes the way that various passes with cape and muleta are made, rather than the effect of those passes (66). This modern emphasis upon "manner" or technique results in some "pretty tricks" that seem "gay and lighthearted" but that "smell of the theatre" (167). Hemingway appreciates the "grace, picturesqueness and true beauty of movement" as a matador plays a big gray bull as "delicately as a spinet," but he criticizes him because the bull's horn does not brush the matador's belly, and so reduces or avoids "the dangerous classicism of the bullfight" (212). Hemingway objects, then, to "flowery work," "interior decoration," and "picturesqueness" because of his conviction that technique, even at its best, can only produce "pure spectacle" that lacks tragedy (213).

The final part of Hemingway's critique of traditional arts faults their tacit subscription to an Aquinian definition of beauty: that is beautiful the apprehension of which pleases.[19] As my next chapter argues, Hemingway modifies that definition in *Green Hills*. But here he takes direct issue with it. To accept Aquinas's definition leads, he implies, to valuing arts whose pursuit of beauty abstracts, minimizes, or attenuates reality by attending to preeminently pleasant experiences. That Hemingway scorns such experiences is clear, not only in his own fiction and the artists he values, but also in his focus here on so many "unpleasant" experiences: the "unbearable clean whiteness" of Hernandorena's thigh bone, visible through his gored-open thigh (20), vindictive, testicle-eating totemism (25), Aranjeuz's "dusty gauntlet" of horrors (40), Chaves's "big-stomached pinwheel around" a bull's horn (45), and, in compressed form, "A Natural History of the Dead" (133–44).

To accept Aquinas's definition of beauty, Hemingway again implies, also leads to valuing only the "proper" arts, those which, as Joyce's Stephen Dedalus translates, generate a static esthetic emotion, arrest the mind, and raise it above desire and loathing (Joyce, 205). To Hemingway such restrictiveness must diminish art by granting higher status to permanent arts that, frozen temporally or spatially in language or images, allow esthetic contemplation, intellectual analysis, and emotionally detached reconstruction. Aquinas's exclusion of improper art from his sanctuary of beauty implicitly asks one to accept the role of a patient spectator, awaiting but not judging "the luminous silent stasis of esthetic pleasure," "the instant wherein that supreme quality of beauty, the clear radiance of the esthetic image is apprehended luminously by the mind which has been arrested by its wholeness and fascinated by its harmony (Joyce, 213).

As Hemingway repeatedly shows, the bullfight, like a "proper" art, can be an esthetic experience. It permits contemplating a moment of beauty, say an esthetically executed veronica. And it can afford a patient, informed spectator with a complete faena that will make that spectator feel immortal, that will give him or her an ecstasy that will be "as profound as any religious ecstasy" (206).

The bullfight, though, like "improper" arts that lean toward either pornography or propaganda, also excites desire and loathing, approval and disapproval, awe and ridicule. To the extent that Hemingway is utilitarian, he rejects cerebrally static and esthetic emotions. Beauty not only should "be" but should be responded to. Those who apprehend beauty should not become rapt in a "luminous silent stasis," he implies, but should express their rapture, articulate their appreciation. In this regard, the appeal of the bullfight—and to a similar extent sporting events in general—lies, not in its display of aggressive competitiveness, decadent technique, or violent death, but in the opportunity and obligation it gives a spectator to judge the performers as artists. At a low level, of course, he may participate crudely, booing contempt or whistling approval. At a high level he carefully analyzes the antagonists' behavior and technique, functioning as Hemingway does all through *Afternoon*, as an art critic. Hemingway declares that regardless of his criticism of the state of bullfighting, he continues to attend to know the good from the bad, to appreciate new techniques without confusing his standards (162). An art experience, in short, should be like all other experiences, an occasion for active judgment, not arrested rapture.

Finally, Hemingway's critique of spectator arts commends the bullfight because it is alive. Its true beauty lies in actions, images of humans and animals in movement rather than in luminous static instants. But the matador, unlike two of his counterparts, the Olympic gymnast or the ballerina, does not offer a well-rehearsed choreographic display of varying bodily attitudes—exquisite though they may be. Instead his display is a strategy for confronting the unpredictable advances and threat of an individual bull, a strategy that he can never adequately rehearse for every exigency.[20] The crisis precipitating his movements is real then, not simulated. And each passing moment can draw from his frame sublime or ridiculous postures. But above all, for the matador the "moment of beauty" is also a "moment of truth."

Hemingway's discourse on bullfighting is partly self-serving. By writing it he vaunts the catholicity of his views and his disinclination to retreat from a dynamic and violent world. He may also hope that in his own interests and esthetic we will see his resemblance to—and so accord him the tribute he writes for—Goya, an artist who believed "in blacks and in grays, in dust and in light, in high places rising from plains, in the country around Madrid, in movement, in his own cojones, in painting, in etching, and in what he had seen, felt, touched, handled, smelled, enjoyed, drunk, mounted, suffered, spewed-up, lain with, suspected, observed, loved, hated, lusted, feared, detested, admired, loathed and destroyed" (205). But ultimately Hemingway tries sincerely to make the case for seeing the esthetics of athletics, realizing, as he must have, that his earlier fictions on the bullfight and sporting events failed to make his point cogently enough.[21] Reacting to the emotional and artistic parochialism of his day, here, then, he tries to merge his father's out-of-doors activities and his mother's thirty-by-thirty music room. And though the "Paris years" were enormously valuable to his artistic development, clearly they spoke to only one-half of it. For the other half he had to go south to Spain. Its dominant cultural event gave him the integrating experience necessary to keep his own art vital.

A Trophy Hunt: *Green Hills of Africa*

Green Hills should not be a difficult work to understand. As a "true" presentation of "a month's action"—as Hemingway's foreword declares—it ought to be little more than a travel book coupled with true adventure story, hunting manual, and slice of autobiography. And within those classifications it ought to follow their conventions. But because he ignores generic expectations, creates problems with his self-portrayal, and links beauty and killing, artists and trophy hunters, Hemingway has created a work that is difficult to understand and to appreciate.

As a travel writer Hemingway duly records former British East Africa's terrains, animals, and peoples. Occasionally he even generalizes, remarking that Mohammedanism was fashionable among the socially superior camp natives (38-39). But as a travel book *Green Hills* is unsuccessful. It provides neither useful and interesting information nor entertaining impressions, two expectations a travel book ought to fulfill. Hemingway, for instance, offers no systematic account of British East Africa's different people and customs. Nor does he include a map or a sense of the land's topography, forcing his reader to spend time in an atlas. And Hemingway's references to animals, particularly the various species of exotic antelope, further force his reader to burrow in an encyclopedia to discriminate among them. Given any such traditional expectations of a travel book, *Green Hills* is less successful than *The Sun Also Rises*. Edmund Wilson concluded correctly: *Green Hills* "tells us little about Africa."[1]

Looked at as a true adventure story the book is even less successful. The excitement that comes from danger and suspense is minimal. An adventure story that begins with a hunter sitting in a blind near a road down which a truck can—and does—come has little concern with adventure and "bold undertakings." Any adventure story that then unfolds a lengthy interview about writers and authorship shows little regard for "stirring experiences." Even the sustaining excitement of "suspense" here hinges not upon how the hunter will free himself from a threatening situation, but only upon whether he will shoot a kudu in the few days left before the safari ends. Hemingway gives more space to the fatigue than to the heroic hazards of pursuit, as caught, for example, in one sentence fragment of over one hundred words in which he registers the seeming endlessness of clambering up steep ravines and along the shoulders of mountains, of hiking across slopes and many small hills to return to camp (58). And an adventure story of big-game hunting ought to hunt "dangerous animals." Yet the animals Hemingway stalks are mostly antelope. The rhinoceros and buffalo he kills are brought down with wellplaced distant shots, eliminating their potential danger.[2] But whatever its shortcomings as a true adventure story are, I do not share another of Edmund Wilson's conclusions about *Green Hills*: "[Hemingway] has produced what must be one of the only books ever written which make Africa and its animals seem dull."[3]

As a hunting manual *Green Hills* offers still less. Hemingway's "Shootism versus Sport: The Second Tanganyika Letter" tells how to shoot a lion much better than the brief account of the lion "shot" by Pauline Hemingway, called P.O.M., in *Green Hills*.[4] Hemingway gives here none of the close analysis of, nor justifies actions as he had in, *Death in the Afternoon*. And though he names the rifles he uses to hunt big game, it is without the specifics of, say, his 1949 article, "The Great Blue River," in which he itemizes and specifies the tackle needed to fish for marlin.[5] Nor does he explain such things as why and when to use certain shells. His posthumously published *African Journal* knows no such reticence. Preparing to kill a wounded leopard that has just entered a "thick island of bush," Hemingway there remarks that "Ngui had been loading the Winchester 12-gauge pump with SSG, which is buckshot in English. We had never shot anything with SSG and I did not want any jams so I tripped the ejector and filled it with No. 8 birdshot cartridges fresh out of the box and filled my pockets with the rest of the cartridges. At close range a charge of fine shot from a full-choked shotgun is as solid as a ball and I remembered seeing the effect on a human body with the small hole blue black around the edge on the back of the leather jacket and all the load inside the chest."[6] Hemingway's penchant for the role of the ex-

pert, preeminent in *Death in the Afternoon* and crucial for someone writing a manual, is subdued in *Green Hills* by his status as
student. In the book's coda Hemingway, still the novice, gets ready
to ride off with strange natives into some new country for his last
chance to shoot kudu. When told that he might also have a chance
to shoot a sable antelope, he admits his ignorance, asking Pop, the
white hunter in charge of the safari, whether the females are
horned and hard to kill (209). Even earlier he had declared his
wish to write about what the country and the animals are like " 'to
someone who knows nothing about it' " (194).

It is perhaps as autobiography that, to many readers, *Green
Hills* is least satisfying—if not most annoying. It has few facts of
Hemingway's life. Instead are some wishes, some observations
about the United States and the Gulf Stream, and some opinions
of fellow writers and the effects good writing can achieve, the portions of the book that normally receive critical comment. Worse,
the book fails to answer the question an autobiography ought to
address: "why . . . a major writer should give so much of himself
to the killing of animals."[7] Worst, as autobiography it portrays a
character whose fulsomeness has given a chorus of critics its alli-
terative song, objecting as it does to the "belligerence," "boastfulness," "braggadocio," "bravura," and "bloating egoism" of
Hemingway-the-hunter, "the worst-invented character to be
found in the author's work," declared Edmund Wilson.[8] Wilson
actually indicted Hemingway's "monologues in well-paying and
trashy magazines," referring, of course, to the *Esquire* "letters."
But the chorus indicts Hemingway's self-characterization in
those letters, in *Death in the Afternoon*, and in *Green Hills*. To
ignore differences among those self-characterizations invites two
errors that have contributed to the misreadings of *Green Hills* and
to its assessments as "inferior," "minor," "trivial," "his least sat-
isfactory work."[9]

One error—let me call it "carryover"—brings to *Green Hills* conclusions derived from Hemingway's other work. If we hear "chip-
on-the-shoulder exhibitionism" in *Death in the Afternoon*
(1932),[10] then when we come to the *Esquire* letters we may well
misidentify their expository voices. Rather than hear a studied
attempt at anonymity in the voice of the informative report on
marlin fishing in the first letter, "Marlin off the Morro" (Autumn
1933), we may instead classify it as more exhibitionism. Instead of
hearing the nostalgic voice in the opening section of "A Paris Let-

ter" (February 1934), we may hear only the smugness in the second section's catalogue of French boxers on whom Hemingway passes judgment. Similarly unheard may go both the nostalgic voice of the Key West letter, "Remembering Shooting-Flying" (February 1935), and the sincere voice of the Gulf Stream letter, "On the Blue Water" (April 1936), Hemingway's attempt to explain the thrill and excitement of marlin fishing. If "carryover" inclines us to expect a swaggering voice in the letters to address us again in *Green Hills*, we will scarcely note or appreciate its different cadences, varying tones, unexpected attitudes, emotional shifts, self-deprecatory ironies, or vocal range. Assuming that *Green Hills* is more journalism, an extended *Esquire* letter, we are also likely to read it casually, the way we usually read that presumably unimaginative mode, nonfiction.

The other error caused by ignoring differences among Hemingway's self-characterizations is oversimplification. Ignoring the distance and difference between Hemingway-as-author and Hemingway-as-narrator-character, oversimplification reduces Hemingway to a caricature of belligerence and boastfulness. He can indeed be belligerent, but not gratuitously. His anger at M'Cola, for instance, has cause. The native tracker has neglected his duty to clean Hemingway's Springfield rifle on the penultimate eve of the hunt for kudu. And he has endangered Hemingway's life by imprudently carrying the cocked Springfield directly behind him when they stalk in high grass a wounded buffalo. Hemingway's belligerence at another native, Garrick, is also just, for the incompetent, theatrical "guide" never confesses his ignorance.

Even the belligerence in Hemingway's "interview" with Kandisky about writing and men of letters is defensible. The usually ignored dramatic context of this exchange occurs just after the explosive clankings from Kandisky's poorly maintenanced truck have ruined Hemingway's chance of shooting a kudu bull at the salt lick he has patiently—and quietly—hunted at for ten days. When Hemingway says that he would have gotten his kudu had Kandisky and his noisy truck not come along (8), Kandisky insensitively proffers no apology. He is intolerant of " 'this silliness,' " big-game hunting. An unwelcome intruder, he is impolitely inquisitive. And he makes no attempt to be diplomatic, expressing his respect only for puritanical materialism, commercial organization, and " 'the best part of life. The life of the mind' " (19). These attitudes explain to me the belligerence in Hemingway's literary declarations: they rechannel his dislike of Kandisky. Some of his un-American sentiments have a similar dramatic context. So when Pop asks him what is happening in America, Hemingway answers, " 'Damned if I know! Some sort of Y.M.C.A. show. Starry-eyed bastards spending money that somebody will have to pay' " (191). This colloquy takes place on the evening of the twelfth day of kudu hunting, a day whose frustrations have again been exacerbated by Garrick, who, having assured Hemingway that the kudu they were tracking was a huge bull, led him to an "enormous cow." As in other instances, Pop and P.O.M. sincerely engage Hemingway-as-character in dialogue to ease the tensions of hunting by giving him a chance to ventilate his emotions rather than, as props, invite him to issue arrogant ex cathedra pronouncements.

Some of the displays of Hemingway's belligerence result also from the surly competitiveness of his fellow hunter, Karl. Indeed, he is the book's figure of belligerence. Continually bitter, edgy, and paranoid, he forces Hemingway, P.O.M., and Pop to treat him indulgently. In one scene Karl is rancorous, returning empty-handed again from hunting kudu. "Very cheerfully" P.O.M. assures him that he will shoot one in the morning at the salt lick (167). Hemingway "very cheerfully" concurs, publicly overlooking that he had luckily drawn a long straw to hunt the salt lick first, but privately astonished at her presumption.

Likewise, the label of boastfulness—and its Latin cousins, braggadocio and bravura—fits the native guide Garrick, not Hemingway. Whether theatrically miming his previous bwana's prowess, strutting pompously beneath an ostrich-plumed head-dress, or self-consciously overreacting to every disappointment and achievement, Garrick nicely outflanks any vaunting that tempts Hemingway. And much of Pop's role is to puncture any hunting that would let Hemingway indulge in the "evening brag-gies." Hemingway banters with Pop about his distance shots on rhino, buffalo, and oryx and about his skill as tracker and bird shot. The banter gives levity to *Green Hills* and shows a detachment not normally granted Hemingway.

To oversimplify Hemingway as belligerent and boastful over-looks a range of feelings, attitudes, and responses in Hemingway's self-characterization. Neither belligerent nor its parodic opposite, stoical, the Hemingway of *Green Hills* is someone who has idyllic dreams. So he languorously wishes to return to Africa just to lie and watch buffalo, elephant, kudu, and sable feed on the hillsides.

But he is also a realist who knows well the dream-ruining realities —crop-eating locusts, fever-giving insects, and droughts (282–83). He is also someone responsive to the marvelous (being in "virgin country" where a warthog does not bolt at twenty yards), to unique pleasure (seeing the tall, handsome, light-hearted Masai village men run alongside his vehicle out of "quick disinterested friendliness" [218–21]), and to exhilarating laughter (the "Chaplin comedy" of himself, M'Cola, and an old native repeatedly falling down with the two kudu heads on their return in the dark to camp [236–37]). Likewise, more frequent than boasts are Hemingway's self-deflating confessions: of stubborn foolishness for firing some ten shots at a Grant's gazelle without correcting his sights (82); of premature judgment for condemning "Droopy's country," which turns out to be " 'great looking country' " (96); of remorse for gut-shooting the sable bull (281); of shame for ignoring P.O.M.'s objections to a pair of ill-fitting boots (95). He confesses his inferiority to M'Cola as a tracker (269) and his "profound personal relief to turn back" from stalking a lion with only M'Cola (141).

Most persuasively refuting the charge that Hemingway is belligerent and boastful are his responses to the horned animals he hunts, responses that suggest the identity and intent of *Green Hills*. Impressed with a rhinoceros he has just shot, Hemingway returns to camp. There he sees Karl's rhino and exclaims at "this huge, tear-eyed *marvel* of a rhino, this dead, head-severed *dream* rhino" (83–84; italics added here and in the rest of this paragraph). Oryx impress him because of their "beautiful straight-slanting black horns[,] . . . the *miracle* of their horns" (126). While hunting kudu he refuses a shot at a young bull because it no more resembles a real bull than a spike elk resembles a "big, old, thick-necked, dark-maned, *wonder-horned*, tawny-hided, beer-horse-built bugler of a bull-elk" (138). Hemingway is moved by the smaller of the two kudu he eventually kills to call its horns a "*marvel*." But then he describes the horns of the larger bull as "great dark spirals, wide-spread and *unbelievable*" (231). The smaller kudu, he reflects, became insignificant next to the "*miracle* of this kudu" (232). Yet his kudu's horns are inferior to Karl's, whose "were the biggest, widest, darkest, longest-curling, heaviest, most *unbelievable* pair of kudu horns in the world" (292).

In a writer noted for understatement, Hemingway's diction here is markedly unrestrained. No artistic lapse, the diction is integral to the esthetic orientation of *Green Hills*. Indeed, the marvel, wonder, and miracle of unbelievable horns represent but a small sample of the images of beauty with which Hemingway fills the book. He looks at trees filled by white storks that are "lovely to see" (287). He watches the passing of locusts that fill the sky and turn it to a "pink dither of flickering passage" (184). He watches, awestruck, as the sudden rising and settling of an "unbelievable cloud" of flamingoes pinks a lake's entire horizon (133). In the " 'great looking country' " of a native hunter, Hemingway stands in a canyon, shaded by smooth-trunked trees whose bases are circled by artery-like roots, whose yellow-green trunks rise to great, spreading, leafed branches. And in the sun-drenched stream bed, "reeds like papyrus grass grew thick as wheat and twelve feet tall" (96). The "wonderful country" where Hemingway gets his kudu is the "loveliest" country he has yet seen in Africa: the green, smooth, short grass and the big, high-trunked trees with turf-green undergrowth made it resemble a "deer park" (217). The larger kudu so epitomizes beauty that Hemingway must touch him to believe his reality: "big, long-legged, a smooth gray with the white stripes and the great, curling, sweeping horns, brown as walnut meats, and ivory pointed, at the big ears and the great, lovely heavy-maned neck the white chevron between his eyes and the white of his muzzle" (231). Indeed, Hemingway also notes ugly images and includes many visually disappointing scenes. So should any study in esthetics, discriminating as it ought between pleasing and displeasing perceptions. But Hemingway emphasizes the beautiful, using the word itself no fewer than twenty-one times, a rather high count for a writer whose esthetic judgments usually come in the monosyllables "clean" and "fine."

Perhaps the book's beauty is in its landscapes. After all, Hemingway tells Pop that any writing he might do about these experiences would only be "landscape painting," for until he knew more about Africa, his experiences would be more valuable to himself than to others (193). This may explain why many readers disparage the work: if the experience is meaningful only to himself, then the book is another example of romantic egotism, one that presumptuously assumes that a writer's every activity deserves his pen. But it is significant that the Austrian Kandisky knows of Hemingway only as a *dichter*, a poet. Seizing upon this, I think *Green Hills* shows that although hunting provides the literal context for Hemingway's pursuit—the term common to the book's four section titles—his broader pursuit is poetic, to render the beauty accessible to a trophy hunter. This esthetic preoccupation not only unifies his experiences and gives them artistic rather than factual shape, as his carefully rearranged chronology makes plain. But it also universalizes the meaning of trophy hunting by translating the pursuit of animals and the act of killing them into a pursuit of beautiful images and an act that arrests them so that they can be visually appreciated. Hemingway is too much an artist to engage in the historian's duty, "to write an absolutely true book."

Neither of the two books on Hemingway's knowledge and use of pictorial arts gives much notice to *Green Hills*.[11] An obvious reason is that except for P.O.M.'s comparison of the trees in one deep valley to some of the trees in André Masson's works, no other artists are mentioned. And yet the book is replete with landscapes, tableaus, portraits, close-ups, and cinematic scenes. Truly a picture book, it even includes Edward Shenton's fine "decorations." But more important than its general visual delights are the specific trophies that Hemingway pursues, those various heads with their wondrous horns, "spiralled against the sun" (5).

To better show the significance of those horned heads, I need first to distinguish briefly among eight kinds of big-game hunters. Setting aside the first two, the poacher and the bounty hunter, whose economic reasons for killing game are fundamentally alien to most hunters, the oldest kind of hunter, Paleolithic man, killed "for pot," to get the food he needed for survival.[12] Hemingway kills reedbuck and gazelle for meat, but focuses only slightly upon such hunting. The defensive hunter kills animals that destroy humans or their property. Hemingway does none of this kind of hunting in *Green Hills*, but it motivates some of the hunting in *African Journal*: the lion Miss Mary must shoot is a cattle killer and a threat to Masai villages, and the leopard Hemingway must shoot has reputedly killed some seventeen Masai goats. *Green Hills* watches the best-known kind of hunter, the sportsman, who, if he's a "good sport," finds happiness in knowing that, successful or not, his efforts have given him a chance to show that a hunter must be intelligent, skillful, and lucky. But Hemingway goes beyond being a sportsman in *Green Hills*. To some readers he is yet another kind of hunter, the self-validating hunter who finds in hunting a ritual mystique of self-definition, who kills big game either to be initiated into or to continue to prove his manhood. To validate themselves may explain what motivates the short-lived

Francis Macomber and the Miss Mary of *African Journal*: "Everyone understood why Mary must kill her lion."[13] But I find little
proof that in *Green Hills* Hemingway "can preserve his integrity
as artist-hero, he can assert his manhood, only by conquering big
beasts."[14] Even less is he the obsessive hunter for whom the violence of killing releases neurotic tendencies, as my afterword to
this phase will explain. Instead, Hemingway is that kind of hunter who keeps the heads of the animals he kills for a taxidermist to
mount. He is a trophy hunter.

Hemingway's competition with Karl for better game heads confirms that he should be classed among trophy hunters. *African
Journal* also confirms that classification: "When I had first been
in Africa we were always in a hurry to move from one place to
another to hunt beasts for trophies. . . . The time of shooting
beasts for trophies was long past for me."[15] Still, why does Hemingway want trophies?

A hunter's trophy, conventionally a memento of triumph, testifies to his past prowess, aggrandizes him. But it can also illuminate a moment of past experience. *African Journal* comments on
this function of a trophy, Hemingway remembering a buffalo
"which had a pair of horns worth keeping to recall the manner of
the small emergency Mary and I had shared."[16] And Pop, looking
at Hemingway's two kudu heads and trying to mollify Hemingway's envy of Karl's superior kudu's head, similarly tells him that
what a hunter truly gets from the hunt is the remembrance of the
way he shot his game (293). Yet Hemingway boasts a memory too
good to need trophies as memory boosters, claiming that he remembers every animal he ever shot, "exactly as he was at every
moment" (235).

Hemingway trophy hunts in *Green Hills* neither to aggrandize
himself nor to capture memories. Rather he hunts to capture objects whose evocative power transcends both self and memory,
objects whose autonomous value is their beauty. Killed and
mounted, his trophies preserve, rather than destroy, images of
beauty, pay homage to, rather than triumph over, esthetic objects.
As the Spanish philosopher Ortega y Gasset concludes, "the greatest and most moral homage we can pay to certain animals on certain occasions is to kill them with certain means and rituals."[17]

The animals Hemingway chooses to hunt for trophies verify his
esthetic intent. Were he trying to gather testimonials of his prowess and courage he would likely have elected to hunt "dangerous
game," the lion and leopard of *African Journal*. But *Green Hills*

includes only one lion hunt, P.O.M.'s, and it had been "confused and unsatisfactory" (40). Instead of hunting dangerous game—carnivores, predatory felines—Hemingway hunts horned herbivores. With superb shots he first kills rhinoceros and buffalo. But these beasts, as his descriptions indicate (79, 115), little please his eye.[18] Not so the dozen exotic antelope he hunts: kongoni, gerenuk, oryx, impala, wildebeest, gazelle, eland, kudu, sable, bushbuck, reedbuck, and waterbuck. Neither "tiny" like the rhino's nor "little" like the buffalo's, their large eyes delight him. So does their gracefulness, the shapes of their necks and muzzles, and their ears, "big, graceful . . . beautiful" on the kudu. But the essential beauty of their heads derives from their horns: the sable's "scimitar-like horns" (255) that "swept up high, then back, huge and dark, in two great curves nearly touching the middle of his back" (258); the kudu's "slow spirals that spreading made a turn, another turn, and then curved delicately in to those smooth, ivory-like points" (276); the oryx's "marvellous, long, black, straight, back-slanting horns" (156). There are also the horns of the gazelle, short, ringed, lyrate; the eland, twisting straight back on a plane with the muzzle; and the impala, outward-jutting, then inward-bending and upward-sweeping.

Appreciative of these antelope, Hemingway nevertheless criticizes some of their features. The "rocking-horse canter of the long-legged, grotesque kongoni, the heavy swinging trot into gallop of the eland" (156–57) displease him. So too does the gerenuk, "that long-necked antelope that resembles a praying mantis" (160). Even oryx would look like Masai donkeys, were it not for their "beautiful straight-slanting black horns" (126). Such demurrals emphasize, however, the visual delight Hemingway finds in the linear grace of the antelopes' horns, in contrast, say, to the branched antlers of deer, elk, and moose. His esthetic preference for a clean, orderly "purity of line" could pursue no animals better endowed to oblige him.[19] That these antelopes' horns are also not deciduous adds to their symbolic value.

To take visual delight in such horned heads and to kill the creatures bearing them are clearly two separate acts. And the latter, a destructive act, seems anathema to the former, an esthetic act. But Hemingway yokes them, thereby showing the kinship between trophy hunter and artist. For whether imposing order on space or wresting permanence from the flux of time, every artist violates reality in the creative process. This conventional paradox also explains, I think, the interdependence of the trophy hunter's violent and esthetic acts. We cannot expect him to capture exotic antelope in his mind's eye or with his Graflex camera. That is like asking a sculptor to express in words or oils his artistic vision, to limit the dimensions of his art. Neither can we marvel at the trophies a trophy hunter refrained from killing any more than we can acclaim an artist for conceiving but not producing a work of art. The patience, skill, work, luck, knowledge, imaginative anticipation, and violence required of the trophy hunter have their counterparts in the artistic process. The writer's mot juste and the trophy hunter's well-aimed bullet, for instance, try to arrest an elusive, fleeting vision. Pop's insistence that Hemingway hunt alone for kudu suggests the analogous activity of an artist practicing his craft by himself. Much of the book's "literary talk," be it Kandisky's interview, the naming of Garrick, Hemingway's reminiscences of vicariously enjoyed books, or his instructions in the art of telling literary anecdotes, nudges us to overhear a correspondence between art and trophy hunting. Indeed, early in the book Hemingway expresses his belief that the ways to hunt, paint, and write are to do so for as long as one lives and as long as there is game to hunt or colors and canvas to paint on, and pencils, paper, ink, or machines to write with—and subjects that one cares to write about (12).

Equating trophy hunters and artists seems to catch Hemingway, once again, overvaluing athletes and sportsmen. One way to deflate his clichéd attitude has been to describe his hunting in *Green Hills* as a "slaughter of a wide variety of animal life."[20] A better tactic has been to fault Hemingway's taste—without defining the terms of one's argument: "The defect [of *Green Hills*] lies in [Hemingway's] values and tastes, which are displayed to their worst advantage."[21] Both tactics raise esthetic objections that only Leo Gurko has articulated. After citing other "unpleasantnesses" in *Green Hills*, he quarrels with Hemingway's admiration of the kudu bull and with his "rhapsodic tribute: 'He smelled sweet and lovely like the breath of cattle and the odor of thyme after rain.' There is something revolting about a *slayer* glorifying the dead body of his deliberately selected *victim*. This is a lapse not so much of morality as of taste. To hunt is one thing. To deliver aesthetic funeral sermons over the *corpse* is quite another."[22] Overlooking Gurko's humanization of the scene with terms that distort it to insinuate homicide, I think he expresses the conventional notion that a proper concern with beauty should find death and esthetics immiscible. As Hemingway did in *Death in the Afternoon*, in *Green Hills* he again tries to disabuse that acquired, genteel habit of mind that would resrict the topics beauty may come under. He characterizes that habit in Kandisky, who regards hunting as a "silliness," who will label as art only that which either hangs from the walls of such places as Madrid's Prado or gets printed in such literary periodicals as *Querschnitt*. To Hemingway the kudu's head, when mounted, will also hang from a wall and, as a prospective object d'art, deserves a "rhapsodic tribute." "Lapse of taste" would be a just charge, I think, had Hemingway exulted in the triumph over the kudu as a foe, or expressed remorse for taking the life of the noble beast, or stoically accepted its death as a matter only to be factually recorded.

The trophy hunter shares with the athlete, the bullfighter, and the sportsman Hemingway's regard for performing artists. But his trophies can acquire the additional value of becoming an art object. That is certainly the status of Hemingway's exotically beautiful antelope. Like the enabling act of violence that freezes their beauty, these trophies possess lineaments whose doubleness suggests paradoxical qualities. To mobile, expressive faces are fixed pairs of rigid horns, a coupling that evokes such antitheses as tenderness and danger, natural grace and geometric abstractness, the known and the fantastic. Particularly evocative is the head of the long-sought-after kudu. The gyrelike lift of high, wide-spiraling horns from its slender, bovine forehead conjures the mythic counterpart that filled men's imaginations for centuries—the unicorn. And the virgin country, whose green hills harbor the kudu that Hemingway finally finds, may allude to that mythic beast's chaste garden. To Hemingway the kudu's head may even offer the rare occasion to be "arrested by its wholeness and fascinated by its harmony," to achieve what Joyce, "a great writer in our time" (71), has Stephen Dedalus regard as "the luminous silent stasis of esthetic pleasure."[23]

Afterword

Death in the Afternoon may well challenge conventional esthetic ideas by asking how well they address a performing art whose stage is a sandy arena where blood spills. And *Green Hills of Africa* may also challenge such ideas by claiming space on gallery walls for the art objects a hunter's rifle creates. Nevertheless, both books are about killing. That alone ought to suggest that Hemingway is preoccupied not with esthetics but with violence and death, topics that are a symptom of his "pathological state of mind," evidence that "Hemingway can no longer manage his neurotic impulses."[1] Yet do critics' aspersions of both books reflect Hemingway's or their own neurotic tendencies?[2]

An interest in death and violence is not necessarily a symptom of neurosis. After all, it extends from an interest in aggression, a drive in all people. We may, of course, prefer that Hemingway either suppress his interest in aggressive drives or displace it by writing of some more socially approved substitutes than death and violence. His apparent refusal to sublimate his interest threatens some critics who, like many people, dislike him for stirring up their deeper anxieties. When so threatened, they react predictably. Repression causes them to distort or falsify the particulars of Hemingway's narrative so that they can deny its threat and their anxiety. Reaction formation causes them to censure harshly his interest in, and treatment of, death and killing so that they can conceal its secret allure for themselves. And projection causes them to allege excess aggression in him so that they can ignore it in themselves. Those defense mechanisms, I think, have contributed to critics' failure to see that whether writing of peoples' collective and vicarious involvement at the bullring or of their individual and participatory involvement in hunting, Hemingway sublimates these aggressive activities by treating them esthetically. I doubt that a neurotic would treat them so.

Were Hemingway pathologically obsessed with death and killing, *Green Hills* should demonstrate that he attends exclusively to them. Perhaps the tally of no fewer than forty-one slain animals, not to mention the countless waterfowl, does. Yet he gives less space to killing and death than to pursuing and life. And he includes various aggressive acts, nudging us to see resemblances between matters venatic and matters domestic, occupational, even academic. Competing with Karl for better trophies translates easily as an aggressive act common in every family. And Hemingway's anger at M'Cola's failure to oil the barrel of his Springfield and irritation at Garrick's histrionics have their analogue in our being vexed at a spouse's neglect or at an associate's grandstanding. Even Hemingway's pleasure in a well-placed distance shot that hits its target has an aggressive parallel in a well-fired verbal volley, an epigrammatical riposte.

Critics who "respect life," however, regard as outrageous Hemingway's deliberate killing of noble animals. And they find further proof of his "sickness" in his admission that as long as he killed cleanly he felt no guilt for interfering in such a minute way with the nocturnal and seasonal killing of animals that goes on daily (272). Rationalization, to be sure. But so is the assumption that the hands of those who find killing morally repugnant are immaculate. For although Hemingway manifests some of his aggressive drives by killing animals, nonhunters merely displace or sublimate theirs at the bridge table or on the tennis court, in the office or bedroom or stadium or shop or classroom. Hemingway's psychic health, then, is partly demonstrable in that he acknowledges his aggressions rather than conceals their destructive impulses.

Perhaps the remarks of someone who has thought deeply on the nature of hunting can also put into perspective Hemingway's behavior:

> . . . Hunting is counterposed to all the morphology of death as something without equal, since it is the only normal case in which the killing of one creature constitutes the delight of another. This raises to the last paroxysm the difficulties of its ethics. . . . I have indicated that a sport is the effort which is carried out for the pleasure that it gives in itself and not for the transitory result that the effort brings forth. It follows that when an activity becomes a sport, whatever that activity may be, the hierarchy of its values becomes inverted. In utilitarian hunting the true purpose of the hunter, what he seeks and values, is the

death of the animal. Everything else that he does before that is merely a means for achieving that end, which is its formal purpose. But in hunting as a sport this order of means to end is reversed. To the sportsman the death of the game is not what interests him; that is not his purpose. What interests him is everything that he had to do to achieve that death—that is, the hunt. Therefore what was before only a means to an end is now an end in itself. Death is essential because without it there is not authentic hunting; the killing of the animal is the natural end of the hunt and that goal of hunting itself, *not* of the hunter. The hunter seeks this death because it is not less than the sign of reality for the whole hunting process. To sum up, one does not hunt in order to kill; on the contrary, one kills in order to have hunted.[3]

As we should expect to find, Hemingway's two books provide the most persuasive refutation to the charge that he exhibits a "pathological state of mind" and "can no longer manage his neurotic impulses." Consider one criterion of authorial control, structure. The manual-like sequence of *Afternoon* testifies to a coherent structure. And even a crude viewer of *Green Hills* must concede that in Horatian terms it begins well, "in the midst of things." In Aristotelean terms its clear beginning, middle, and end also show that it is "an imitation of an action that is complete and entire." Other critics commend *Green Hills* for more sophisticated structural excellences: for Hemingway's craft in unifying the book "by inculcating a journey or quest design" and in manipulating the time scheme so as to "add a level of suspense and density not intrinsic to the material itself "; for his "careful planning" of "contrasting emotional atmospheres" that leads both to the "crown of the book," the killing of the kudu, and to the "structural anticlimax" of pursuing the gut-shot bull sable; and for his sustained focus on diminishing competitive and magnifying fraternal feelings.[4] These interpretations of coherence, both in the materials and in the shape given them, show that Hemingway "manages" his impulses.

If Hemingway's mind were in a "pathological state," the narrative of *Green Hills* should also offer proof. Its narrator should be blind to an imbalance or pattern of aberrations caused by his lack of detachment. Or his preoccupation with violence should reveal abnormality, perhaps some erotic leers or obsessively minute recordings of the last spasms of just-slain animals. I have already tried to discount the charge of "mental imbalance" in my earlier discussion of Hemingway's alleged belligerence and boastfulness. So here I look at the second charge. Watch how Hemingway repeats the word *feel* in the following quotation. I think the repetition and all of the tactile words show that he is more concerned with having readers vicariously share a tactile experience than that he is indulging an abnormal preoccupation with violence. Hunting with Droopy, a native tracker, Hemingway has brought down a reedbuck with a shot he thinks has killed it, only to find that its heart beats strongly when they reach the animal. Lacking a skinning knife, Hemingway has to use his penknife to kill it:

> I *felt* for the heart behind the foreleg with my fingers and *feeling* it *beating* under the hide *slipped* the knife in but it was short and *pushed* the heart away. I could *feel* it, *hot* and *rubbery* against my fingers, and *feel* the knife *push* it, but I *felt* around and *cut* the big artery and the blood came *hot* against my fingers. Once bled, I started *to open* him, with the little knife, still showing off to Droopy, and *emptying* him neatly *took out* the liver, *cut away* the gall, and *laying* the liver on a hummock of grass, *put* the kidneys beside it. [53–54; italics added]

Not only is this the one time in *Green Hills* that a bullet does not administer a necessary coup de grace, but I see little here that is pathological or even nauseating. Hemingway admits that he is "still showing off to Droopy." But this does not entirely explain his not killing the reedbuck with a rifle shot and his extracting the internal organs. What does explain his behavior is the context. Just before this episode he has told of his difficulties in gaining the trust of his other tracker, M'Cola. Seen in this context, then, Hemingway is also trying to earn Droopy's respect as a hunter, showing Droopy that he knows precisely where to stick the reedbuck and how important it is to remove internal organs. As he does in all the killings in the book, Hemingway also minimizes the gore. From "the blood came hot against my fingers" he omits the details of bleeding out the reedbuck. Tastefully he shifts to several minutes later: "Once bled, I started . . ."

Hemingway's pathological abnormality should also surface when he finally kills his kudu. Yet rather than gloat over the death of the noble beast, he walks away from the skinning-out, thinking that he could better remember his first sighting of the bull (235). But he quickly rejects such delicacy, not because it tarnishes a he-man image, much less because the skinning-out is voyeuristically alluring. Instead he returns to watch M'Cola skin it because that act is integral to the reality of the kudu's beauty, asserting that not watching the skinning out was laziness, like stacking "dishes in the sink until morning" (236). Holding the flashlight while M'Cola skins the second bull, Hemingway enjoys "his fast, clean, delicate scalpeling with the knife" and records the several steps that are necessary for M'Cola to do before the kudu's cape hangs "heavy and wet in the light of the electric torch that shone on his red hands and on the dirty khaki of his tunic" (236). Rather than a gruesome, unnecessarily detailed scene, Hemingway's summary omits grisly specifics and even mention of blood, noting only M'Cola's "red hands." Also, this account is necessary since it climaxes many days' patience, frustration, and hope. Its deletion would imply that only killing the animal was important. And its value as the only skinning-out scene of any length in *Green Hills* comes through the audible rhythms of the entire 230-word sentence. Finally, the scene acknowledges M'Cola's "scalpeling," done swiftly, cleanly, and delicately, the trademarks in Hemingway's work of an action deserving esthetic status. (To better appreciate Hemingway's restraint in this scene, compare it with that work of high chivalric art, *Sir Gawain and the Green Knight*. Its three splendidly gruesome, fully itemized skinning-out scenes of deer, boar, and fox are as necessary to that poem as the above scene is to *Green Hills*.)

There is still the matter of Hemingway's "perverse" delight in watching hyenas' various death agonies, his "foul jokes of mortality."[5] Anyone who looks closely at the three paragraphs on shooting hyenas will find that Hemingway is not a participant in the hilarity. He gives several pictures of hyenas shot in different places. But he does not usually identify who finds them "highly humorous," "mirth-provoking," and "jolly." Or when he does, he specifies that it is M'Cola who finds them funny, that the intestine-devouring hyena was the joke to make M'Cola flutter his hands about his face, turn away, shake his head, and laugh (37). The paragraphs on the hyenas, in short, describe M'Cola's sense of the comic, not Hemingway's. To M'Cola a dirty joke is the hyena, a clean joke is bird shooting and Hemingway's whiskey, and any religion was a joke (38). I do not discount the likelihood that in Hemingway's mind hyenas have their eponymous counterparts, probably critics. But the paragraphs contrast Kandisky's conventional notion of "studying the natives"—learning their songs and dances—and Hemingway's intimate study and report of one native's sense of humor.

To turn back briefly to *Death in the Afternoon*, I find even less evidence to buttress the notion that Hemingway exploits bullfighting to indulge a personal fixation with violent death. Were he a sadist rather than an aficionado, we would see him at *novilladas*, the amateur bullfights where one goes to see tossings and gorings, not to see bulls dominated (17). Or else we would notice that he spends a good share of his time at, or annually attends, the *ferias* of Bilbao instead of Pamplona. Bilbao is the town that terrorizes bullfighters: when Bilbaoans like a bullfighter, they continue to buy bigger and still bigger bulls to pit against him so that eventually he will have either a moral or a physical disaster. That will then justify Bilbaoans' scorn for matadors as the cowards and fakes that big bulls will prove them to be (38). Or again, we would see Hemingway participating in *capeas*, town-square bullfights whose used bulls provide a spectator simply with "great excitement" (23). But they too have little appeal for Hemingway, as he records in an eighty-word sentence, adding that such amateur killing makes for a barbaric mess that has little in common with "the ritual of the formal bullfight" (24).

Were Hemingway obsessed with the violence of bullfighting, I do not think he would devote so much time to so many different kinds of nonviolent details: the pedestrian details of a glossary of terms, a calendar of bullfights, and advice on where to sit and how to buy tickets; the technical details explaining the use of cape, muleta, pic, and banderilla; the esthetic details of beautifully executed *suertes*; the comparative details required by the numerous cameos of matadors; and the catalogued details of his last chapter. A catalogue that Walt Whitman would envy, that chapter is a tribute to Spain's plenitude, a country whose many experiences resist Hemingway's attempts to organize or repress them.[6]

Perhaps Hemingway's idiosyncratic analysis of the Spanish people—singling out for praise their pride, common sense, and impracticality—betrays some neurotic impulse. After all, it is curious that all three traits derive from Spanish appreciation of death: their pride enables them to not mind killing, to feel themselves "worthy to give this gift." Likewise, their common sense enables them to take an interest in, not to avoid thoughts of, death (264). And their impracticality, concludes Hemingway, enables them to respect death as a "mystery to be sought and meditated on" (265).

Biographical determinants suggest private, perhaps unconscious, but not neurotic reasons Hemingway values those three Spanish traits. The household he was raised in did not encourage him to develop a strong or secure sense of pride. If anything, pride in himself was at least triply subdued, raised as he was under the shadow of three successful "fathers": grandfather Ernest Hall, granduncle Tyley Hancock, and Dr. Hemingway. Respectively men of wealth, adventure, and medicine, their competencies, coupled with Mrs. Hemingway's renowned operatic talent, formed a constellation that would make any child feel the inadequacy of his own orbit. We may think that Hemingway's pride had been nurtured, particularly since he was the only male child in the Hemingway house for fifteen years. But both parents were devoted to professions of serving or teaching others besides their own children And they were almost the opposites that D. H. Lawrence's parents were. I cannot exaggerate their actual oppositeness any more than Hemingway does, as his fiction, especially "Now I Lay Me" and "The Doctor and the Doctor's Wife," shows. From such contrasting types a child would have a hard time getting the unified parental approval needed to develop a secure sense of pride that would begin to compare to the pride Hemingway attributes to the Spanish. Indeed, had his pride been properly nurtured, then neither his insecurity and diffidence (masked as both are by defensiveness) nor his pugnacious (because compensatory) competitiveness nor his compulsiveness would have been so marked.

Biographical factors may also explain Hemingway's reason for valuing Spaniards' common sense. The trauma Hemingway suffered from that Fossalta shelling, his subsequent insomnia, and his alleged obsessions with death and violence might have been less severe had he not grown up in a country whose religious traditions and cultural taboos fed the illusion of personal immortality, a country that scorned familiarity with death, with seeing "it being given, avoided, refused and accepted in the afternoon for a nominal price of admission" (266). Surely Hemingway's boyhood hunting and fishing experiences acquainted him with death. Yet his father hunted only small game or fowl, caught only small fish. And so Hemingway's early familiarity with death was relatively sheltered, for nothing seriously threatened his own life. As the son of a hunter-doctor Hemingway must have indulged in the childhood illusion that his own life was doubly protected. If his father's marksmanship could not protect him from threatening situations, then his father's medicinal or surgical skills could deal with them. Perhaps reaction to that precise fantasy partly motivated Hemingway to write of Nick Adam's first encounter with death in "Indian Camp," for the story mocks Nick's naive confidence when he and his father return to their camp: "He felt quite sure that he would never die" (*Stories*, 95). Little in Hemingway's background encouraged him to think of "morbid" ideas or to develop a common sense that could take "an intelligent interest in death." Dr. Hemingway's interests as a naturalist, his postdoctoral work in obstetrics when Hemingway was nine, and his later appointment as head of obstetrics at Oak Park Hospital emphasize that his children were raised with "an intelligent interest" in life, not death.

Hemingway appreciates Spanish impracticality in reaction to the domestic environment that nurtured him. His parents led busy lives. When not giving voice lessons or practicing medicine, they were charitably training church choirs or serving the needs of others, suggesting that impracticality had little value in the Hemingway household. Marcelline Hemingway poignantly records the severity of Dr. Hemingway's work ethic, recalling his habitual reaction to finding his children reading or idly daydreaming: " 'Haven't you children got anything to do? Haven't you any studying or mending?' "[7] Surely many things contributed to Hemingway's becoming a writer. But would he have pursued his profession had Dr. Hemingway been tolerant of his children's indolence? After all, Hemingway's impractical career partly reacts against his father's insistence upon being pragmatic, doing something useful.[8]

His reaction against his father puts Hemingway on terrain where psychoanalytic critics find him most vulnerable. For them his aggressive drives clearly indicate that his fascination with the bullfight and with big-game hunting expresses his latent urge to slay his father.[9] To them such Oedipal hostilities illuminate his neurosis, his "pathological state of mind." I agree that dangerous animals figure in our minds as father surrogates. And not only do they appear as the frightening beasts that visit a child's dreams, but they are also Little Red Riding Hood's wolf and Odysseus's Cyclops, Polyphemous; that beastly troublemaker Grendel, whom Beowulf dispatches by wrenching off its "arm," and the leering little gnome squatting atop the swooning woman-in-white in Fuseli's painting "The Nightmare." This equation makes it easy to interpret bullfighting and big-game hunting as thinly disguised parricidal acts.

I agree too that parricide plays a leading role in both *Afternoon* and *Green Hills*. In the former, for instance, by devoting so much time and energy to studying and writing about the bullfight, Hemingway shows hostility against the "fathers" of Western civilization who fastidiously coached their sons to disparage the vital, rich, and healthy experience of the bullfight.[10] Hemingway's attitudes toward art and death also assault his culture's paternally approved values. But his parricidal impulse is most easily seen in the displaced Oedipal drama of the bullfight itself. The matador-as-son—youthful, gorgeously arrayed, accompanied and encouraged by his brothers—dominates and slays the bull-as-father to receive the enamored approval of the spectator-as-mother.[11] In *Green Hills* the impulse is equally transparent, since Hemingway hunts male animals whose protruding horns are phallic. And he is openly hostile to those proxies of the father's different roles: the angry, competitive Karl; the intellectually condescending, insensitive, and intolerant Kandisky; even the ignorant, pompous Garrick. Offset though they are by the benevolent, passive Pop, Hemingway is unconsciously hostile even to him. For though Hemingway assigns Pop the status of big-game guide, he dramatizes him as the stay-at-home, ineffectual, grandfather type; from him the active son easily wrests Poor Old Mama.

Several things show that Hemingway's parricidal tendencies are not abnormal. Since the Oedipal complex means that parricidal wishes are universal, then they will get expressed in various forms of aggression. But the aggression will rarely be pure. An erotic wish may accompany it, as in the son's incestuous desire to "rescue" the mother whose well-being the father endangers or, in a homoerotic version, the son's desire to "struggle" with his male opponent. As in any violent act, then, parricide will complexly mingle love and hate, demonstrating the ambivalence in all strong behaviors.

This ambivalence partly explains and shows the normality of Hemingway's attitudes toward matadors in *Afternoon*. He commends those who are genuine valor artists, who exhibit esthetically that ethic of "grace under pressure."[12] Besides representing an ego ideal of his own deeper fantasies, a wishful double of himself, from one angle they act out his normal parricidal wish in a sublime way by killing those bull-fathers. Yet *Afternoon* apotheosizes no matador. Take Maera, the Manuel of "The Undefeated." Often touted as the archetypal Hemingway hero, he does not get Hemingway's imprimatur in either the story or *Afternoon*. He is courageous and persevering while trying to kill the bull " 'made out of cement.' " But Maera's performance is no esthetic treat: *pundonor* without grace is cuisine without wine. Besides, Maera usually had wrist trouble (80). Hemingway professes to regard highly another matador, Gallo. But he undercuts him, too: he would refuse to kill a bull if the bull gave him a certain look (157), for when looked at that way, Gallo will leap the barrera and refuse to fight. Hemingway even looks askance at the great Belmonte—a practitioner of "the decadent, impossible, the almost depraved style" (69). He even finds a grave fault in the matador who receives his highest marks, Joselito: he did everything so easily that he could not convey the emotion that the physically inferior Belmonte always managed to convey (212). Hemingway discusses these and other individual matadors to imply that modern matadors, the "sons," are no match for their predecessors, their "fathers," the matadors of old, who "had served a real apprenticeship, knew bullfighting, performed as skillfully as their ability and courage permitted with cape, muleta, banderilla, and they killed the bulls." Modern matadors are specialists, "good with the cape and useless at anything else" (85).

Since matadors can be seen as Hemingway's doubles, then his criticism of them must be self-criticism. To interpret the matador-bull relationship this way suggests that a good share of Hemingway's latent sympathies are with the bull. From this angle, then, his wish is not parricidal but affiliative, to ally himself with the bull-father whom the matadors symbolically try to slay. Indeed, still another reading of the matador-bull-spectator relationship supports this view. When looked at as symbolic of the sexual act, with the matador as an exquisitely frocked woman who lethally flirts with the bull-as-male, three conclusions suggest Hemingway's unconscious wish to ally himself with his father. First, if the bull is father, then the spectator is son, privy to a scene that symbolically shows the encounter in the arena to be, at the very least, castrative. And though Hemingway would be unable to believe that his father had ever been an awesomely aggressive "bull," unconsciously he would sense that Clarence's submissiveness to Grace resulted from her castration of him. Since the bullfight would then represent the violent encounter of sexual mating, Hemingway would also unconsciously feel grateful for his father's willing participation in that encounter: that noble sacrifice had begotten Hemingway. Second, if the bull is son, then the spectator is father, witness not only to the incestuous implications of the son's actions but also to his sacrifice. Hemingway's unconscious wish for alliance with his father would be evident in the bull-as-son's confrontation with, and acceptance of, death at the hands of the matador-as-mother. Here Hemingway would unconsciously identify with the bull-as-son's ability and intent to preserve his father by slaking his mother's aggressive thirst. Third, whether the bull be father or son, Hemingway's criticism of matadors-as-women would conceal his wish to curry approval from the real object of his affection, his father.

There is, of course, yet another way to interpret the dynamics of the richly ambiguous bullfight. Besides the earliest formulation I cited—which sees matador-as-son, bull-as-father, and spectator-as-desired-woman or -mother—and the formulation I have just discussed—which sees matador-as-mother and either bull-as-father, and spectator-as-son or vice versa—we can also formulate the bull-as-mother. To so equate the bull as mother still confirms Hemingway's unconscious wish for alliance with his father. For matador and spectator share antagonism, however sublimated, for the bull. Grace Hemingway's size and domination in the Hemingway household could surely trigger Hemingway's unconscious to make that equation, as could, for that matter, his marriage to an aggressive woman who "unrelentingly" (*Feast*, 209) stalked him—Pauline Pfeiffer.

Hemingway's attitude toward the antelope in *Green Hills* should modify the tidy conclusion that his hunting big game expresses only parricidal aggression. For one thing he shows no "Oedipal fury,"[13] no Ahab-like rancor or obsessive enmity toward any antelope he kills. For another, he does not treat those antelope-as-fathers as objects to slay and either eat, extract profit from, or cast aside to rot. Nor does he present them as the animals that besiege his fictional Francis Macomber, vicious beasts that, as they rush angrily at him from dense undergrowth, he must annihilate to prove his manhood. Exotic rather than threatening, Hemingway's surrogate fathers poeticize rather than melodramatize his parricidal wish. And by memorializing in trophies and prose the beauty of those bull antelope, Hemingway expresses filial guilt, thereby compensating for having acted out parricidal wishes.

If *Green Hills* truly revealed Hemingway's "pathological state of mind," the book would manifest some singular obsession like parricide. Yet other latent wishes overlap parricide. Consider the striking femininity of those hooved herbivores. Their large eyes, deer-shaped faces, and graceful movements link better to female than to male traits. Hunting such bovine creatures suggests matricidal tendencies, a suggestion that Hemingway's commonly known attitude toward his mother supports. And the value Hemingway places on his Springfield rifle—its "sweet clean pull . . . with the smooth, unhesitant release at the end" (101)— invites, of course, the view that it is phallic. That correspondence between the pleasures of shooting and ejaculating expresses as strong an erotic as a parricidal wish in any killing he does. And Hemingway's descriptions of numerous landscapes call for the standard identification in dream interpretation of landscapes and female anatomy. The safari's movements into increasingly "new country" buttresses that identification of land and body contours: the "grassy hills" (48) where Hemingway and Droopy first hunt rhino, the "steep grassy ridges" (75) of the "new country" where Hemingway shoots a buffalo, the lake Manyara terrain where each shot at game birds pinks the entire horizon of the lake with the sudden rising and languid settling (133) of flamingoes, the "new miraculous country" where Hemingway hunts kudu at the salt lick, and the "deer park," "virgin country" (218) where he shoots kudu and sable. By carefully recording the sequence of terrains he and his Springfield move into, Hemingway reveals a wish for sexual penetration that is at least as pronounced as his parricidal wish. Even the association between "green hills" and the fertile Mounts of Venus adds to his erotic wish.

As with most hunts, aspects of this one suggest homoerotic impulses that vouch for another unconscious wish, Hemingway's wish for his father's approval. Hemingway enjoys, for instance, the male camaraderie of not only Pop, M'Cola, and Droopy, but also of his competitor, Karl. And late in the book he withdraws from the domestic society of Pop and P.O.M., the parental pair, to find the ecstatic feeling of brotherhood the book climaxes with. He enjoys the friendliness shown by the Masai village men who race alongside his car. And he exults in the unusual thumb-shaking ritual accorded him after he shoots the kudu, Pop telling him that it is like an act of " 'blood brotherhood' " (293).

The crown of affiliative feelings, however, occurs during the sable hunt, showing that these feelings speak to Hemingway's wish for father-son accord. That is, old M'Cola's loyalty to Hemingway through the rigors and disappointments of tracking the gut-shot sable demonstrates that Hemingway has finally earned the approval of the father who has withheld it. Hemingway had acknowledged early that M'Cola was initially indifferent toward him (40). And when they pursued the wounded buffalo, it was out of disregard for Hemingway that M'Cola carried his Springfield cocked, endangering Hemingway's life. When they stalked the lion, M'Cola deeply disapproved of the adventure and expressed relief when Hemingway gave it up. M'Cola began to approve of Hemingway when Hemingway shot fowl and hyenas to delight M'Cola and when he showed the patience and persistence of a good hunter while hunting the kudu. M'Cola's failure to oil the

Springfield on the penultimate eve of the hunt for kudu, though, expressed refusal to sponsor him. Only after Hemingway shot the pair of kudu does M'Cola confer his approval, borne out in his unflagging efforts to track the bull sable with Hemingway the next day. M'Cola's paternal benediction is seconded by the devotion of the nameless old man who participates in the last hunt and who resists parting from Hemingway during the return to camp.

I believe that Hemingway's dominant wish in both *Afternoon* and *Green Hills* is ultimately to gratify his father. I infer this principally from his having written two such works of nonfiction. Even though Dr. Hemingway took pride in his son's writing, he did not find it significant. Part of what would have prompted Hemingway to suspend his efforts as a novelist and to write these two books, then, would have been a desire to address the memory of his father and to show allegiance to his values. Dr. Hemingway might have faulted his son's choice of subjects in *Afternoon*. But he would not have failed to see the discipline, study, and discernment that went into a book about the historically real art of bullfighting. Nor would he have failed to feel his son's tacit agreement that a man fares better if he involves himself in activities that exclude or minimize women's importance than if he does not. He would also have enjoyed the antifeminism tucked into his son's colloquies with that veiled caricature of his wife, Grace, Old Lady. And "an absolutely true book" about hunting would have appealed to the doctor's moralistic and scientific pledge to truth. Hemingway's selective trophy hunting defers to yet another of his father's values: "Father had the greatest contempt," Marcelline recalls, "for so-called sportsmen who killed ruthlessly for the fun of killing or to boast about the size of the bag."[14] And Hemingway would have further pleased the doctor by fulfilling his—and probably every hunter's—dream of seeing and stalking Africa's big game. But to know that Hemingway prized and commemorated the hunting skills first learned from him would have especially gratified the doctor.

Hemingway's wish to gratify his father is also evident in the different unconscious implications in the works of this and the previous phase. The two novels of the thesis phase express filial aggression toward paternal values and, through their love stories, standard erotic drives. But the male camaraderie of aficionados and hunters as well as the conscious striving to subdue his competitiveness in *Green Hills* suggest that these two nonfiction works try to overcome filial aggression. To this end Hemingway sublimates erotic drives, partly visible in the homoerotic tendencies of these two books but more so in their preoccupation with esthetics. Relinquishing his interest in direct erotic pleasure, he forfeits his claim as the father's rightful rival for the favors of their mutually desired woman, he declares that he has found a substitute beauty in bullfighting and hunting antelope, and he solicits the father to be his ally. Emancipated from carnal bondage to women, the books wishfully murmur, father and son can discover refined pleasures, pursue esthetic ecstasies.

THE ARISTOTELEAN PHASE

3

A Classical Tragedy: *To Have and Have Not*

" 'No matter how a man alone ain't got no bloody fucking chance' " (225). These words, Harry Morgan's last, are his anagnorisis. They make that utterance required of any classical tragic hero, his recognition, and so they establish the genre for correctly assessing this novel: tragedy. Hemingway generates neither a Shakespearean nor a Sophoclean catharsis. But this is due partly to his creation of a questionable hero, someone whose actions seem too saturated with villainy for us to discern tragic qualities in them. It is also due to our expectations: the last thing we expect to find in Hemingway's realistic canon is a tragic protagonist. Our unpreparedness, then, may thwart a purging of our emotions of pity and fear. Inclined to regard the words spoken over Harry's dead body as ironic, we overlook the diction that points at that quality every tragic hero shares, excessive suffering:

"He didn't suffer at all, Mrs. Morgan," the doctor said. Marie did not seem to hear him.
"Oh, Christ," she said, and began to cry again. "Look at his goddamned face." [256]

Customarily cited as the novel that signals Hemingway's thematic shift from individualism to brotherhood,[1] *To Have and Have Not* better signals his artistic shift from the autonomous forms of his earlier fictions to the prescriptive form of tragedy. The novel deserves to be faulted for its structural flaws, perhaps caused by its interrupted gestation.[2] But its problems wane and its achievement waxes if, with formulas of tragedy in mind, we look at its species, its protagonist, and its dramatic structure.[3]

Let us speculate upon the novel's species: the characteristics of "common" tragedy seem tailor-made for it. Harry Morgan is con-

cerned with a most rudimentary human problem—economic survival in a society that offers him debasing options. He can starve,
dig sewers for relief wages, operate a filling station with one arm,
or make money by unlawful means. A "conch," by definition
Harry has a place in the social order—among its "dregs," its "sed-
iment," its "leftovers." Proud and resentful of such status, he
struggles to slip no lower. And though superficially adventurous,
Harry's actions are domestic, pragmatically concerned with providing for his family without injuring his self-esteem.[4] Commonplace though he is in this regard, he has what Arthur Miller defines as the "flaw" shared by all tragic heroes, an "inherent
unwillingness to remain passive in the face of what he conceives
to be a challenge to his dignity, his image of his rightful status."[5]
And the catastrophe that ends Harry's life also reveals his dignity
because, citing Miller again, his "destruction in the attempt [to
evaluate himself justly—that is, as more than the negligible
means to others' ends] posits a wrong or an evil in his environment." Hemingway emphasizes Harry's commonness by having
him die by a stomach wound, thereby focusing upon Harry's major concern—that his wife and daughters have enough to eat (96).
Inasmuch as the novel dramatizes several forms of "starvation"—
social, sexual, political, and psychological—Harry's lethal stomach wound is the common denominator of those hungers.

Several of the novel's features also show its kinship to Renaissance tragedy. Particularly apt is the "tragedy of blood," that variation of revenge tragedy that specializes in murder, mutilation,
and morbid excitement as means to bring about revenge and retribution. An inheritance from Senecan tragedy, one of this species'
traits is amply present: the blood-and-lust motif of sensational
scenes and "unnatural" crimes. Harry's actions and the supposedly digressive episodes on the Gordons, the vets, and the
yachters show adultery, perversion, brutality, and sadomasochism. But revenge motivates most of the novel's action.

Harry's murder of Sing, the go-between for illegal Chinese immigrants, is usually read as an unmotivated, cold-blooded act.[6]
But it is an act of revenge that Hemingway carefully prepares.
After all, the novel begins with Harry watching the Chicago-style
gunning down of three Cubans who have just solicited him to boat
them to the States and threatened him with the fate of *lengua largas*, betrayers. The novel indicates that their deaths were politically motivated, for they were antigovernment rebels, as their
conversation with Harry establishes, telling him that later, when

things are different, his having served them now would benefit him (4). To this milieu of revenge Hemingway adds Johnson's treachery. He leaves Havana before paying the eight hundred twenty-five dollars he owes Harry for carelessly lost tackle and three weeks of chartered fishing. By the time Sing propositions Harry and tells him that he may land the Chinese wherever he wants, the odor of double cross is strong. So to prevent treachery to himself and subsequent Chinese, Harry, with some justification, murders Sing. No champion of the Chinese, Harry identifies with them since their naive trust of a profiteer mirrors his earlier trust of Johnson. Knowing Sing's deceitfulness, then, Harry murders him as a compensatory act of revenge, Sing being Johnson's scapegoat.

Sadistic though it seems, Harry's later killing of the four Cuban revolutionaries also fits a revenge motif. Even before Harry manages to knock overboard Roberto's submachine gun, Roberto has indicated that he intends to kill him gratuitously, justifying Harry's retaliation as self-defense. The loss of Harry's arm and boat, directly caused by Cuban officials who had been ignoring Harry's post-Prohibition rum-running operation only to shoot at him unexpectedly, also gives him reason to avenge a recent wrong by gunning down these also treacherous Cubans. And still alive in Harry's mind, too, may be the sense that their intent to betray him traces back to, and makes good, the early threats against him as a *lengua larga* (49). To the complexity of his motive must be added the wish to avenge Albert's, if not Bee-Lips's, death. In sum, like many a Jacobean hero, Harry has to grapple "with the question of how virtuous action can be taken in an evil world when that action itself must be devious, politic, or tainted with evil."[7]

The most compelling evidence of the novel's generic lineage is in the presence of so many of the elements that Aristotle found in classical Greek tragedy.[8] Harry has all the qualities required of a tragic hero. His superiority to the novel's other characters gives him stature. For instance, people turn to him when they need something done well: Eddy and Frankie, Johnson and Sing, Albert and Bee-Lips, the Cuban trio at the novel's beginning and quartet at its end. Satiric butt though she is, even Mrs. Laughton instinctively responds to his stature, calling him "wonderful," "Ghengis Khan," her "dream man" (130, 136, 149). King of the conchs, Harry aptly dies upon a boat named *Queen Conch*. He is "not a paragon of virtue and justice," as well he should not be; but the "nobility" of Harry's actions is questionable only if we discount the nobility of every man's struggle for survival. Harry's hamartia, "an ignorance or mistake as to certain details" (i.e., that he had slain his assailant), is "a 'big' mistake, one pregnant with disaster for the hero" (Else, 383), for his hamartia dramatizes his "overweening pride" that he alone can handle the four Cuban revolutionaries. As it should, Harry's hamartia causes the peripety of events, the sudden reversal of fortune necessary to his ultimate downfall. And his hubris, proud belief in his self-sufficiency, is precisely what his anagnorisis sees as his blind spot: " 'No matter how a man alone ain't got no bloody fucking chance.' " Proairesis, or the belief in choice and free will, is also here. Harry thinks fatalistically about transporting the Cubans: "I don't want to fool with it, but what choice have I got? They don't give you any choice now" (105). Still, he does choose to transport them, conscious of the potential calamity that can result from his voluntary decision.

To add a word about catharsis, the novel's catastophe should arouse pity and fear: fear because Harry "is like the rest of us" (Else, 365), his struggle for economic wherewithal replicating ours; pity because Harry "suffers undeservedly" (Else, 370). Certainly he must suffer punishment for murdering the Cubans. But the slow agony of his twenty-four-hour death exceeds justice. Moreover, he has done nothing to deserve the promise of being shot by the Cubans. His acceptance of the inevitable confrontation requires him to fire upon them first and exculpates his "motive from polluted intent" (Else, 447). Because of circumstances, then, Harry's act is neither morally repugnant nor a cold-blooded act, and he deserves our pity for his excessive suffering.

The novel houses other elements of classical tragedy too. Setting aside for the moment the structural problem of Hemingway's inclusion of the Gordons, the vets, and the decadent yachters, I find the novel otherwise meeting the Aristotelean criterion of unity. Its plot is "complete and a whole" (Else, 282), not episodic, for it follows the rise and fall of Harry's fortunes. The seasonal sectioning of the novel (spring, fall, winter) also suggests this completeness to me, despite the omission of summer, a season whose bounty seems properly deleted from the novel's bleak landscape. The novel even has the spatial magnitude required of tragedy, literally encompassing not an Aegean but a Gulf archipelago, from Cuba to the Florida Keys. The novel's events also show the "logical sequence, continuity" (Else, 297) required of tragedy. For as Johnson's double cross causes Harry to transport the Chinese and to murder Sing, the economic depression causes him to transport rum. The loss of arm and boat—the means for Harry's normal employment—causes his dangerous exploit of transporting the Cuban revolutionaries for a mere two hundred dollars. The consistency of these variations upon the single action of Harry's occupation as transporter underscores the novel's unified action. So does his transporting Cubans at the novel's beginning and end.

The novel seems flooded with unexpected events—the sudden deaths of the first Cubans and Sing, the abrupt defection of Johnson, the unanticipated gunfire that Cuban authorities give Harry and Wesley, the untoward arrival of Frederick Harrison, the swift reconfiscation of Harry's boat, and the unforeseen bullet from Harry's assailant. Yet these further accord with Aristotle's inductive conclusion that a tragedy's events must "happen contrary to our expectation" and "possess the quality of surprise" (Else, 323). Though Hemingway rejects the dramatic mode of tragedy, the dramatic monologues by Harry, Albert, and Marie approximate the methods and the effects of the chorus in Greek drama. The digressive chapters might even be there as choric commentary upon the environment within which Harry must fulfill his destiny. And Hemingway's decision to end the novel in Marie Morgan's consciousness might also conform to some choric function: "the chorus," Aristotle says, "should be considered as one of the persons in the drama; should be a part of the whole, and a sharer in the action."[9] In any event, her thoughts provide a fitting kommos, the lamentation with which a classical tragedy often concludes.

As readers or spectators of a tragedy, ultimately we are concerned less with its obedience to a prescribed formula than with its ability to generate those complex emotions that only tragedy can. And those emotions occur only when a hero performs an act that paradoxically "runs counter to man's deepest moral instincts" but is "purified" because its motive is not morally repugnant (Else, 420, 439). This criterion lets us justly dismiss *For Whom the Bell Tolls* and *A Farewell to Arms*, although both are often called tragedies. Robert Jordan is too admirable a lover and patriot to cross the bridge of that criterion, and his martyr's death is neither a terrible deed nor a consequence of one. Similarly, Frederic Henry performs no morally repugnant act, unless we wish to so regard his shooting of the engineering sergeant. More a victim of—rather than an agent in—the world's manifold irrationality, he elicits only pity. And neither Colonel Cantwell's nor Thomas Hudson's suffering approaches Harry Morgan's, leaving him as Hemingway's only novel-length hero who undergoes the violent death necessary to tragedy, the sole hero whose acts are steeped in, but purified of, moral repugnance.

It is, of course, tempting to label a work "tragedy." An honorific label, it often confers status upon an otherwise negligible piece of writing. Worse, specious elevation of a negligible work harms the whole concept of tragedy, reducing it to an intellectual pradigm or using it as a label for any pathetic situation.[10] So I set aside the prescriptive formula of classical tragedy and look instead at what finally matters in tragedy, the quality of life invested in the tragic hero. Despite assessments of Harry Morgan as an amoral tough,[11] I find in him those qualities that any hero who asks to be dubbed "tragic" must have. He is divided and intelligent.[12]

The three episodes of part 1—the Cubans' solicitation, Johnson's defection, and Harry's murder of Sing—chart Harry's rapid change from law-abiding charter-boat fisherman to ruthless murderer. This change might be too swift for credibility or easy proof of Harry's basic villainy. But the change outlines Harry's dividedness. He has a strong sense of decency and morality, but he also inclines to let circumstances lure him into lawless acts. Harry's past activities indicate this dividedness. He boasts about the exact number of cases of rum his boat will hold and so tells of experiences as rumrunner. But he also admits he was a policeman in Miami. Again, greed seems to prompt him to smuggle a dozen Chinese into the States. But he had earlier refused to smuggle in three Cubans for considerably more money. And again, he appears to relish the death of Sing: "He was flopping and bouncing worse than any dolphin on a gaff. . . . I got him forward onto his knees and had both thumbs well in behind his talkbox, and I bent the whole thing back until she cracked. Don't think you can't hear it crack, either" (53–54). But because Harry mentions his former employment as a policeman in Miami (44) while preparing for this job, it is Harry's desire for justice, not homicidal glee, that surfaces in the situation. Sing's death, that is, compensates for his indirect murder of countless Chinese whose betrayal has provided him for two years with the means to wear, as Harry observes, a white suit, a silk shirt, a black tie, and a one-hundred-twenty-five-dollar Panama hat (30).

Harry's treachery to Sing, congruent with the novel's world, seems to be Harry's basic character trait. Yet it is at odds with his trustworthiness, the trait that Johnson exploited by pulling out before paying Harry. And deaf Frankie's loyalty to Harry and the first Cubans' request that he be the one to ferry them to the mainland also speak for his trustworthiness. Even Sing testifies to it. After all, he is surprised that Harry is willing to smuggle his compatriots, beginning to ask what circumstances have made Harry consider the assignment (31). And he knows Harry's reputation well enough to trust him with a two-hundred-dollar down payment. So when Harry asks, " 'Suppose I went off with the two hundred,' " Sing replies, " 'But I know you wouldn't do such a thing, captain' " (34). Sing's unpreparedness for Harry's murder of him confirms Harry's guess, "Maybe he just trusted me" (60). Traitors, criminals, and commoners respect Harry's moral responsibility.

Emphasizing his dividedness, the several episodes of part 1 converge upon Harry's dilemma of whether to kill Eddy, witness to his killing of Sing. Tempted also by his assumption that Eddy is not on the crew list and so will cause complications with customs officers when he reaches Key West, nevertheless Harry dislikes doing something he would regret later (60). No inveterate killer, Harry has already dismissed the notion of massacring the dozen Chinese, realizing that only "a hell of a mean man" could "butcher a bunch of Chinks like that" (57). He even ignores the impulse to silence the Chinaman who keeps calling him " 'Goddam crook' " (58). Nor does heavy drinking on the return to Key West skew Harry's dilemma. Waver though he does, Harry's interior debate makes unlikely a homicidal intent, even had Eddy not been saved by being on the crew list.

The seeming sensationalism of Harry's masculine action and lawless self-expression in part 1 creates the distorted mug shot many readers see. Yet Hemingway draws a balanced and complex portrait, for the rest of the novel dramatizes Harry's equally strong obligations to domestic security and moral decency. Like Hemingway's fine counterpointing of Jack Brennan's fisticuffs and tightfistedness in "Fifty Grand," here Harry's violent actions play against his middle-class values, his domestic pleasure. After all, upon his return to Key West at the end of part 1, he spends the evening as many a domesticated man does. He sits in his living room, smokes a cigar, sips on a whiskey and water, and listens to Gracie Allen on the radio (64).

The motive common to all of Harry's hazardous exploits, to provide for his family, may seem a sleazy rationalization that allows him to indulge his penchant for violence.[13] But the novel's setting during the depression and the frequency of Harry's financial anxieties authenticate his motive. Thinking of the dangers of transporting the Cuban revolutionaries from Key West, he considers not getting mixed up with them. But he promptly chastens himself with the idea that there would be no money to feed and support his wife and daughters (147). The narrative silence about Harry's motive for smuggling rum in part 2's fiasco seems again to focus the view of him as merely an outlaw by nature. But since this is a post-Prohibition run, Harry's venture will not bring in a huge profit, even though it will avoid import duties. And to testify that Harry does not run rum for the criminal thrill of thwarting the law, Captain Willie Adams correctly defines his motive. Belittling the idea that Harry is a "lawbreaker," he declares that Harry is simply trying to earn money to feed his family (81). Essentially a homebody rather than an adventurer, before Harry leaves his home for the last time, he sits at the oak table and looks at the objects in the room—piano, sideboard, radio, pictures on the wall, table, chairs, and window curtains—and thinks, "What chance have I to enjoy my home?" (127).

Lying in the cockpit of *Queen Conch* mortally wounded, Harry also wonders what his wife will do. He hopes that she will get some reward money or some of the bank money on the boat (174). Besides showing Harry's monogamous loyalty, his wondering also shows his considerateness of others, an odd quality for someone regarded as an amoral tough. Thinking about the driver who will taxi the Cubans to the boat, he earlier tells Bee-Lips to get one who has no "kids" (134). And when he comes home late one night, he leaves the light off, removes his shoes, and quietly climbs the stairs in his stockings (112). Just as Harry tolerates Wesley's whining, he rejects Albert's help in transporting the Cuban quartet, silently trying to shield him from foreseeable danger: " 'I'm sorry, Albert, I can't use you,' Harry said. He had thought it out that far already" (122).

Harry's dividedness, in tune with the novel's paradoxical title, also reflects the intelligence required of a tragic hero. To convey Harry's intelligence may well have prompted Hemingway to begin the novel with his dramatic monologue, articulateness a corollary of intelligence. "You know how it is there early in the morning in Havana," Harry begins his story, demonstrating his doubleness as a man of words and a man of action. His role as narrator of part 1 is particularly crucial to its moral ambiguity and accounts for the sparseness of his moral reflectiveness, even though these subtleties have gone unnoticed, the habitual fate of Hemingway's first-person narrators. When Eddy asks what he had against Sing, Harry answers, " 'Nothing,' " and adds that he killed him " 'to keep him from killing twelve other Chinks' " (55). Ruthless as both statements sound, Harry is telling this conversation, as the idiom makes clear, to a chum. Because he is, then either he is modestly muting his real motive, or he is indicating that he sees little point in revealing his motive to a rummy, or he knows better than to bore a friendly, lower-class listener with the niceties of Jamesian moral desiderata. Neither vainglorious nor defensive, Harry is justly proud of the exploit that let him recoup his loss and serve up justice. And he knows well that his listener is interested in the "what" of the adventure, not in its "why." His intelligence is also evident in his implied reason for turning away the Cuban trio at the novel's beginning. His fear of having U.S. customs officials catch him and seize his boat is legitimate enough. But equally important is his desire to avoid the cross fire of Cuban political warfare. By being unruffled by the fates of both the trio and *lengua largas*, Harry silently indicates the commonness of such events and the wisdom of his refusal to charter the Cubans.

Unlike Hemingway's usual hero, who says he does not want to think, Harry enjoys thinking, especially about difficulties, be it landing a marlin, unloading sacked liquor with one arm, double-crossing Sing, deciding Eddy's fate, or planning for the contingencies of his last exploit: "Suppose they figure about me and Albert. Did any of them look like sailors? . . . I have to find out about that because if they figure on doing without Albert or me from the start there's no way. Sooner or later they will figure on us. But in the Gulf you got time. And I'm figuring all the time. I've got to think right all the time" (106–7).

Despite the outcome of this last episode, it fully brings out Harry's shrewdness. Wary of its dangers, he conceals from the Cubans his knowledge of Spanish, hides his submachine gun, bumps Roberto's gun overboard, and ingratiates himself with Emilio to better surprise him. When Harry realizes the murderousness of the foursome, the now-omniscient narrator observes that he "had abandoned anger, hatred and any dignity as luxuries, now, and had started to plan" (159). He has even concealed from friends his knowledge of the specific job. Pretending to be chartering just another fishing party until commandeered by the Cubans, Harry causes the sheriff and Coast Guard retrievers to regard him as a victim. But Harry victimizes himself as tragedy demands.[14] For he has guilefully nudged overboard Roberto's machine gun and so has inflamed the Cuban's resolve to kill him. And he begins the fatal shooting. Most important, he makes that error in judgment expected of all intelligent tragic heroes: he ignorantly assumes that his assailant, the shoulder-wounded Cuban, is dead. Linked to his earlier mistakes—trusting Johnson, anticipating no difficulties running rum, and overlooking the visibility of his stolen boat from a tall truck—this error contributes to the inevitability of his tragic death.

More evidence of Harry's tragic stature sifts out of the sociopolitical matter that seems to clutter the novel. Hemingway does not paint a backdrop of war vets and Cuban revolutionaries, of Marxist portraits and depression-era weltanschauung so that we can facilely catalogue another social protest novel. Rather he paints it to objectify Harry's dilemma, that being another yardstick for measuring any candidate for tragedy. Harry's impulse is for individual freedom and independent action. However, it butts up against an imperative, whether we see it as family duty or as the call to be his brother's keeper. Indeed, Harry's dilemma mirrors clearly the dilemma on which the novel's social problems pivot. And so, loner though Harry would like to be, his dependence upon such "dregs" as deaf Frankie, rummy Eddy, whining Wesley, and wife-nagged Albert makes him admit early that loners are doomed. Thinking about whether to enlist Albert to help him transport the four Cuban revolutionaries he registers, "It would be better alone, anything is better alone but I don't think I can handle it alone. It would be much better alone" (105). Although Harry denies the label of "radical" (97), he refuses to endorse existing social or political structures, for they strip Cuban, *conch*, and vet of dignity, rather than serve them as brother's keeper. Even the revolutionists' pragmatic rationale—that the end justifies the means (166)—serves self rather than others, to Harry's way of thinking: "What the hell do I care about his [Emilio's] revolution. F— — his revolution. To help the working man he robs a bank and kills a fellow works with him and then kills that poor damned Albert that never did any harm. That's a working man he kills. He never thinks of that. With a family" (168).

Harry does think of Albert, his attitude toward Albert further clarifying Harry's dilemma. Given their discussion of family obligations (95–96), Harry's decision to reject Albert's help expresses conflicting wishes: to act independently and so be beholden to no man, and to protect a family provider and so be his brother's keeper. When Harry later reverses this decision, he does so not as an act of betrayal. Rather in preparation of his last words, he admits that just as Albert needs money, he himself needs help, that he alone may not be able to cope with the hazardous voyage. Those fears confirmed by subsequent events, Harry understands the obsolete and fatal luxury of autonomy, aptly comparing it to " 'trying to pass cars on the top of hills. On that road in Cuba. On any road. Anywhere' " (225). And Hemingway understands the artistic need to make ambiguous Harry's final illumination: " 'No matter how a man alone ain't got no bloody fucking chance.' " Harry's repetition of "man" nine times before this utterance italicizes properly its universal truth. And though the imperative of brotherhood lies at its core, it does not remorsefully exhort us to join ranks with our downtrodden brothers, thanks to its failure to specify how involved we must get. Nor does it guarantee that because men alone have no "chance," collective efforts will—as the dead bodies of the four Cubans indicate.[15] Finally, the rich imprecision of "chance" leaves open what "a man alone" will lack the opportunity to do: eke out a living? reform social inequities? express meaningfully his individuality?

Significant though Harry's stomach wound is to seeing the representativeness of his economic struggle, the loss of his right arm is equally significant. It is a synecdoche of those personal and—as the novel's maimed world insists—social handicaps all men must live with, handicaps that compel interdependency. The loss of Harry's right arm, long a symbol of assistance, reliability, and dependence, shows Hemingway, like a latter-day Hardy, reprimanding Harry's flagrant individualism, making compulsory his dependence upon others. Yet it is only by literally achieving his wish to operate single-handedly that Harry recognizes the limits of single-handedness and man's need of assistance from either literal or figurative right arms, brothers.

Politically unsophisticated though his rude environment requires him to be, Harry's illegal activities still amount to an individual protest against the social injustices of every age. Like Lear and Oedipus, who flout communal dictates, Harry's actions similarly express his need for a measure of security, autonomy, and dignity. Indeed, Harry is the avatar of the Cuban revolutionaries, the downtrodden *conchs*, the betrayed Chinese, and even the dispossessed vets—of all societies' "leftovers." Their frustration with, or anger at, social injustice incites them all to violent, illegal, or impotent action. But Harry fails to recognize his brotherhood with such people. And that, unfortunately, muffles the novel's tragic resonance. Tragic pleasure, says Aristotle, best emanates from a horrible act performed by a hero initially ignorant of the kinship between himself and his victim (Else, 413–15). Harry's massacre of the Cubans is justified as an act of self-defense, to be sure. Yet both the terror and the pity of the act would have been heightened had Hemingway found a way for Harry to express a realization that he resembled the Cubans. After all, their claim to social justice echoes his. And their ethic (illegal means to achieve noble ends) is his as well. They are, in effect, his brothers. But Harry gives no sign that he has unwittingly committed fratricide.

One matter yet remains: the novel's digressions. To be bold about it, of all of Hemingway's novels, this is structurally his tightest. Its discrete episodes are fully developed, its sequence easy to recall, and its outline transparent, even to an eye not apprised of its generic roots. In fact, it obeys the conventional formula of a tragedy's "dramatic structure," dividing unequivocally into the seven components of the classical Freytag pyramid.[16] It has an introduction, an exciting force that generates the rising action, a crisis or turning point, a tragic force that precipitates the falling action and, of course, the catastrophe. (I too was inclined to think that such a stock, dramatic structure would be totally alien to Hemingway's artistry. Then I remembered that the work that followed this novel is his play, *The Fifth Column*.)

The scene in the Perla cafe with the solicitous Cubans is the tragedy's *introduction*. It provides the setting of a world in the throes of social warfare and it quickly establishes the novel's tone or mood—distrust, treachery, and violence. Johnson's defection constitutes the *exciting force*. His double cross defines the "conflict of opposing interests" between the haves and have-nots, the trustworthy and deceitful, the brotherly and egocentric, the lawbreakers and law-abiders. The episode also "sets in motion the *rising action*," Harry's murder of Sing. As the witches' prophecy stirs Macbeth into scheming for kingship, Johnson's betrayal motivates Harry's scheme to recover his losses and avenge himself on double-crossers. True to the pyramid, Harry returns to Key West "in the ascendency." Part 2 is the *crisis* or *turning point*, "the point at which the opposing forces that create the conflict interlock in the decisive action on which the plot will turn." Harry's fate as rumrunner shows an individual in conflict with collective forces. His conflict is duplicated in Captain Willie's verbal tussle with Harrison, " 'one of the three most important men in the United States today' " (80), and in his defense of Harry as family provider against Harrison's charge of "lawbreaker." Prohibition over, Harry anticipates no genuine danger in transporting liquor. Yet "interlocking" with the Cuban government he loses his arm, and with the U.S. government, his boat. Inasmuch as in the rest of the novel Harry tries to wrest a living without boat or arm, this episode's "decisive action" locates the "incident wherein the situation in which the protagonist finds himself is sure either to improve or grow worse." Not to be confused with the climax ("the point of highest interest at which the reader makes his greatest emotional response"), this turning point results in events "which produce climactic effects without themselves being of compelling interest." That is, Hemingway selectively ignores the three events of "compelling interest" in part 2—the escape from the Cuban harbor, the confiscation of the boat, and Harry's amputation. He centers instead on the single event that contains them. The *tragic force*, the single event "closely related to the crisis," is when customs officers reconfiscate Harry's boat. The event also "starts the *falling action*," Harry precipitously resolving to rent Freddy's boat and to carry the Cubans across. "A moment of final suspense," Harry's stomach wound answers to the falling action, for that event "delays the *catastrophe*," "seems to offer a way of escape for the hero," and "often is attended by some lowering of interest since new forces must be introduced."

Central to understanding the novel's structure are the ancillary functions of falling action, since they explain the novel's apparently disintegrating focus on Harry. If Hemingway did not sense the need to magnify Harry's world, then one ingredient of falling action instructed him, for he "stress[es] the activity of the forces opposing the hero." Into the novel, that is, Hemingway brings characters who represent those opposing forces: self-indulgent rich and violent poor, perverse egocentrics and self-deceiving incompetents. A grotesque version of Harry's conflict, the episode in Freddy's bar portrays the vets as creatures who have submitted to society's dehumanizing forces. And so their sense of brotherhood enslaves them to a collective drudgery that allows them no more dignity than what they can express through the anarchy of their sadomasochism. Hemingway keeps tragedy's proper focus by dramatizing their self-victimization. Equally grotesque foils are the well-to-do. Hemingway's catalogue of the rich on their yachts exhibits a social system that protects wealthy self-indulgence. The rich are targets of Hemingway's scornful pity because they too lack the intelligence or courage to seek a dignified existence. That they mimic Harry's conflict is seen in Hemingway's juxta-positions of the perverse "brotherliness" of Johnson and Carpenter's homosexuality and the destructive individualism of the sixty-year-old grain broker, of the domestic security of Frances's family, the frivolous thirst for adventure of the Esthonians, and the narcissism of Dorothy Hollis. Further stressing "the activity of the forces opposing the hero," Hemingway places in the center of these vignettes the family whose security comes from selling a three-cent liquid for a dollar a pint, fit analogue of Harry's rum-running and indictment of government double standards.

One other trait of falling action helps explain the novel's structure: "Relief scenes are often resorted to during the Falling Action, partly to provide emotional relaxation for the audience." Mrs. Tracy's farcical remorse for Albert is surely such a "relief scene." Though it lacks tragedy's proper dignity, its comedy has precedent in the scenes of Lear's fool, Hamlet's gravedigger, or Macbeth's gatekeeper. And despite her fraudulent grief, she parodies the lament Harry deserves and receives in Marie's novel-ending soliloquy. A finer relief scene is the brief chapter 20. Its matter-of-fact description of the damaged *Queen Conch*, drifting in the Gulf Stream, nicely modulates to a catalogue of the various fish feeding upon the blood that oozes from the boat's splintered bullet holes and trails in the water (179). Only then does Hemingway turn to the phantasmagoria of Harry's muted agony.

Avoid them though I would prefer, the "relief scenes" that ask for justification are those with Richard Gordon. Artistically indefensible, they show Hemingway trying to convey and unify the social and moral context of the novel by creating a character whose distorted resemblance to Harry will clarify the novel's issues. To that end Hemingway parallels Gordon's social protest novel and Harry's protesting illegalities, Gordon's impotence with Helène Bradley and Harry's unsuccessful one-armed struggle with the Cubans, Gordon's misreading of Marie and Harry's misjudgment of Johnson, Gordon's rejection of MacWalsey's fraternal help and Harry's strident self-sufficiency, Gordon's rapid disintegration and Harry's demise. If Hemingway intended these parallels, the bald contrast between a pathetic and a tragic character excessively augments Harry's stature or, as the novel's reputation sadly confirms, severely detracts from its achievement.

Looking at *To Have and Have Not* harshly, I find that its obedience to ancient paradigms of tragedy and to rigid rules of dramatic structure suggests a derivative quality in Hemingway's imagination. Surely this novel catches him engaged in an epigonic act. Yet every writer who seriously courts the Tragic Muse must defer to her preestablished criteria. And the dearth of modern tragedies testifies to the difficulty of those criteria. So it is to Hemingway's credit that he silently accepted the self-imposed challenge to compose a tragedy. Equally commendable is his artistic integrity, refusing to justify his novel or to castigate disparaging critics by declaring it to be a classical tragedy.[17] But the measure of his achievemet is another matter. That Harry Morgan's tragic lineaments have been mistakenly interpreted as villainous ones shows that Hemingway skillfully wrought him. But whether Harry's dividedness and intelligence are enough to raise him even to the level of Macbeth, his closest cousin, cannot be decreed by critical fiat. For most readers they are not. Perhaps they need to hear again that cryptic statement in Hemingway's Nobel Prize acceptance speech: "Things may not be immediately discernible in what a man writes, and in this sometimes he is fortunate; but eventually they are quite clear and by these and the degree of alchemy that he possesses he will endure or be forgotten."[18]

A Classical Epic: *For Whom the Bell Tolls*

I find as little merit in the notion that Hemingway was a Johnny-one-note as in the similar notion about Jane Austen's "husband-hunting" novels.* *For Whom the Bell Tolls* should have laid to rest the notion. Glaring dissimilarities between it and his other novels brought it immediate attention and have continued to do so. But the attention has created two bands of commentators who regard the novel as though it were a replica of that bridge in the Guadarrama mountains. And they are determined to preserve or to detonate it. One band hurls "concentrated action" against the other's volley, "diffuse digressions"; "political orientation" against "contradictory politics"; "stylistic range" against "strained and verbose language"; "in-depth characterization" against "stereotyped puppets"; "positive theme" against "forced conception"; "tragedy" against "melodrama."[1] One cause for the conflict between these bands is that they have not identified the object that has stimulated their responses. Certainly *For Whom the Bell Tolls* deserves classification under the rubric "novel." But it has alloys alien to Hemingway's other novels and to most novels. Those alloys are nothing less than epic machinery.

In *Death in the Afternoon* Hemingway disarmingly cautions, "Remember this too: all bad writers are in love with the epic" (54). *For Whom the Bell Tolls* finds even a good writer unable to resist its allure. And within at least three years of its publication the novel was described as epical, as it has since been, both in derogation and praise.[2] But as Carlos Baker's representative discussion shows, the term gets used loosely. Indeed, his scant catalogue of

---

*An earlier version of this chapter appeared under the title "Epic Machinery in Hemingway's *For Whom the Bell Tolls*," *Modern Fiction Studies* © 1971 by Purdue Research Foundation, West Lafayette, Indiana 47907 U.S.A.

epic traits—timelessness, heroic allusions, heightened language, and characterization—uses the term *epic* honorifically, not substantively. He conveys a subjective impression that Hemingway toyed casually with the epic, tantalized by a few of its mechanics. I find that Hemingway must have studied its machinery thoroughly. But although he superimposes that machinery upon the novel's materials, he carefully camouflages it. We can, of course, ignore its presence and proceed to judge the novel as a success or a failure on the conventional grounds of theme, plot, characterization, and the like. But once we hear the whir—or perhaps the clank—of that machinery, we should judge the novel on the grounds of Hemingway's intent—to create an epic. And we should be able to see clearly Hemingway's craft and craftiness. For he offers to his reading public what seems like a realistic, historically based war novel wrought only of personal experience, observation, and creative imagination, when in fact it was wrought also of the antique machinery of a classical, literary mode.

The first signal of any epic is that celebrated trope, the "extended" or Homeric simile. Given a writer who studiously avoided tropes as ornaments of bad taste, their frequency in this novel should surprise us. When Robert Jordan and Maria walk hand in hand through the heather, Hemingway writes that her touch was "as fresh as the first light air that moving toward you over the sea barely wrinkles the glassy surface of a calm, as light as a feather moved across one's lip, or a leaf falling when there is no breeze" (158). In chapter 27 (Sordo's hilltop fight) El Sordo considers that the hill is a chancre, of which he and his men are the very pus (310). Thinking of his inevitable death, he then rhapsodizes on living in a sequence of metaphors, likening it to a "field of grain blowing in the wind on the side of a hill," to a "hawk in the sky," to an "earthen jar of water in the dust of the threshing with the grain flailed out and the chaff blowing," and to a "horse between your legs and a carbine under one leg and a hill and a valley and a stream with trees along it and the far side of the valley and the hills beyond" (312–13). After Pablo first rejoins the guerilla band, Jordan considers the entire series of events as a merry-go-round (225). But the novel's most forceful and truly Homeric simile is Pilar's harshly criticized description of the smell of death (254–56).[3] Certainly her enumeration of the four smells that one must mix together to experience its smell is a tour de force that calls excessive attention to itself. But such verbal embellishments are obligatory to an author composing an epic.[4]

The four ingredients of the smell of death also show a second epic convention, the catalogue. Jordan's thoughts on pleasant smells (260, 200 words), on snowstorms (182, 144 words), on what he has learned in war (236, 108 words), and on the odors of the cave (59, 175 words) are all epic catalogues. So, too, is Pilar's reminiscence of Valencia and the food she and Finito ate there, Pilar reciting a salivating menu that detracts from the novel only if we overlook it too as catalogue:

> "We ate in pavilions on the sand. Pastries made of cooked and shredded fish and red and green peppers and small nuts like grains of rice. Pastries delicate and flaky and the fish of a richness that was incredible. Prawns fresh from the sea sprinkled with lime juice. They were pink and sweet and there were four bites to a prawn. Of those we ate many. Then we ate paella with fresh sea food, clams in their shells, mussels, crayfish, and small eels. Then we ate even smaller eels alone cooked in oil and as tiny as bean sprouts and curled in all directions and so tender they disappeared in the mouth without chewing. All the time drinking a white wine, cold, light and good at thirty centimos the bottle. And for an end; melon. That is the home of the melon." [85, 142 words][5]

The catalogue of truly epic size is Pilar's story (twenty-five pages) of the ceremonial execution of the six Fascists in Pablo's town. Often deplored as excrescent, it too adds to the novel an episode whose proper enjoyment requires that we be attuned to the novel's epic orchestration.[6]

Other epic features described by the ancients are also visible. For one thing, Hemingway "rushes his hearer" in medias res, as Horace maintains a proper epic ought. That is, Hemingway opens the novel with Robert Jordan already reconnoitering the road at the mountain pass. But that moment chronologically follows the beginning event, Golz and Jordan's discussion of the mission two nights before, recorded in a flashback. And that event has been preceded by many more events, we learn. For another thing, by focusing upon the three days it takes Jordan to accomplish his mission, Hemingway obeys Aristotle's dictum that the epic should center "around a single action which is whole and complete and has beginning, middle and end, so that like a single whole creature it may produce its proper pleasure."[7] Third, Hemingway's economical treatment of "The Spanish Civil War 'Story' " is as deserving of Aristotle's applause as Homer's treatment of "the Troy Story." Not only does Hemingway avoid the pitfall of writing a biography or a chronicle, but he too "has picked out one portion of the story and used many of the others as episodes, with which he intersperses his composition" (581). The episodes of Sordo's death, of Andrés's trek to Golz, of Pilar's experiences with Finito, of Gaylord's on the eve of the offensive are but a few of the diversifying episodes that, fourth, enlarge the scope of the novel and provide its special quality of *megaloprepeia*, or "elegance." Readers who fault Hemingway for subordinating larger political issues to a single guerrilla skirmish or to a single character's actions would, fifth, disregard a similar subordination in Homer's *Iliad*, whose subject is "the wrath of Peleus' son Achilles / and its devastation," not the Trojan War.

Hemingway's formal transliteration of Spanish into archaic English also complies with conventions of the epic. The "thees" and "thous," that is, add the diversity, solemnity, and strangeness excepted of epics, and they elevate language to a heroic meter. Such a meter, notes Aristotle, is "most proper" to the epic, which "is particularly receptive of 'glosses' [i.e., archaic or dialectal words] and metaphors" (614, 619).

Another of Aristotle's observations tempts my epic hunting. Among improbabilities in the novel, the most objectionable is the character of Maria, her love-at-first-sight romance with Jordan, and their ability to share in the near-mystical experience of making the earth move.[8] But one of Aristotle's distinctions between tragedy and epic may be worth noting. Although the marvelous should be incorporated in a tragedy, he says, "the epic has more room for the irrational (which is the chief source of astonishment)" (622). Hemingway more than likely expected Jordan and Maria's relationship—as well as the late-May snow—to be acceptably realistic. But if its impulsiveness seems irrational and astonishes us, that may have been Hemingway's intent, a sought-after effect of another convention of the epic. At the very least we might allow that Hemingway has chosen "impossibilities that are (made) plausible in preference to possibilities that are (left) implausible" and so has not made his basic plot depend on "irrational incidents" (623).

Finally, Hemingway's choice of the kind of epic he wrote might also show that he had studied Aristotle's *Poetics*. Of the two kinds, the novel resembles the kind that Aristotle says characterizes the *Iliad*, the simple and disastrous, as opposed to the complex and moral, found in the *Odyssey*. The novel is simple because its straightforward narrative emphasizes inevitability rather than peripety and discovery and because it pivots around a unified action rather than the episodic adventures characteristic of the *Odyssey*. The novel is disastrous rather than moral because its outcome is fatal rather than fortunate.[9]

The lack of factual proof that sometime between March of 1939 and August of 1940 Hemingway carefully read the *Poetics'* sections on the epic certainly hobbles my attempt to be scholarly. I can only point at strong correlations between Aristotle's observations and the novel. And, once again, records of Hemingway's reading and library turn up little more than evidence that he owned and took with him to Finca Vigía—among the forty-five crates of books—a copy of Homer's *Iliad* and several books of literary criticism.[10] But these same records fail to show that he read Herodotus's *History of the Persian Wars*, which he did.[11] And traits enumerated in nearly any handbook of literary terms urge the conclusion that Hemingway intended to create a "literary" or "secondary" epic.[12] He has Jordan consider, for instance, that the "bridge can be the point on which the future of the human race can turn" (43). With this single thought Hemingway makes the setting for Jordan's mission "important to the history of a nation or race," "vast in its scope." And the novel's double actions—war and love—generate themes of "universal concern" that contribute to the didactic element so characteristic of an epic.[13] For example, Jordan repeatedly states his beliefs, as when he tells himself that he is no Marxist, that he believes in liberty, equality, and fraternity, in life, liberty, and the pursuit of happiness (305). While his credo indicates personal motives for being involved in the Spanish Civil War, it also inserts a recurrent theme of "universal concern": man's obligation to be his brother's keeper. This is, I trust, one reason the epigraph from Donne so strongly appealed to Hemingway when he was searching for a title.[14] The brother's-keeper theme also accounts for Jordan's thoughts on the eve of the attack. He feels that he has spent his entire life in the Guadarrama hills, that his oldest friend is Anselmo, that Agustín is his brother, and that Maria is his "true love," his wife, his sister, and his daughter (381). Jordan's obedience to duty and his patriotic sacrifice for Republican Spain also testify to his brotherly impulses, fighting in the war because he loves Spain and believes in the republic (163). When Maria, Pilar, and Jordan meet Joaquín, who tells them of his slain family, Hemingway again insists upon the brother's-keeper theme, for Maria sympathetically kisses him and tells him that she is his sister, that she loves him, and that they are all his family. Jordan confirms the sentiment by insisting that all of them are brothers (139).

To undercut this heady selflessness and its deference to noble principles and the future of the race, Hemingway adds the complementary theme of another "universal concern," man's duty to respond individually to each day's sensory realities. Jordan's romance with Maria, which provides him the erotic gratifications of the present moment, acknowledges that duty. And so he considers himself lucky to trade a life of seventy years for one of seventy hours, declaring that "now is the thing to praise and I am very happy with it. *Now, ahora, maintenant, heute. Now*, it has a funny sound to be a whole world and your life" (166). Not antithetical, the two themes merge. Hemingway insists upon this when Jordan professes his love to Maria, telling her that he loves her as " 'I love all that we have fought for,' " loves her " 'as I love liberty and dignity and the rights of all men to work and not be hungry,' " loves her " 'as I love Madrid that we have defended and as I love all my comrades that have died' " (348). In sharp contrast to the subtleties of Hemingway's earlier fiction, the frequency of overt, thematic expressions here should not cause us to regard them as evidence of artistic propaganda, of technical ineptness, or of failing imagination in Hemingway. Rather we should regard them as hallmark of an epic: statement of theme.

A writer whose allegiance seems to have been with fiction's realistic mode would presumably balk at concocting the required hero of an epic, someone "of heroic stature, of national or international importance and of great historical or legendary significance."[15] Yet Hemingway makes an epic hero of Robert Jordan. On no parochial mission, Jordan's belief that the "bridge can be the point on which the future of the human race can turn" (43) partly vouches for his potential "national or international importance," even though his efforts ultimately have no impact upon the outcome of the war. By yoking the complementary values in the themes of "universal concern," and by having internationalist associations with Spaniards and Russians, he also shows his stature. But is he of "great historical or legendary significance"? Well, the specific mission Golz-Hemingway assigns him has such potential, even though the job of detonating a bridge near a mountain pass seems common enough in a modern wartime situation. Hemingway gives it epic overtones by the specific allusions he allows Jordan when he contemplates his task: "He would abandon a hero's or a martyr's end gladly. He did not want to make a Thermopylae, nor be Horatius at any bridge, nor be the Dutch boy with his finger in the dyke" (164). Although Jordan rejects such heroics, his mission weds Spartan Leonidas's defense of the

mountain pass at Thermopylae against Persians to Roman Horatius's defense of the bridge over the Tiber against Etruscans. And
Jordan's final act, waiting at the pass to deter Lt. Berrendo's cavalry, emphasizes again the importance in an epic's "heroic plot"
of defending a mountain pass or a bridge. Surely that rearguard
action evokes the *Song of Roland*, with which Hemingway was
familiar.[16]

Perhaps Hemingway's efforts to ensure Jordan's heroic stature
account for some of his superhuman traits: his ability to ignite
Maria's instant love and the guerrilla band's (excepting Pablo)
quick approval of him, his Olympian range of experience and
knowledge, and his being entrusted with such an important mission despite his brief activity in the war. Most superhuman is perhaps his erotic power. While loving Maria he can—within seventy-two
hours—make the earth move twice out of the three times possible
in one lifetime. Jordan's ancestry also recommends his stature.
He descended from a Chiron-like grandfather whom a Civil War
general described as "a finer leader of irregular cavalry than John
Mosby"; and Jordan's grandfather in turn had praised Mosby as
"the finest cavalry leader that ever lived" (339). Among Jordan's
possessions back in Missoula, Montana, is his "Grandfather's
saber, bright and well oiled in its dented scabbard" (336), conjuring the legendary arms that heroes of epic mold usually have. Indeed, a suicidal father mars Jordan's noble lineage. But I read
Jordan's reminiscences of that father as a psychological "descent
to the underworld," for such journeys traditionally feature conversations with the dead.

Because it accepts Jordan's mission as its own, the guerrilla
band acquires the elevated position also expected of an epic cast.
And unlike the realistic characters of Hemingway's earlier fictions, who have no easily schematizable function, the band, a
spectrum of classic types, does.[17] One pair in that spectrum is
naive youth (Andrés) and sententious *senex* (Fernando). Another
pair is the obscene soldier (miles gloriosus–like Agustín) and the
wise humanist (Anselmo). There is also the gypsy-hedonist (Rafael), the ingénue (Maria), the man of feeling (Primitivo), the cynically intelligent journalist (Karkov), the paranoid chief commis-
sar of the International Brigade (Comrade Marty), and the realist
(Golz). I grant that such labels may oversimplify Hemingway's
dramatization of his characters. But I do not ignore the artistry in
his more complex creations of Pilar and Pablo. And I see his use of
single-faceted characters serving his design, for it is the only way

he can get the number of characters epic magnitude requires. And it contributes to epic elegance, achieved, as it must be, by breadth and variety rather than economy and intensity. By making most of his characters simple types, Hemingway avoids subplots that would blur the plot's unified action. Think of Milton deftly stereotyping the military attitudes of Moloch, Belial, Mammon, and Beelzebub in book 2 of *Paradise Lost*. Hemingway also stereotypes the military attitudes Andrés encounters while trying to deliver Jordan's message to Golz: the distrustful line captain; the enthusiastic battalion commander, Gomez; the indifferent brigade officer; the concerned Lt. Col. Miranda; the paranoid Comrade Marty; and the contemptuous Karkov.

The formidable problem for a realist writing in the epic mode would be how to present credibly those gods and supernatural forces who "interest themselves in the action and intervene from time to time."[18] Hemingway denies them the limelight that epic writers traditionally give them. But he does hint that they may be just offstage. On a military level, for example, Jordan and the guerrillas are subordinate to superiors whose larger views and petty rivalries determine events in much the way Homer's canopied gods do. On a symbolic level, Jordan and Maria's discovery of a true love that enables them to feel the earth move, the "miracle" (392) of Pablo's return with men and horses on the eve of the bridge blowing, Jordan's sense of luck at having his leg nerve crushed, the unexpected late-May snow, Andrés's thwarted odyssey to Golz, and even Jordan's inevitable death—all these might be construed as tokens of some supernatural intervention. But Pilar better shows supernatural forces at work in the novel. Her superstitions (the smell of death), palm-reading (Jordan's imminent death), and intuition (Maria's *gloria*) suggest a preternatural force that dallies with the supernatural. The agents of the air that literally intervene in the action are not gods, of course, but Fascist airplanes. And they are as partisan as Homer's Olympians, Milton's angels, Vergil's Fate, or the Beowulf-poet's *wyrd*.[19]

Ancillary epic traits are also in the novel. Trying to portray his hero objectively, Hemingway gives Jordan frequent internal debates that bear comparison with those of Odysseus (e.g., *Iliad*, 11:404–10), Satan, or Adam. He also lets Jordan get angry at his mission of trying to organize two "chicken-crut bands" to help him "blow a bridge under impossible conditions" so as "to abort a counter-offensive" that has probably already begun (167). As this quote suggests, Jordan succumbs to several rages—against the snow (178–81), against Pablo for stealing the detonator (369–70), and against the death of Anselmo (447). Perhaps these are meant to vie with the outsized anger and wrath typical of Achaians, Trojans, and devils. Hemingway also has several "extended formal speeches by the main characters": Pilar's accounts of the slaying of the Fascists and of Finito's conduct at the banquet in his honor, Jordan's and Anselmo's discussion of killing (chap. 3), and Jordan's *alba*, persuading Maria to leave him at the pass. Stories of other heroes' valorous deeds take their appropriate place in an epic: Finito's bullfighting, Sordo's combat, Pablo's raid of Otero (chap. 15), Jordan's grandfather's Civil War experiences, mention of Custer, Rafael's account of the train-blowing and rescue of Maria, even Jordan's trainblowing with Kashkin (149) and delivery of a tank for Montero's attack at Carabanchel (239–42). The narrative point of view is, as an epic requires, duly omniscient and focuses mainly upon the hero. But the narrator, alas, fails to invoke the muse. Mindful of Milton's diffident invocation two dozen lines into book 7 of *Paradise Lost*, I wonder if it is to reflect similar authorial diffidence and to acknowledge some superior power that prompts Jordan's several writing references. He mentions other writers, his desire to write about his present experience, and his envy of Pilar's bardic narrative of the slaying of the Fascists. And he remarks on Karkov's belief in his writing abilities, despite an unsuccessful, earlier book on Spain.

Parallels between *For Whom the Bell Tolls* and the *Iliad* are the last way I infer Hemingway's intention to compose an epic. Similar to the emotional wrangling in book 1 of the *Iliad*, discord dominates the early chapters of the novel. And so Pablo's disapproval of Jordan's mission and of Pilar's wresting control from him gives rise to *Iliad*-like angers, recriminations, vauntings, insults, and public embarrassment. Even the usually mild Anselmo berates Pablo, calling him a brute and a beast, brainless, even thising and thating in the this and that of Pablo's father (11). Pablo's refusal to assist in the bridge-blowing and his defection create the same anxiety for Jordan and the guerrilla band as Achilles' withdrawal creates for the Achaians; without the two men, each effort is doomed. And the skulking, crafty Pablo jealously resents Jordan's taking of Maria, much as Achilles resents Agamemnon's taking of his "prize," Briseis. Even Pablo's return, caused by his realization that he found himself lonely (390), parallels Achilles' return to battle, caused, among other things, by loneliness due to Patroclus's death.[20] Also included are *Iliad*-like accounts of the slaying of suppliants (the six Fascists) and of kin (both Maria's and Joaquin's). Finally, I hear in the novel's heroic futility an echo of the suffering and doom in the *Iliad*.

My catalogue of epic traits should crowd out any belief that it was beneath Hemingway's literary dignity and ability to use an ancient literary mode. If anything, such an imitation enhances his stature. It shows that his impulse for experimentation did not collapse with the stock market in 1929. And it compels respect for the very considerable effort that had to go into composing an epic. Surely it took a good bit of reading and research before he launched into it.

Yet some readers may be morally offended by Hemingway's deviousness, hiding as he does an epic beneath the skirts of a "realistic" war novel. And others will be esthetically offended by the amount of creative energy Hemingway must have spent to soundproof the epic machinery. Still others, if they give credence to my reading, will rush to his defense with the idea that all great art conceals itself. But for me the knowledge that Hemingway fashioned *For Whom the Bell Tolls* as an epic invites evaluating his novel as he must secretly have wished it to be evaluated, as rival to the great epics. And in this competition his novel fares poorly.

One defect in Hemingway's novel is owing to his partial commitment to epic machinery. I grant that hearing its machinery requires a heavy gloss. But once heard, it should dominate everything Hemingway attempts in the novel. Yet his commitment to writing in a realistic mode interferes. The epic stamp, for example, seems ubiquitous. It seems to compel Hemingway to rely heavily, say, upon the internal debates so common to the epic. But because Hemingway will not engage that convention completely, his internal debates lack the intensity, complexity, and psychological depth—in a word, the *brio*—of those wrought by Homer, Vergil, and Milton. And consider Jordan. The epic tradition seems to dictate many of his features, values, and actions. Yet in Hemingway's hands he becomes, ultimately, a schematized character, a genetic cross of duty-ridden Aeneas and will-forging Odysseus. Hanging back from a full commitment to the epic, Hemingway ignores Aristotle's advice, that an epic hero not be "eminently virtuous." Yet regardless of Jordan's several "rages" and his lovemaking, he is. Even his capacity to make love and to be aware, without distress, of the approaching hour of his mission (378) shows an emotional shallowness and lack of moral dilemma that he needs to rival the dimensions of Achilles, old Beowulf, or Adam. A martyr, Jordan is a fit figure for hagiography, not epic.

A more serious defect is the novel's structure. Because the authors of great epics do not try to conceal its conventions, accepting them without embarrassment or apology as a minor aspect of a larger design, they can apply themselves to the significant creative problems of invention and construction. And most evaluations of the construction of epics will find the *Iliad* and *Paradise Lost, Beowulf* and the *Odyssey* massive and delicate, *For Whom the Bell Tolls* mechanical and reductive.[21] Its own structure, not the suprastructure of the epic, makes it so. For Hemingway overuses the single metaphor of civil war to construct his novel. He writes of Spain's civil war and, in turn, of the civil war between the ideologies of opposing political extremes, fascism and communism. And he writes of the civil war within the guerrilla band and even within Jordan, as seen in Jordan's numerous internal debates and in the civil war between his values: love, pleasure, self, cynicism, and the present on the one hand; war, duty, others, idealism, and the future on the other.

But Hemingway overworks the metaphor of civil war in the novel's sequence. Almost predictably the novel moves back and forth across that symbolic bridge from plot to flashback, as nearly every chapter reveals. Chapter 1 shifts from Jordan's arrival at the pass to the scene with Golz two nights earlier, and then back to his meeting with Pablo. Andrés's journey to Golz later keeps the narrative deliberately double. Hemingway also develops many chapters by contrasting character types: chapter 1, Golz and Pablo; 2, Rafael and Pilar; 3, Anselmo and Agustín; 11, Joaquín and El Sordo. Or else chapters contrast ideas: Pablo's attitudes contrast with Pilar's about the bridgeblowing mission in chapter 4; the views at Gaylord's contrast with those at Velasquez's in chapter 18. Sometimes chapters contrast emotions. In chapter 14 Finito appears festive while secretly spitting blood, is horrified while the banquet honors his courage. In chapter 15 Anselmo wants to leave his post in the snow and return to the comfort of the cave, but he stays, obedient to Jordan's request. In chapter 27, Joaquín shifts from Communist cliché and Pasionara to Catholic ritual and the Virgin Mary. Or in chapter 34 Andrés feels both pride and shame for his annual act of biting the bull's ear during the bull-baiting. Hemingway's use of Spanish even gives the novel two styles that maintain the metaphor of civil war. And certainly the conventions of a realistic novel and those of a stylized epic seesaw on the metaphor.

The novel's various features, then, show Hemingway turning continuously to civil war as subject and metaphor for the novel's structure. By so doing he achieves a sustained focus upon the dilemmas, the ambivalencies, the internal and external civil wars characteristic of all human experience, an apt focus for an epic.[22] And the novel gives flesh to Hemingway's belief that "civil wars are the best wars for writers." But his ambitiousness to bridge symbolically all experience results in a novel without an organic pulse. Or at least the rigorously superimposed grids of epic conventions and of civil war structure subdue the novel's pulse. For as soon as I found these grids, there was little left of "The Undiscovered Country"—the novel's provisional title—that did not conform to one or the other of them. To tidy the sprawl of his concealed epic and to enforce the novel's unity, Hemingway reduced the novel to a pattern that he repeats and repeats. He forgot to allow for the residual unexplainables, the intransigent materials, the trace elements or just-heard rhythms that a living work of art, one with an organic pulse, has.

In George Plimpton's *Paris Review* interview Hemingway makes a distinction that has always struck me as more defensive than descriptive: "Though there is one part of writing that is solid and you do no harm by talking about it, the other is fragile, and if you talk about it, the structure cracks and you have nothing."[23] Hemingway makes this statement, let me note, while discussing the craft of writing rather than the craft of a finished piece. But except for matters of authorial intention and interpretation, I find it hard to imagine anything so fragile or private that an author would harm it by discussing it. Besides, to talk about a structure that can crack refers more to an object than to a process, to a written, finished work, rather than to the craft of writing. In any event, I can not see how a good piece of writing, however paradoxical, can be preciously schizophrenic and yet simultaneously integrated, as Hemingway's division of writing into solid and fragile parts implies. Nor can I see how any author who asks to be considered major can also ask to have his works only partly talked about. That is like asking that they be left on the bookshelf, that they not be tested for their durability. Much less can I see how a writer who prides himself on his outdoorsman's image can be so anxious about fragile things—unless his writings conceal delicate structures whose discovery he feared would cause them to shatter. Clearly Hemingway's hidden epic in *For Whom the Bell Tolls* confirms his statement about the two parts of writing. And detecting that hidden, fragile epic may crack the novel's solid structure, whether *structure* refers loosely to the plausibility of the novel as a realistic story or refers literally to the novel's all-too-conscious construction and architecture. Still, the detection leaves more than nothing. It leaves a modern experiment in an ancient mode. And that experiment will surely survive, if only as a rarity, a fascinating museum piece.

Afterword

Maybe what prompted Hemingway to write the novels of this phase was simply his need to keep rank as one of America's foremost novelists, some years having elapsed since *A Farewell to Arms* was published. Maybe he was answering the call for fiction with a social theme. Morgan's dying words and Jordan's actions and beliefs heed it. Maybe Hemingway was trying to refute the charge that he was a Johnny-one-note. Any truth in it would be overwhelmed by the ancient literary modes orchestrating *To Have and Have Not* and *For Whom the Bell Tolls*. Maybe Hemingway was hoping to restore for modern readers those classic modes of tragedy and epic, just as he had hoped to restore the esthetic dimension of spectator sports and hunting. Maybe his concern with esthetics in those two nonfiction books prodded him to pursue esthetics in a disciplined way in these two novels. Aristotle's *Poetics* is not an unlikely starting place for an autodidact like Hemingway. Its interest in discerning those elements of a literary work that yield its distinct pleasures, after all, would appeal to him, and because he loves concealing, omitting things, he would enjoy putting to use knowledge that few readers or acquaintances would suspect he had. Perhaps Hemingway's remark about studying Cézanne applies to Aristotle as well: "I was learning very much from him but I was not articulate enough to explain it to anyone. Besides, it was a secret" (*Feast*, 13). Or perhaps Hemingway's interest in the rules, codes, strategies, and techniques of sports and war led him to spend time acquainting himself with some of the older rules, formulas, and conventions of the craft by which he earned his living.

Maybe what prompted the two novels of this phase was Hemingway's fear that his artistic vision and imagination had gone dry. To discover him using old literary conventions should certainly also see his adventurousness. But it can also find him resorting to those conventions to charge his imagination, to get his own creative juices pumping. If one of Hemingway's perennial problems was that he was better endowed to write short stories than novels—a fine sprinter but no long-distance runner—then the criteria of tragedy and the epic would set a task big enough to require a novel-length effort. And if Hemingway did not have that problem, then his use of those older literary modes still asks whether these two novels were internally or externally inspired, whether they are original or derivative works, whether they are organic or mechanical. To me the latter term in each pair seems the more likely answer, especially when I ask myself whether Morgan and Jordan are human beings on whom Hemingway has lavished detail and attention because of their intrinsic worth or whether they are characters subservient to a formula, cogs in some intricate literary machinery.

My maybes may answer why Hemingway wrote the novels of this phase. But I find more compelling the answer that Hemingway was driven to express in them a specific form of his fixation on his father. Deeply wounded by his father's suicide on that Thursday morning of 6 December 1928, Hemingway here tries to exorcize his preoccupation with it by assigning it to Robert Jordan, perhaps still believing that " 'you'll lose it if you talk about it' " (*Sun Rises*, 245). But even more, Hemingway's anger at his father's weakness erupts in these novels' strong parricidal wishes. At the same time, those wishes are offset by the fraternal impulses of Harry Morgan and Robert Jordan, impulses that reveal an equally strong wish to save the father-as-brother. The marked ambivalence in this pattern of desiring both the death and the rescue of the father correlates with Hemingway's feelings about his father during this period.[1]

Whether the tragic protagonists are Oedipus, Antigone, Hamlet, or Macbeth, their recurrent adversary is the father, displaced though he may be as stepfather, uncle, or king. Harry Morgan's father, of course, is never mentioned in *To Have and Have Not*. But he is present, however fragmented and displaced, in his treacherous acts. He guns down three young Cubans, defaults on the money he owes a fisherman, and betrays a dozen of his racial kinsmen. Mr. Sing, Harry's literal victim, succinctly typifies the terrible father, acting out the treachery of Johnson and the Cubans' two assailants. By slaying Sing, Harry avenges the wrongs a "father" has done him, the three young men and the other twelve "sons," the trusting Chinese. He also avenges the wrong done the third parties of the perennial triangle—mothers, wives, and daughters—be they the Cubans', the Chinese's or Harry's.

Harry's specific adversaries, Johnson and Sing, however, are proxies for an even more treacherous father, the political system. It makes have-nots of Harry and his fellow dregs, haves of people who sell for a dollar a pint something that costs them only three cents per quart (240). A capitalistic system that permits such economic inequities becomes the unjust father whose authority lets him tyrannize over his weak or malcontent sons.[2] Denying that he is a radical, Harry nonetheless admits that he has been sore at the government for a long time, adding that it is trying to starve out the conchs, burn down their shacks, and build apartments to make it a tourist town (96–97). Cynically defining the government's attitude toward the vets, Nelson Jacks declares that President Hoover forced them out of Anticosti flats and President Roosevelt shipped them to the keys to get rid of them " 'because we are the desperate ones. . . . The ones with nothing to lose. We are the completely brutalized ones' " (206). Jacks's Communistic convictions and Harry's outlawry are like the revolutionaries' efforts to overthrow Cuba's dictatorship. All three express hostility toward the misconduct of government-as-father. Its arrogance is sketched in Frederick Harrison, one of the top men in the administration (80). Its ruthlessness is typified in the piratical sixty-year-old grain broker whose paternal greed, unrestrained by government policy, makes the many "sons" who compete with him commit suicide (237–38). Its castrating power is dramatized in the harm it inflicts upon the vets and Harry, costing him an arm and a boat.

Harry's hostility toward Eddy is a different matter. Witness to Harry's murder of Sing, Eddy gives Harry reason to kill him, a relatively useless, untrustworthy parasite who might blab or try to blackmail Harry. Part of the reason Harry does not kill him is that he knew him back when he was still a good man (43). Harry's considerateness is like his regard for deaf Frankie, whimpering Wesley, and wife-nagged Albert. And Harry's considerateness seems motivated by fellow feeling for his downtrodden brothers, by his apparent wish to help these feckless men regain some shred of dignity. But Harry's altruism is compensatory at best. That is, to compensate for his parricidal acts against the treacherous fathers, he tries to rescue from complete degradation men who are no longer what they once were, who are, like Albert, browbeaten by their wives. But when the Cuban Roberto shoots Albert, Harry is not angry just at Roberto, another bullying father. Nor is he angry just at himself for failing to protect Albert. He is also angry at Albert for being so defenseless, so resourceless, so deficient, in effect, as a father.

The pattern here, then, is that parricidal wishes find their conventional outlet against treacherous, strong fathers, and an unconventional one against the fathers whose weakness is also treacherous because it betrays the traditional role of the self-sufficient, masterful male. Concealed behind a mask of fellow feeling, Harry wishes them dead too. Among them only Albert actually dies. But though Eddy is only threatened and Wesley only wounded, they unaccountably disappear from the novel, suggesting Hemingway's wish to rid his world of them. Again, the novel seems to solicit pity for the brutalized vets and for those men Hemingway's narrator numbers as suicides (237–38). But the tone of both sections is hostile, attuned to "the mess they [suicides] leave for relatives to clean up" (238). Little wonder that Harry wants to do things singlehandedly. He wants freedom from tyrannizing, weak, and suicidal fathers because they all stir up parricidal wishes in him.

Parricide notwithstanding, Harry also wants paternal understanding and approval. This motive partly explains his narration of part 1 of the novel. To whom does he tell the exploits of that section? Not just to any chum, any friendly listener, as I mentioned earlier. Rather to someone he trusts, whose regard he seeks. His wife, Marie, meets these criteria. But the last page of Harry's narration discounts her as listener. He would not tell her what he said to her upon his return to Key West. The only character who deeply respects Harry is Captain Willie Adams. Surprised to see Harry's boat after the night's storm, he thinks, "So Harry crossed last night. That boy's got cojones. He must have got that whole blow" (78). Captain Willie's defiance of Frederick Harrison, his attempt to protect Harry, and his admiration of Harry as equal suggest that he may be the unidentified listener of part 1, the father figure who bestows understanding and approval upon Harry.[3] But he too is weak, unable to safeguard Harry. And perhaps his disappearance from the novel in part 3 suggests Hemingway's unconscious doubts about whether Captain Willie is a trustworthy or a treacherous father.

Because Hemingway faulted his father for being an authoritarian father, a weak husband, and a suicide, it is easy now to translate some of the unconscious origins of *To Have and Have Not*, rooted as they are in Hemingway's hostility toward all three traits. To vent that hostility could well prompt creating the novel's three kinds of bad fathers and, of course, Hemingway's wish to project himself into a tragic hero. But his regard for his father's positive traits—charity, responsibility, and self-discipline—may also explain Hemingway's sympathies in the Oedipal triangle of Professor MacWalsey, Richard, and Helen Gordon.

Hemingway's satiric treatment of Richard Gordon is consciously directed at contemporaries who write formulaic, social-protest novels. But unconsciously it is self-directed. The near-duplication of Jordan, Morgan, and Gordon's rhyming surnames might imply that idea, since all three are self-projections of Hemingway. But even more, Gordon's betrayal of his wife Helen and his adultery with Helène Bradley retrace Hemingway's betrayal of Hadley ten years earlier for the seductive wiles of Helène-like Pauline, " 'that dirty rich bitch' " (186), as Helen calls her.[4] Hemingway's regret shows up in the contempt he lets Wallace Johnston voice against Helène-Pauline—" 'She represents everything I hate in a woman' " (229)—and in Gordon's recall of his afternoon with her. The reason Gordon-Hemingway leaves her bed is not, I suspect, fear of her supposedly impotent husband, but disgust for Helène and shame at being caught by a father figure *"standing heavy and bearded in the doorway"* (189). Hemingway projects his self-loathing upon Gordon by allowing Helène to slap and mock him: " '*I thought you were a man of the world*' " (190). Hemingway compounds his self-punishment by having Gordon unjustly slap Helen and take drunken punches at MacWalsey. Helen's fondness for MacWalsey is reciprocated, acknowledging Dr. Hemingway's fondness for his first daughter-in-law and his disappointment in the son who betrayed her. So to his guilt for marital wrongs Hemingway adds more for betraying his father, portrayed as he is partly by MacWalsey. Though no ideal, Helen respects him: " 'He's a man. He's kind and he's charitable and he makes you feel comfortable and we come from the same things and we have values that you'll never have' " (187). Hemingway respects him too; so MacWalsey's paternal attempt to care for the stupid, belligerent Gordon seems an oblique confession of Hemingway's blindness and filial ingratitude. As Gordon lurches away from the taxi MacWalsey had been taking him home in, the driver asks, " 'Is he your brother?' 'In a way,' said Professor MacWalsey" (221).

Hemingway's ambivalent feelings toward his father prompted *For Whom the Bell Tolls* too, for the novel's motif of suicide and Jordan's struggle with his father's suicide consciously acknowledge Hemingway's similar struggle.[5] Indeed, the information on Robert Jordan's father and grandfather is an anomaly in Hemingway's fiction. The familiar pattern of his novels is to omit a clear account of his hero's family background, but here Hemingway breaks that pattern. His literary reason may be to defer to the requirement that an epic hero have a lineage of some stature. Though Jordan's father is a minus on that score, his grandfather's stature as "a finer leader of irregular cavalry than John Mosby" (339) (and as a member of the Republican national committee [66]?) is a plus. Hemingway's personal reason for breaking his pattern may be either to show that he can face his father's suicide without flinching or to exorcize its stigma: "If he wrote it he could get rid of it. He had gotten rid of many things by writing them" (*Stories*, 491).

The information on Jordan's background lets us infer the complex reasons Jordan is in Spain. His putative reason, of course, is idealistic: to fight for a country and a way of life he values. His Communist and Republican sympathies both express his presumed fraternal ethic. And they show that beneath his altruism is a normal hostility toward the repressive, dictatorial father, which fascism represents. Figuratively the Spanish Civil War acts out the classic struggle between the brothers and the father for possession of Mother Spain. But Jordan's fraternal allegiance seems questionable, since the four men he kills—Kashkin, the cavalryman, the sentry at the bridge, and, we are to assume, Lt. Berrendo—are his "brothers." Berrendo and the cavalryman come from Navarre, a region Jordan is especially fond of, Kashkin shares Jordan's military skills, and they are all young.[6] As his killing of the sentry at the bridge suggests, Jordan wishes to slay fraternal rivals who interfere with his erotic pleasures of making the earth move, be it with sexual orgasm or dynamite explosion. Jordan's killing of the young cavalryman who comes upon him and Maria in their sleeping bag reinforces that interpretation.

I am more persuaded, however, that Jordan's fratricide reveals his unconscious sympathies with his father, circuitous though they are. After all, Jordan's fundamental reason for going to

Spain is to deal with the disgrace of his father's suicide. As his recurrent internal dialogues indicate, that act has so traumatized Jordan that he can only regain self-esteem by proving to himself that he is like his grandfather, not his father.[7] He has pledged himself to the Republican cause, for example, as proof that he is not selfish; by contrast his father was so wrapped up in his own problems that he selfishly took his own life. Also, Jordan has learned the skills of a dynamiter so that his military duties will require hazardous assignments to test whether he will buckle under crisis and commit suicide too.

This view of Jordan's reason for being in Spain explains his relationships with several of the novel's characters. Rather than see Kashkin as Jordan's double, a brother whose nervousness, anxiety, and diffidence deeply unsettle his comrades, he is one displacement of Jordan's father. Kashkin represents a truly disgraceful father, someone whose self-preoccupation breeds worse results than did Mr. Jordan's. A suicide at least has the dignity of dying by a self-inflicted wound. But Kashkin, a "rare one," requires Jordan to shoot him, imposing guilt upon Jordan as a parricide or a fratricide.

Another displacement of Jordan's suicidal father is Anselmo.[8] A benevolent man, the old guide's nonviolent ways are admirable. He is the obedient subordinate who stays at his post despite the snow. He is the meek elder who serves a violent cause despite his ethic of peace. He is the tenderhearted soldier who weeps upon killing the sentry at the bridge. Winsome though he is, he is also, like Jordan's father, weak and submissive to more dominating, self-assertive people: " 'I will do as thou orderest' " (410), he tells Jordan, just as Mr. Jordan took orders from the woman who bullied him (339). Anselmo's failure to flatten himself behind the high stone road marker that has been hiding him lets a fragment of steel kill him when the bridge is blown. But since he pulls one of the detonating wires, perhaps, like Mr. Jordan, he dies by his own hand. Jordan, however, has a hand in Anselmo's death, and not just because he pulls the other wire. Rather he has not told or ordered Anselmo what to do after they pull the wires. And he has been around Anselmo long enough to know that the old man needs orders. Whereas Jordan directly shot the anxious and weak father, Kashkin, here then he indirectly slays the benevolent, meek father, Anselmo.

Jordan's relationship with his father is displaced in other characters too, as consideration of Fernando, Primitivo, or El Sordo would show. But it is Pablo who makes most visible Jordan's effort to deal with his suicidal father. A warrior turned soft, a revolutionary gone domestic, a leader who leads now only to the wine bowl, Pablo is the clearest counterpart to Jordan's father—a disgrace. His sullenness and resistance to Jordan's mission are shameful to the band and prompt Pilar to become the maternal, domineering force in this adopted family of Jordan's. Pablo's theft of the caps and detonators and his murder of the band of men who help him overcome the soldiers at the mill below the bridge amplify our moral outrage toward him. But Jordan refuses to kill him. The father figure most deserving of Jordan's parricidal impulses, Pablo rides out of the novel unscathed. To be sure, there are good reasons for Jordan's refusal to shoot Pablo. If he is to be shot, the band should do it. If he is so "inutile," there is little need to kill him, for he will not hinder the band's plans. If Jordan were to shoot him, Jordan might alienate the guerrillas and jeopardize the mission.

But these are rationalizations. Jordan refuses to kill him because he wishes instead to redeem a disgraced man, both Pablo and the man Pablo represents, Jordan's father. Jordan's redemptive role is visible, I think, in several ways. His relationship with Maria shows it. His romantic act of loving her and figuratively making the earth move, the first miracle, renews her self-esteem, shattered, disfigured, and dishonored as she has been by her parents' death, her shaved head, and her rape. Jordan's mission also shows his redemptive role. His revolutionary act of blowing the bridge and literally making the earth move, the second miracle, renews hope for the republican cause, disgraced as it is by the cynicism of Gaylord's, by its poor leadership, and by such brutalities as Pablo's execution of the Fascists. But Jordan's redemptive role serves his filial wish to make the earth move beneath Pablo, to redeem him by reigniting his manliness, self-esteem, and leadership. Jordan's success is testified to by the third miracle, Pablo's return. He brings five men to replace El Sordo's band and to help accomplish Jordan's mission. Later he shoots those same men to provide the horses his "family" needs for their escape to Gredos. And he leads the remainder of the band away from the pass where the wounded Jordan awaits Berrendo's cavalry. Pablo thereby honors Jordan's wish, confirmed as it is when "their two hands gripped in the dark. . . . Pablo's hand gripped his hard and pressed it frankly and he returned the grip. Pablo had a good hand in the dark and feeling it gave Robert Jordan the strangest feeling he had felt that morning" (404). The handshake, which partly precipitates Jordan's recall of the first time he went away to school (405) and of his father's good-byes, again identifies Pablo with Mr. Jordan, Jordan as redemptive son.

That Jordan's mission of redeeming his father is of primary importance to him and to his author is also seen in Jordan's willingness to remain at the pass at the novel's end. I grant that Jordan's leg injury may be mortal. But no external evidence, neither blood nor agony, verifies that it is. And the guerrilla band is not a mercenary lot who would ride away from an injured comrade. Their rescue of Maria has borne that out. They could have put a splint on Jordan's leg, dumped the supplies from the pack horse Rafael had caught, and secured Jordan so that he would not seriously hamper their escape, even were he to lose consciousness. But Hemingway ignores these alternatives. Instead, Jordan, seeing Pablo shake his head, nods at him (461), apparently signaling that death is too certain for any rescue attempt.

I would like to suspend my disbelief and be confident that Pablo and Jordan have the medical savvy to size up Jordan's situation at a glance. And when Jordan tells Pablo, " 'Listen. Get along. I am mucked, see?' " (462), I would like to believe that his rapid and decisive resolve argues his heroism. But in the exchange between them Jordan implies that he should not go with the band, now that the father has been restored to his rightful role. And Pablo tacitly accepts Jordan's offer. After the band has ridden off, Jordan is confident that Pablo has a sound plan, is certain that Pablo has left him nothing to worry about (466). Jordan's confidence in Pablo, in short, leaves him no further reason or wish to live, his real mission accomplished. Pablo makes no gesture of gratitude or praise to commend the son's sacrifice. But his stand-in, Agustín, does. The "old one," reluctant to leave Jordan, stays behind with him for a few minutes, offering to shoot him if he suffers, weeping, making sure that he has what he needs, cursing the war and respectfully bidding him farewell. Coming as this display of paternal approval does from a character who has been portrayed as a tough, obscene soldier, Jordan's redemptive influence seems amply confirmed.

For all its presumed romance, Jordan's relationship with Maria better reveals the primacy of his relationship with Pablo-as-father. Had Jordan truly loved Maria, he would have made some effort to escape at the end of the novel. Had he truly loved her, he would have let her remain with him at the pass where they could have died together in a romantic finale. It is not Hemingway's or Jordan's realism that rejects both options. Rather Jordan does not want any sustained heterosexual involvement. His bachelor's status and his military commitment bear this out, declaring as they do his unwillingness to court female favors or domestic entanglements. And his acts of becoming only briefly involved with Maria and then casting her off also bear it out. Having been sure all along that his mission will be fatal to him, Jordan's leg injury propitiously and honorably gratifies his secret suicidal wish, a wish that allies him with his father. But the leg injury also gives him an honorable way to terminate his romance. The phallic implications of his wound suggest not only Jordan-as-son's willing relinquishment of both the sexual and leadership roles to the resurrected Pablo-as-father, but also repudiation of Maria-as-daughter-sister, for whom the two men have tacitly competed.

There are other reasons Jordan rejects Maria. Despite his protestations of true love, his love is for a woman whom none of the men in the band have sexually known. Obviously her recent traumas have kept any of them from trying her favors. And it is fortuitous that Jordan arrives just when enough time has elapsed for her to be over the shock of her experiences and for her hair to have grown out enough to make her attractive, especially to an American who would not be bothered by her short hair. But her specific traumas make her repugnant to the band, however lovely she is to their eyes. Not only has she been massively deflowered of hair and virginity, but as she tells Jordan, it is probable that she will never bear him a child, no issue having come from her rape (354). And her traumas have affected her personality. Her infantile innocence and unrestrained love for Jordan clearly suggest that to me. So, sexually dishonored and sterile, psychologically regressive and dependent, she is a woman to be avoided, not a dream maiden to be desired. Flanked as she is by the dominating, aggressive Pilar, the two might threaten even a normal male and cause him to desire only a temporary relationship with them and then to redirect his amorous desires into homerotic channels.[9]

Even more, to Jordan, Maria is ultimately loathsome. Beneath his apparent ardor lie feelings of self-congratulation for sharing his bed with a ravaged girl. Beneath that lie feelings of repugnance for her easy surrender, for the experiences that have deeply soiled her body, and for the incestuousness of their love, Pilar having said early that they looked like brother and sister (67). And beneath that lie feelings of guilt for having taken what belonged to Pablo, if not to the rest of the band, whose rescue of her revealed their erotic desire for her. Jordan's unconscious contempt for Maria surfaces in his rejection of her when they part. Magnanimous to appearances, its wound is more savage than all her earlier experiences. For though the triple trauma of seeing her parents executed, being shorn, and being raped is inflicted by enemies, here it is her lover who rejects her. Hemingway does not ask us to consider the effect this will have on Maria. But I find no reason to be sanguine about her psychic condition after Jordan, the dynamiter, sends her riding off with the explosive force of that rejection in her mind. At the novel's beginning Pilar had declared, " 'I do not want her crazy here after you will go. I have had her crazy before and I have enough without that' " (33).[10]

Despite Hemingway's parricidal wish in *To Have and Have Not* and *For Whom the Bell Tolls*, his contrary wish to redeem his own father outweighs it. And whereas the two nonfiction works of his previous phase express filial allegiance by commemorating his father's values, the novels of this phase sustain it by projecting Hemingway's willingness to sacrifice his life for him. Like Harry Morgan, mortally wounded by one of the Cubans, Robert Jordan will be shot by Lt. Berrendo's cavalrymen who survive his machine gun. Firing upon and being slain by their brothers, both men essentially immolate themselves for a father, whether he is the formerly disgraced Pablo or the wife-nagged, weak Albert whom the Cubans have ruthlessly slain. The other fictitious heroes of this period further bear out Hemingway's wish. Hemingway's decision to have Philip Rawlings in *The Fifth Column* abandon Dorothy Bridges for the certain death of an espionage agent mirrors it. His choice in "The Snows of Kilimanjaro" of letting Harry die reveals it too. After all, Harry's failure to nurse the slight wound that eventually causes his death expresses Hemingway's analogous guilt, his failure to heed a set of values summed up as "the doctor's orders." The clearest instance of Hemingway's wish is "The Short Happy Life of Francis Macomber." What makes Francis's life happy is not his brief adulthood but his endorsement by the story's father figure, Wilson. Even more deeply gratifying to Hemingway's unconscious would be the paroxysm of pleasure derived from allowing Francis to die at the hands of the mother, Margot. That immolation puts her under Wilson's thumb and gratifies Hemingway's wish of helping his father acquire what he most lacked, masculine domination of a woman.

THE IMITATIVE PHASE

4

A Dantesque "Imitation":
Across the River and into the Trees

I imagine many readers scratch their heads after browsing through a shelf of Hemingway's works. Why, there is a play, a parody, and a guidebook there, they find. Now, why would a writer of realistic fiction wander into such literary byways, they might well ask. Sampling the short stories, they might also wonder what to make of such oddities as "A Natural History of the Dead," "One Reader Writes," or "Homage to Switzerland," so different from his better-known stories. And should they read "Old Man at the Bridge" and "The Chauffeurs of Spain" as news releases or as fiction? Among the curiosities in Hemingway's canon, *Across the River and into the Trees* would perplex them most. Its realistic story, a dying ex-general on his last weekend pass to hunt ducks and to romance a nineteen-year-old Venetian girl, does not have much promise. Nor does its fantasy, that a princess can draw rancor out of an aging soldier and purify him before he dies. And its many nonfictional references would make them wonder whether a library should classify it under fiction, history, or autobiography. Carlos Baker's explanation of many aspects of the novel would make my imagined readers decide in favor of autobiography: Hemingway's interest in nineteen-year-old Adriana Ivancich, his recurring illnesses during 1948 and 1949, the deaths of several friends, the 1949 winter sojourn in Italy, and the appearance of Sinclair Lewis at the Gritti.[1] And my readers' decision would be encouraged were they to read other critics who, biographically inspired, unsympathetically dismiss the novel as a satire of middle-aged adolescence, a wish-fulfilling fictional interview, a "senile version" of "vanquished heroes," or a self-indulgent daydream.[2] But I would have my imagined readers, whom I let return to their busy reality, hear Hemingway's own classification of his novel, cryptic though it is: " 'In writing I have moved through arithmetic, through plane geometry and algebra, and now I am in calculus.' "[3]

If the recipes for tragedy and epic went into making *To Have and Have Not* and *For Whom the Bell Tolls*, and if they help us read those novels a bit more knowledgeably, then why not ask if any recipe went into making *Across the River*, too? Taking Hemingway's mathematical metaphor in good faith, I answer that the calculus of the novel—its special symbolic method of analysis—is his conscious "imitation" of Dante's *Divine Comedy*.[4] I put the word in quotation marks because Hemingway does not imitate the design, specific scenes, or even crucial strategies of the poem; he is too good an artist to copy blatantly. I use the word in its renaissance sense to suggest, rather, that Hemingway "follows classical models," writes "in the spirit of " the *Divine Comedy*. He borrows some of its modes and devices. He incorporates several Dantean effects. And he duplicates enough features to make discernible a conscious parallel.[5] Unaware of the novel's indebtedness to the poem, we may find little more than a novel of character, a quite muddled novel at that. But by hearing in one ear the poem, we may hear in the other Colonel Richard Cantwell—whose name invokes the cantos—a Dantesque sinner whose imminent death weighs heavily upon his failing heart. We may even hear Hemingway's experiment, his Dantesque yoking of mimetic fiction, historicity, and dream.

Four months before *Across the River* was published, Lillian Ross's notorious interview with Hemingway appeared. In it Hemingway declares that his writings compete against literary predecessors: " 'I started out very quiet and I beat Mr. Turgenev. Then I trained hard and I beat Mr. de Maupassant. I've fought two draws with Mr. Stendhal, and I think I had an edge in the last one.' "[6] No reference to Dante, of course. And some posturing and exaggeration as well. But this statement reiterates what Hemingway had said fifteen years earlier in "Monologue to the Maestro: A High Seas Letter":

> Listen. There is no use writing anything that has been written before unless you can beat it. What a writer in our time has to do is write what hasn't been written before or beat dead men at what they have done. The only way he can tell how he is going is to compete with dead men. Most live writers do not exist. . . . The only people for a serious writer to compete with are the dead that he knows are good. It is like a miler

running against the clock rather than simply trying to beat whoever is in the race with him. Unless he runs against time he will never know what he is capable of attaining. [*By-Line*, 218–19][7]

One sign that Hemingway is competing with Dante is the novel's most conspicuous but most ignored feature, its mixture of fiction and nonfiction. No work of literature more effectively yokes historical and imaginary experience, actual and legendary characters than Dante's great poem. Likewise, along with its fictitious characters *Across the River* alludes to no fewer than sixty actual people, ranging from Ingrid Bergman and Margaret Truman to Giotto and Piero della Francesca, from Custer and General Walter Bedell Smith to Frederick the Great and T'Sun Su, from Gene Tunney and Stonewall Jackson to Gabrielle d'Annunzio and Red Smith. And to the novel's imaginary world Hemingway ties military campaigns of both world wars, odd things for a novelist to hitch to a fiction—unless, of course, he has the esteemed precedent of a literary work that contains Florentine civil strife among Guelphs and Ghibellines, warfare between papal and temporal rulers, and many historical events that predate 1310. Like the poem, the novel is riddled with arcane and topical allusions, both to people—Benny Meyers, Lightning Joe, Cripps—and to places—the Rapido, Grosshau, Eylau, and Cooke City, Montana. In this respect the novel competes with the poem for annotations, should it ever be properly edited for future generations.

Not only does Dante's name occur a dozen times, but many minor features also suggest that the Italian's poem lurks in the novel. Dante's love of the city-state, despite his censure of Florence's degeneracy, has its parallel in Cantwell's love of Venice. Intimate with its history and former inhabitants, its nobility and working people, he regards it as his city (26). Cantwell fulminates against many things, recalling those grand diatribes that erupt throughout the one hundred cantos too. Thinking of France, for instance, he notes that "there you fight your way into a city that you love and are very careful about breaking anything and then, if you have good sense, you are careful not to go back because you will meet some military characters who will resent your having fought your way in. *Vive la France et les pommes de terre frites. Liberté, Venalité, et Stupidité*" (26). Though scaled down, Col. Cantwell also mirrors Dante's encyclopedism. He knows birds, wines, fish, the history of Venice, writers, artists, architecture, fuels, and, above all, military history. Dante's topophiliac style may have encouraged Hemingway's already strong penchant for writing about landscape, terrain, place names, and rivers; and so

Cantwell relishes thinking, for example, about cities—Torcello, Burano, Caorle, Mestre, Noghera—and rivers—Tagliamento, Piave, Sile, Brenda, and Dese. The novel's narrative point of view is also Dantesque. Cantwell is a character narrated about and a persona who narrates interior monologues, just as Dante is author-commentator and pilgrim-participant.[8] The novel's several boatmen and Venetian bridges call to mind the ferrymen and angels who assist Dante's progress, the bridges across the pits of hell, and even the metaphoric motif of the Dantean journey: "O you who in your wish to hear these things / have followed thus far in your little skiffs / the wake of my great ship that sails and sings, / turn back and make your way to your own coast. / . . . / My course is set for an uncharted sea" (*The Paradiso*, 2:1–4, 7).[9] The title of the novel, *Across the River and into the Trees*, ascribed to Stonewall Jackson, evokes those rivers Dante's pilgrim crosses: Acheron, Styx, Phlegethon, Lethe, and Eunoe. Particularly apt to the memory-ridden Cantwell would be the river Lethe. Its waters of forgetfulness wash away memory and so lead to the "everlasting forest," the sacred wood of the earthly paradise. Least to be overlooked is the "sparse, direct, and idiomatic language" of both writers, a quality noted by Hemingway's middle son: "Though I have never read it anywhere in the critics, I do think that the deceptively simple style of Dante was as much a model for Papa as anything else he may have read."[10]

The poem's best-known volume, *The Inferno*, deals with a place that figures prominently in the novel too: hell. While the cornices of purgatory and the spheres of paradise have their share of historical personages, Dante especially delights in populating the circles of hell. So does Cantwell. He relegates generals Walter Bedell Smith, Bernard Law Montgomery, and Jacques Leclerc to the Inferno's vestibule, telling Renata, who dreads having to know such men,

> "We won't have to know them this side of hell," the Colonel assured her. "And I will have a detail guarding the gates of hell so that no such characters enter."
> "You sound like Dante," she said sleepily.
> "I am Mister Dante," he said. "For the moment."
> And for a while he was and he drew all the circles. They were as unjust as Dante's but he drew them. [245–46]

Neither Cantwell nor Dante disparages only military figures. Of professional writers who fraudulently write of combat Cantwell acknowledges that he is uncertain of how to categorize that sin (137). But anyone familiar with *The Inferno* could easily assign stations for several of the novel's fictional characters. Cantwell's boatman on the duck shoot will go among the wrathful and sullen in the inferno's fifth circle. *Pescecani* (i.e., sharks), the fat, wealthy Milanese in the bar at the Fiat garage, will go into bolgia five among the grafters of the eighth circle, his mistress into circle two among the carnal. Brusadelli, the Milanese profiteer who had gone to court against his young wife, claiming that her inordinate sexual appetite had caused him a severe loss of judgment (57), will go into circle nine among Cain's fellow traitors against kin. But Cantwell, like Dante's pilgrim, praises people. He wishes he could live half his time in hell (250) with Rommel, Ernst Udet, and Col. Buck Lanham, historical figures. And if he had his way he would probably like to elevate Renata to paradise's sphere of Venus among the amorous.

A more telling parallel between the poem and the novel is the shared aim of both works' heroes. Aware of his spiritual sloth and fearful of the afterlife awaiting him, Dante's pilgrim flees the dark wood to seek his soul's salvation. Richard Cantwell similarly fears his approaching death. And his desire to reform acknowledges both spiritual sloth and the need to purge his soul for salvation. He admits to being a bastard, brusque and brutal; wishes that he were kind, good, and had less of what he regards as wild boar blood; and asks, "God help me not to be bad" (65).

Entrenched in many of the deadly sins, Cantwell's salvation is not easy. Gluttony, that hedonism of the palate never absent in a Hemingway novel, is one of Cantwell's major vices. It is closely followed by pride. Cantwell tells himself, for instance, that nobody on the duck hunt shoots better than he (292), and he immodestly congratulates himself for being correct in more than ninety-five percent of the military decisions he has made (294). While thoughts of his ex-wife, the *pescecani*, and the Fascist hall porter easily stimulate the deadly sin of wrath, his admission that he disparages the successful (251) shows envy too. Rather than adduce the other cardinal sins, I would note the impress of Dante's poem on the novel by pointing out that though fraud is not among those sins, Dante regards it as the worst of sins, giving it the two lowest circles in his inferno. By having Cantwell counterfeit his heart condition during the medical examination, Hemingway makes him a potential inhabitant of circle eight's "simple frauds." Cantwell's passion for Renata might invoke the sin of lust. But Dante's scheme would locate him among the carnal of the second circle, for Cantwell's relationship to Renata is like that of such other warrior-lovers as Paris, Tristram, and Achilles.

Dante's pilgrim learns that for his salvation he must obey the confessional formula: candid confession, mournful contrition, and burning gratitude. Hemingway's thirty-odd years as a "Catholic" would make him no stranger to that formula, and Cantwell complies with it, though he does not believe in an afterlife. He confesses that he has made three wrong decisions that have cost the lives of many men (94) and that he has lied to his own advantage precisely four times. His war reminiscences, Hemingway's narrator insists, are not military swagger: he was "confessing," not lecturing (222). Cantwell is also contrite. Acknowledging his wish to attain and keep the rank of general, he admits "I have failed and I speak badly of all who have succeeded. Then his contrition did not last . . . " (251). The sincerity of his contrition shows through the three memories that plague his conscience. He had arrogantly assumed that Ardennes was safe for his best friend George, who died there (292–94). He had let many of his troops be killed by obeying SHAEF military orders during the Westhall Schnee-Eifel campaign (233–35). And he had obeyed more SHAEF orders on the Hurtgen Forest assault, which decimated his regiment, causing him to be "completely desperate at the remembrance of his loss of his battalions, and of individual people" (242). Cantwell is remorseful even for something as minor as wasting electricity, regretting that just "as he regretted all his errors" (180). Though it is not "burning," he finally expresses gratitude that he has been such a "lucky son of a bitch" who ought to be sad about nothing (254). Moments before he dies he reiterates this last step in his confession, again grateful for his lifetime of luck (307). Much of Cantwell's talk, memory, and action may find him among the ditches of hell or, in the novel's terms, in "the oaken staved hogshead sunk in the bottom of the lagoon" (3). But he hopes to ascend to some ledge of purgatory.

Like Dante's pilgrim's quest for spiritual salvation, so too is Cantwell's assisted by a guide, a young woman who fulfills the courtly convention of being Christ's secular analogue. Lying with Cantwell she consoles him and encourages him to talk, thereby purging his bitterness and trying to help him " 'die with the grace of a happy death' " (240). Handmaiden to Cantwell's need for spiritual housecleaning, Renata is the confessor-therapist who hears his unorthodox confession.[11] Repeatedly she admonishes him to be good, gentle, and cheerful, not angry, rough, or brutal; to ignore those things that, like the pockmarked American writer, evoke his malice. He tries to comply, beseeching God to help him "avoid brutality" (85). His supine position during much of the novel, especially the long sequence on his bed during which he "educates" her about the war, also shows her role as therapist. To further suggest her role may have been why Hemingway included Cantwell's five-chapter conversation with Renata's portrait: he behaves as virtuously before her image as Dante's pilgrim does before Beatrice's. Cantwell's salvation, then, depends upon Renata's ability to teach him *caritas*, the charitable love of others. Reflecting this, her gifts help him see their value as gestures of love and of willingness to serve. He reciprocates by buying her the turbaned, ebony-faced brooch, symbol of a "confidential servant" (105).

Clearly the novel lacks the poem's scholastic thinking, theological and anagogical framework, allegorical method, and intricate architecture. But it shares the poem's historicity. Dante-as-pilgrim, walking among the "dead," allows Dante to reminisce, declare his historical biases, and give dramatic voice to such authentic people as Ser Brunetto Latino, Farinata degli Uberti, Publius Papinius, Guido de Guinizelli, or Forese Donati. Cantwell, on the brink of death, similarly allows Hemingway to remember things past and to make historical footnotes on people, places, and events. Both the poem and the novel, as testaments, then, settle accounts with friends and enemies, dramatize personal beliefs and values, and bear witness upon time past and present.

The novel's historical references and reminiscences, assignable as Hemingway's actual experiences, might suggest that he is experimenting with the historical novel. Yet that kind of novel tries to portray realistically the social milieu, events, or crises of a historical place or period and to represent, to one degree or another, actual persons. Or it tries "to portray the kind of individual destiny that can *directly* and at the same time typically express the problems of an epoch."[12] In contrast, Hemingway's novel and Dante's poem are not fixed to one place and time. And they dramatize the private historical biases of fictional characters who, removed from a typical milieu, are preoccupied with personal problems that relate to more than one historical period. But unlike Dante, Hemingway never dramatizes the actual people Cantwell cites. Instead, he generates the novel's historicity by alluding to, rather than dramatizing, actual people. Admittedly the immediate effect is that Hemingway is merely name-dropping, for he fails to give substance to people who apparently have meaning to Cantwell. Yet the allusions fulfill their expected literary function. By drawing together and establishing a relationship between dissimilar experiences, they amplify an individual experience and make it representative. For example, when Cantwell thinks of "Marbot's Lysette who fought, personally, at Eylau" (52) during the Napoleonic War of 1805, the allusion to the French general's fierce mare may parallel both his own combat with death and a female's attempt to rescue him.[13] Allusions to such past and present persons as Robert Browning and Custer, Eisenhower and Margaret Truman, du Picq and Degas reflect Cantwell's praise or scorn of lifestyles and values that mesh or clash with his own. A form of historical shorthand, such allusions let Hemingway create a hero who overlaps fictional and historical realities.

Because nonfiction theoretically defers to truth rather than beauty, and because both Dante's poem and Hemingway's novel are strongly autobiographical, the historicity of both works would seem to limit their esthetic effects. On the contrary, by honoring the muse of history only part of the time, both writers secure esthetic effects unobtainable had they adhered to the convention that a work be allegiant either to fiction or to nonfiction. Dante and Hemingway deliberately mix the two and so get the effects accruable both to history and to fiction as well as the enriched ambiguities of the mixture. That is, both poet and novelist satisfy a reader's interest in fact, information, opinion, and truth; gratify his desire to engage in wish-fulfillment, beauty, and the imaginary; and challenge his ability to differentiate history from fiction and to interpret both. The hazard in a historical-imaginary matrix is occasional Dantesque obscurity. And Hemingway succumbs to it, as the vagaries of some of Cantwell's maunderings show. But in so doing, Hemingway is not unique. One of his earliest mentors, Pound, had likewise succumbed to it in his *Cantos*. And the hazard is worth risking since the attempt to synthesize fictional and historical realities prods a reader to engage with the interplay of different realities, to engage his sensibilities more than he does with conventional works. It also acknowledges the long-standing classical debate between Plato and Aristotle of reality versus mimesis. Hemingway renders this debate in Cantwell's recurring colloquies with two objects in his hotel room, Renata's portrait and his mirror. Cantwell admits that the portrait inadequately represents reality, the living Renata: " 'There's no comparison, of course,' he said. 'I don't mean likeness. The likeness is excellent' " (209). But as an artistic creation, the portrait is like the novel's fictitious elements, a mimetic attempt to represent the essential reality of a person. Cantwell's mirror is like the novel's historicity: "Mirror was actuality and of this day" (180).

The consorting of fiction and nonfiction is not an isolated example of Hemingway mingling normally disparate entities. The January-May relationship between a battle-ravaged American colonel and a nubile Italian countess also signals that he overlaps alien worlds. So do the novel's two actions, the duck hunt frame tale and the reminisced day with Renata, and its two times, a single winter weekend set against the entire range of rapidly shifting events that the colonel's memory recalls from the past. But Hemingway's most interesting act of interpenetration is his immersing mimetic experience and historical material into a dream vision.

Although the *Divine Comedy* has a historical dimension, even more noticeable is its dream dimension. After all, the journey of Dante's pilgrim grows out of the medieval convention of the dream vision. Many things suggest that Hemingway's novel is also a dream vision. Renata and the colonel daydream about a trip through the States, knowing full well it will never come to pass. Many of the colonel's memories approach dreams or nightmares that haunt him. Some of his memories even have the tang of fantasy, as does the one of beating senseless two sailors who disrespectfully whistle at Renata. Cantwell's regard for liars also hints that his story may have elements of a tall tale: "A liar, in full flower, the Colonel had thought, is as beautiful as cherry trees, or apple trees when they are in blossom" (278). The novel's lack of physical action also intimates the novel's dream or daydream dimension; for most of the novel's events are Cantwell's reminiscences while lying on his bed or sitting—in the Buick, in Harry's bar, in a duck blind, at the Hotel Palace Gritti restaurant, in a gondola, or on the toilet. Sedentary action, appropriate to the novel's contemplative mood, invites dreams and memories, unreal and real experiences, to blur and mingle. And the novel's setting in the "Sea City" is a good place, Jungians would say, for unconscious dreams to surface.

The novel's dream dimension explains an apparent artistic flaw.[14] At the beginning of chapter 3 the novel's narrator says that Cantwell, sitting in the duck blind on Sunday morning, had been medically examined the "day before yesterday" and that "yesterday he had driven down from Trieste to Venice" (12). In this chronology the exam was on Friday, the drive on Saturday, and the hunt on Sunday. But this omits the day Cantwell spends with Renata. For if he drove to Venice "yesterday" (Saturday) and spent one night sleeping in the Hotel Palace Gritti with a portrait and another night with Barone Alvarito and the other duck hunters—"Last night there had been a fair amount of good lying after the grappa had been passed around" (279)—then the duck hunt would have to have been on Monday. Not a flaw, the extra day is one of Hemingway's "blinds," "any artifice you use to hide the shooter from that which he is attempting to shoot" (278). (Hemingway's narrator gives this definition when the novel resumes the duck hunt in chapter 40.) This blind sustains the blurred demarcations between fictional, historical, and dream materials in the novel. And it conceals Hemingway's use of Renata as a dream maiden.

The literal translation of her name, "reborn," has obvious significance for Cantwell, a man desiring salvation. And several of her features suggest that Cantwell fabricates her, just as Dickens's Mrs. Gamp fabricates her imaginary companion, Mrs. Harris. When Renata describes her portrait looking as though she were rising out of the sea with dry hair (97), her comparison to Aphrodite is as difficult to imagine a real woman saying as it is easy to imagine a middle-aged man feeling proud to be adored by such a young goddess. Similarly, the poetic language that defines her is fantasy-inspired. Her identity? " 'I am only the unknown country' " (155). Her ambition? To " 'run for Queen of Heaven' " (83), offers Cantwell. Her genealogy? " 'The moon is our mother and our father' " (114). We can snicker at such language. But it helps us reject Renata as a credible character, the effect the novel must achieve if Renata is to fulfill the "blessing-bearer" role of Dante's Beatrice.[15] Her solicitousness over Cantwell's maimed right hand, her gifts of the portrait and the emeralds, and her desire that he release the memories and experiences that cause his bitterness—all characterize her as *la belle dame à merci*. But her love for the battered Cantwell, who she knows will soon die, is not sufficiently motivated for a believable love story. Hemingway never even defines the origin of their relationship, letting us imagine that it springs full-bodied from Cantwell's forehead. But its "great miracle" (288) is no less justified than Beatrice's love for Dante. Having abandoned his youthful devotion of her, Dante is unworthy of receiving Beatrice's intercession. That she intercedes for him anyway demands as much willing suspension of disbelief as Renata's love for Cantwell.

What about the novel's tropes? Cantwell's heart turns over inside him when he sees Renata's profile "as though some sleeping animal had rolled over in its burrow and frightened, deliciously, the other animal sleeping close beside" (83). Because Renata is menstruating, Cantwell must search for her clitoris, "the island in the great river with the high steep banks" (153). And after he has manually induced her orgasm, the ecstasy is a "great bird" that "had flown far out of the closed window of the gondola" (154). Pretty poetic for Hemingway. But to approach the metaphoric heights to which the paradisal voyage of Dante's pilgrim and Beatrice soars, he must risk lyrical language. And such lyricisms add to the novel's dream dimension, just as allusions emphasize its historicity.

The novel's dream dimension seems partly aimed at mythopoeticizing Cantwell as the dying hero. That role seems confirmed by Renata's devotion to him and her definition of his narrated memories, " 'Sad stories of the death of kings' " (236). And his formulaic confession, his verbal exorcism of bitterness, his return to and commemoration of the site of his initiation into mortality at Fossalta, and his participation in the mock Order of Brusadelli— all approximate ceremonies that would confer representative stature upon Cantwell. His desire to keep death at bay, evidenced in his continual self-medication and his relationship with Renata, is a universal desire, adding to his stature. Unwilling to succumb to a failing heart, Cantwell subscribes to a life-sustaining belief, declaring, " 'Every day is a new and fine illusion' " (232). And notwithstanding his verbal brutalities, he values the Platonic qualities absorbed in Dante's trinity and esteemed by the race: goodness, beauty, and truth. Acknowledging the first of these, he is ever conscious of his lapses in kindness. When he leaves Renata he pledges that he will continue to try being good (277). Equally noticeable is his esthetic sensibility. He appreciates the beauty of art and architecture, Venice and its market, oxen, Renata and red sails on the country canals (24). He also desires to know and express the truth. Regarding his military experience, he tells Renata that he will tell her the truth, regardless of whom it hurts (225). Even the occupation to which Cantwell has given his life, metaphor of every man's combat against life's continuous conflict, suggests his universality. Like the residents of Dante's postmortal places, then, he is an individual and a type.

But Cantwell is not an archetypal hero. Leave that to Santiago of *Old Man and the Sea*. Santiago's antithesis, he is a more complex character, made so partly by the novel's marriage of fiction, history, and dream. And Hemingway's studied refusal to create a character who invites quick identification adds to Cantwell's complexity. Revamping the conventional types of the soldier—neither miles gloriosus, sadist, nor Homeric model of poetry-inspiring heroism—Hemingway literally demotes him to a prosaic career man who drinks, defecates, and knows his cant well: " 'S-6 wants you to button up and use plenty of artillery. White reports that they are in fair shape. S-6 informs that A company will swing around and tie in with B' " (245). By keeping Cantwell out of heroic combat scenes, Hemingway further deprives him of situations that normally guarantee admiration. No apologist for the career soldier, Hemingway denies Cantwell dignity, force of character, and self-understanding, giving him, instead, vanity, self-righteousness, and vacillation. Like Dante's pilgrim, who immodestly regards his talents as superior to Lucan and Ovid (*The Inferno*, 25:91–94), Cantwell vainly sees himself as Rommel's peer and Eisenhower's superior, and he boasts of his military savvy. Self-righteousness makes both Cantwell and Dante's pilgrim mete out judgments, just or not. And like Dante's pilgrim, who vacillates from sympathy to censure for the various people he encounters, the colonel slides from tenderness to coarseness, divided between his impulse, to extend his public profession of war and violence into his private life, and his self-imposed imperative, to be good. Even more, so insignificant is Cantwell's current military role that his duties in Trieste go unmentioned. Hemingway thereby strips him of valor and patriotism, authority and power, attributes that are vital to any military hero.

Complex though Cantwell's character is, it does not draw together the novel's diverse elements. A character who tries to straddle the worlds of mimetic representation, history, and dream, Cantwell at least confounds my attempts to identify with him. Ultimately he mirrors his own right hand, incurably split. His excursions into paranoia and estheticism, jargon and poetry, history and fantasy, vindictiveness and confessions, obscenity and tenderness portray him at best as schizophrenic.[16] I grant that schizophrenia is consistent with the novel's experimentation. But the novel must also satisfy the primary requirement of all successful fiction, to be narratively engaging. Disingenuous readers and a fond author, I believe, grant the novel that.

The novel might have been successful had Hemingway given firmer clues of its source than those I have gathered. For as it stands the novel's use of autobiographical flashbacks, historical allusions, lyricism, dialogue, and love story seem muddled. And they invite critical disapproval largely because the novel is being measured against the conventions of realistic fiction rather than those of Dante's classical poem. For comparison, one virtue of Joyce's *Ulysses* is that the title serves notice that a reader will benefit from knowing Homer's poem. Hemingway serves no such notice, which may block a reader from seeing that the novel's heterogeneous elements are as yoked by design as are those in Dante's poem.

Had he served notice, however, the novel would suffer from the comparison. Understandably it lacks the poem's scholastic thinking, theological and anagogical framework, allegorical method, and intricate architecture. All but the last of those are alien to Hemingway's art. But it also lacks the subtle psychological resonances of the poem, even though Dante's method of achieving them is usually Hemingway's too. The customary method of both writers, that is, is to dramatize actions and record dialogue objectively to let psychological insights surface of their own accord, without authorial prompting. When, for example, Dante's pilgrim embraces Casella in canto 2 of *The Purgatorio* and admires his song, Dante dramatizes his pilgrim's hedonistic lapse from his commitment to seek spiritual salvation and also mocks his vanity, for the song is one of Dante's own *canzone* set to music. Similarly, in the dialogue between Catherine Barkley and Frederic Henry during their supposedly idyllic retreat in Switzerland, Hemingway brilliantly dramatizes not romance but boredom, tension, and the psychological burden that their desperate dependency upon each other creates. But in *Across the River*, by directly immersing us in the psychological process of Cantwell's mind, Hemingway loses the dimension, interest, and interpretive potential of such drama. Even more, while Dante's pilgrim filters the plethora of Dante's mind because he is student-spectator, a similar pethora splits Cantwell, tutor-participant. Finally, whereas Dante, for all his artistic subtlety, maps his pilgrim's basic journey, Hemingway leaves most readers wandering among the back roads of Cantwell's mind.

Afterword

Hemingway's use of literary formulas and a classical model in the Aristotelean and imitative phases may help assess his stature as an artist. The debts his works owe to precursors may add to Hemingway's artistic dimensions, for they show that he is an artist-scholar, like Pound, Joyce, and Eliot, able to conceal a classic poem or mode within a modern work. But debts may also subtract, for they should oblige us to ask some strong questions about the three novels of these phases. Is his imagination original or bookishly derivative in them? Are the novels experiential or epigonic? Are they organically structured or mechanically dependent upon preexisting forms? Do these novels reflect Hemingway's artistic freedom or his enslavement to a lifelong penchant for ritual and traditions? Do they show that he is motivated by an authentic compulsion to express a genuine artistic vision or by an athlete's desire to compete? And can a major writer also be subtle scrivener or crafty copyist and hypersensitive guardian of his reputation who conceals from ready view the imprints of his models?

Hemingway's debts to literary formulas and a classical model may also help assess his place within the larger tradition of literature. I hold no brief for the virtues of generic criticism; most usually it results in a pedantic catalogue of resemblances between a work and the formula, tradition, or model it follows, usually without addressing the questions of whether and why the resemblance is significant. Nevertheless, good generic criticism evaluates a work by the criteria the author has implicitly accepted, the set of predefined characteristics established by other authors who have written in the same genre or mode. And rather than just classify a work within a specific tradition, generic criticism isolates and compares the shared characteristics among or between works to discover one work's superiority or inferiority to another. In this regard, though I fault Hemingway's three novels during these two phases, I also hope I have established that by attempting them he placed himself among exalted writers, wrote three "gallant failures."

This may partly explain why Hemingway was vexed when Faulkner ranked him below Wolfe, Dos Passos, and even Erskine Caldwell, faulting him for never having risked any experiments, any "gallant failure."[1] It would be tendentious were I to argue that Faulkner's assessment in 1947, the year before Hemingway began *Across the River and into the Trees*, goaded him into writing a "gallant" experiment. But I do not think it is tendentious to say that the disapproval that Faulkner articulated—widely shared by book reviewers and critics alike since as far back as the response to *A Farewell to Arms*—had partly goaded Hemingway into the experiments of not only *Across the River* but *To Have and Have Not* and *For Whom the Bell Tolls* as well.[2] The sting of Faulkner's attitude also echoes some of Hemingway's parents' disappointment in his early literary efforts.[3] And Hemingway seldom responded to disapproval with indifference. Pugnacious challenge was more common: "How do you like it now, gentlemen?" It was his need, then, to prove himself worthy of approval that partly accounts for the literary competitiveness in the three novels of this and the preceding phase.

As I mentioned in my Introduction, artists renovate, parody, or challenge their predecessors in an act of competition that is a form of Oedipal rivalry.[4] Shakespeare, Chaucer, and Milton take predecessors' works to show what geniuses can do with their "fathers' " mismanaged materials. Fielding parodies Richardson and Twain Dumas. Joyce's *Ulysses* tries to rival Homer's. Even a minor writer like William Golding struggles to outdo his "fathers," *Pincher Martin*, for instance, reworking *Robinson Crusoe*. Other artists follow the same pattern. Picasso, for example, competes against his ancestors, his 1955 *Les Femmes d'Alger* reworking Delacroix's 1834 painting of the same title, his 1957 *La Meninas* Velásquez's identically titled 1656 painting.[5]

By adopting epic and tragic modes in his preceding phase, by imitating Dante's *Divine Comedy* in this one, and by talking and writing about having "beat dead men at what they have done," Hemingway shows his conscious attempt to challenge and surpass literary predecessors, proxies for his father. If Hemingway feels that he beats them—" ' . . . I beat Mr. de Maupassant

. . . and had an edge [on Mr. Stendhal] in the last [fight]' "[6]—
then he presumably frees himself to go his own way, independent
of predecessors' restraints, conventions, and values. But his continued competition against those "fathers" also reveals his dependency, his belief in their superiority, his wish to be esteemed as
their worthy rival, in short, his filial respect.

Looked at in this light, Hemingway's parricidal wish to compete against his literary "fathers" is subordinate to his affiliative
wish for paternal approval. Both phases, Aristotelean and imitative, support this idea. Hemingway chooses to compete with
worthy predecessors, not mere contemporaries. The rivals he
selects—"the dead you know are good"—are, then, substitutes for
his father, men he respects and whose respect he seeks, not
"brothers." And Hemingway chooses to write novels whose sim-
ilarities show his reluctance to rebel and to free himself of his fixation on his father. Such labels as "the Hemingway hero," "the
Hemingway code," and "the Hemingway style," for example, are
vague and oversimplified. But they legitimately respond to a uni-
formity in Hemingway's vision and material that signals his
deep-seated unwillingness and inability to be original and autonomous, his wish not to alienate his father: "You could if you
wanted," he writes his father, "be proud of me sometimes—not for
what I do for I have not had much success in doing good—but for
my work" (*Letters*, 259). Hemingway also chooses to resurrect
past modes and models, implying that just as they are still useful
to modern writers, so too is his father's influence still meaningful
to him. And just as Dante honors Vergil's worth by choosing the
Roman poet to guide his pilgrim, so too does Hemingway honor
the worth of both Dante and the paternal guide Dante represents,
Dr. Hemingway. Finally, Hemingway chooses to conceal his resurrection of past modes and models, hopeful that his keen-eyed
father would see and approve of his craftiness. That is, rather
than write fiction that would immediately garner his father's approval, Hemingway's ploy was to write works whose subtle or
ambiguous elements, undiscerned upon first reading, would eventually be discerned by the father whose pleasure would acknowledge that his son truly knew best, would satisfy Hemingway's secret wish to win paternal approval on his own terms.

The text of *Across the River* reveals the strength of Hemingway's affiliative wish for approval and nonerotic love. Superficially the novel purports to be about the love of an old colonel and

a young countess. But the love relationship takes a hind seat to the father-daughter relationship between Cantwell and Renata. Dependent upon her both to rejuvenate him by giving him reason to fight his failing heart and to redeem him by helping him overcome his guilts and hostilities through confession, Cantwell embodies the wish to be approved of as an aging, good father, properly dependent upon a daughter.

From a biographical point of view, the father-daughter relationship seems to address Renata's model, Adriana Ivancich, even though her role in reality little resembled the romantic one Hemingway imagines for her.[7] Indeed, Cantwell and Renata's relationship is not very romantic. Now I grant that as lover she does kiss Cantwell so hard that the inside of his lip bleeds (111). And she seems to enjoy the sexual delights that Cantwell manually provides beneath the blanket in the gondola. But more of her delights come from doting on Cantwell's needs, from soliciting him to tell of his experiences, from consoling him for his guilts, from worrying over his hand, and from bequeathing to him family jewels and her portrait. In effect, Renata gives Cantwell more psychological than sexual release, as his monologues with her portrait suggest. Add to this Hemingway's insistence that Renata be maritally unavailable, that she be menstruating on this last weekend,[8] that Cantwell be suffering from heart and hand troubles, and that the novel's sexual scenes be unusually ambiguous. Summed up, these details suggest that something in the prospect of Cantwell's marrying Renata repels Hemingway. Perhaps it is some sexual anxiety that repels him. Perhaps he deeply senses that Cantwell and Renata's heterosexual relationship is incestuous. Perhaps his anxiety is symptomatic of feelings of impotence, welling up due to the eye injuries and illnesses that accompanied the writing of the novel.[9]

Although these anxieties may partly explain the ultimately nonerotic relationship between Cantwell and Renata, it can be better explained by translating their father-daughter relationship into a father-son relationship that Hemingway tries to keep from being homoerotic. Specifically, Hemingway unconsciously addresses his sons, collapsing all three of them in Renata.

Consider the fiction he was working on just before and after *Across the River*. What we now know as the "Bimini" section of *Islands in the Stream* deals primarily with Thomas Hudson's relationship with his sons, commemorating one of them in particular. The "Cuba" section extends that relationship and so focuses upon Hudson's grief over the death of his oldest son, as does the last section of the novel, "At Sea." Likewise *The Old Man and the Sea* deals essentially with Santiago's relationship with his "son," Manolin, not with the marlin. Some of the sentimental risks that Hemingway takes in those works, by emphasizing a father's love for his sons, he avoids in *Across the River*, emphasizing instead a man's love for a younger woman. But the dynamics of the relationships are quite similar. Cantwell's calling Renata "Daughter" partly shows the similarity, since the narrator notes that the word "meant a different thing" (107) to Cantwell, to the *Gran Maestro*, and to Renata. Even the dialogue shows a father-son relationship. Although there are, of course, Cantwell's declarations of heterosexual ardor, the larger number of his monologues are prompted by questions a son or an ingénue, not a lover, would ask: " 'Did you like many Germans?' " (122). " 'Don't you ever close windows?' " (210). " 'How could you have done such a thing' " (213) as to marry a conceited, ambitious journalist? " 'Can I come duck shooting?' " (142). " 'Richard, what is a jerk?' " (97). " 'Why do you hate cavalry?' " (232). " 'How do you lose a regiment?' " (233). " 'Tell me about the town' " (239). " 'But why do you have to obey other people's orders when you know better?' " (242). " 'Where will we stay in Wyoming?' " (265). " 'Can't I ride with you to the garage?' " (274).

The egocentric monologues that such a parade of queries invites might charm boys who spent relatively little time with their renowned father, especially during the war years. But at the time the novel was written, none of Hemingway's sons had the need, the boyish adoration, or the patience to listen to their worldly father reminisce and utter obiter dicta. John was twenty-six, Patrick twenty-one, and Gregory eighteen. That may explain why Hemingway has Cantwell recite his monologues to a daughter figure rather than to a son; a teenage daughter might still nurse the Oedipal fantasy of adoring a knightlike surrogate father, particularly since Renata's father had been killed in the war. Moreover, Renata's patient adoration would shame Hemingway's sons for their lapses in filial respect. In this light, Hemingway addresses his sons to censure them. This is seen in his portrayal of one group of Cantwell's "sons": the contemptible, comic-book-reading chauffeur, Jackson; the young Fascist hall porter who snoops among Cantwell's belongings; and the "sullen boatman," who treacherously shoots at mallards "coming to the Colonel's blind" (280). It is also seen in Hemingway's portrayal of an exemplary son, Alvarito, properly deferential.

Stronger than Hemingway's unconscious wish to censure his sons is the wish for their understanding, forgiveness, and acceptance. This explains the confession formula the novel appears to follow. For as lover Cantwell has little cause (and less savoir faire) to confess his wrongs and seek therapy from a young woman who supposedly loves him. But Hemingway had reason to apologize to sons harmed by his marital instability, extended absences, and lack of sustained paternal regard. And the frequency of overt father-son relationships in Hemingway's remaining works validates his guilt feelings about his fatherhood.

Cantwell's apologetics, though, aim finally at ears other than Hemingway's sons. They aim at a man who died in his fifties, who had that incurable ailment, diabetes, who suffered from angina pectoris, and who in his last years was particularly moody and embittered: Dr. Hemingway.[10] Renata is not, then, a substitute for Hemingway's sons. Rather she substitutes for Hemingway. And Cantwell substitutes for Hemingway's father.

Like *Green Hills*, dedicated to one surrogate father, Philip Percival, *Across the River* is dedicated to a pair of fathers, Colonels "Buck" Lanham and Charlie Sweeny, men who would appreciate Cantwell's reminiscences, allusions, and jargon.[11] But these fathers are stand-ins for Hemingway's real father. After all, Hemingway's return to Italy in 1948 and his memory of the physical trauma he had suffered at Fossalta thirty years earlier precipitated a special trip to visit the site of that wounding.[12] That visit revivified the psychological trauma he suffered from his father's ignominious suicide, the guilt that he was partly responsible for it. Farfetched? I think not, for at the deepest level of *Across the River* Hemingway fabricates a weekend during which he can reconstruct his relationship with his father, at whose death he had not been present. This reading is partly suggested by the "great miracle" of Renata's love for Cantwell, which literally expresses her desire to give a war-injured older man the love she had been unable to give to the man whose place he takes, her father, killed in the war. It is also suggested by seeing that Hemingway's projection of himself into Renata expresses his unconscious wish that he had been a self-sacrificing son, solicitous of his dying father's needs. He wishes that he had heard his father's confessions, had given him intimate companionship, had boosted his morale. And by transforming himself into a malleable, beautiful noblewomen, he wishes he had been able to provide his father with a woman who could obliterate and avenge his father's relationship with a matriarch who brooked commands from no male.[13] He even wishes he had been able to make his father, like Cantwell, a more aggressive, domineering male to compensate for that lack in Dr. Hemingway. Hemingway wishes he had been able to do all this so that his father might have died, as Renata expresses it, " 'with the grace of a happy death.' "

I suppose the major objection to this interpretation is that there is little in Hemingway's background or known attitudes toward women that would explain a wish to transform himself into a woman. Yet just a few years before writing *Across the River* he had consciously flirted with the idea of transferring the sexual identities of Catherine and David Borne in his unfinished novel, *Garden of Eden*.[14] And his several stories that explicitly deal with homosexuality signal reaction formation, suggesting his attraction to homosexuals and to the idea of receiving the favors of a man whose love and approval he sought. Ultimately, Hemingway's wish to take his mother's place—to be female and to care properly, tenderly, for his dying father—would derive from his impression, while still an infant, that to win his father's approval he needed some female attributes. He would wonder if the trio of sisters who were born into the Hemingway household after him reflected a boy's lesser value and acknowledged parental preference for girls. And he would have been confused by his mother's efforts to make him and his older sister look-alikes, bobbing their hair so that they were neither clearly male nor female children. Finally, Hemingway's ability to create subservient, selfless women like Catherine, Maria, and now Renata shows his wish to provide good men with tender, caring women. His ability, then, to imagine such relationships vouches for his carrying them in his unconscious as variations on his wish to provide his father with such a woman.

Hemingway's wish for a last weekend with his father is full of guilt feelings. He wants to make amends for what he feels was his betrayal of his father. I realize, of course, that Hemingway consciously believed that his father had betrayed *him* by committing suicide. And so Cantwell's remorse for the three errors that brought death to those under his command is Dr. Hemingway's remorse for committing suicide and being treacherous to his dependents. But the doctor's act did not directly cause anyone else's death. So it is more likely that Hemingway felt that it was his own treacheries that contributed to his father's suicide. Like Cantwell, remorseful for assuring his best friend, George, that it was safe for the two of them to venture into enemy terrain, Hemingway had overconfidently assumed that his father would be safe when left at home, enemy terrain too. He concludes otherwise by the time he writes this novel and projects his remorse upon Cantwell, who doubles, then, as Hemingway's self and father. Similarly, Cantwell rationalizes the deaths of the men under his command during the Hurtgen Forest and Schnee-Eifel assaults by claiming that he was obeying SHAEF orders. Hemingway wants to excuse himself from being responsible for his father's death by claiming that he too had been obligated to obey superior orders: to pursue his destiny as an expatriate writer and to follow his instincts by divorcing Hadley and marrying Pauline. But by the time he writes *Across the River* his obedience to those orders undoubtedly causes further remorse, which he again projects upon Cantwell. I find compelling the belief that Hemingway shared his own son's brooding thought: "I never got over a sense of responsibility for my father's death and the recollection of it sometimes made me act in strange ways."[15]

Fortunately Hemingway's desire to "beat dead men at what they have done" died with *Across the River*. Public response to the novel may have taught him that literary experiments, however nobly conceived, were not going to sell—at least two out of three times. And he must have found little gratification in deceiving nonplussed critics, even though he may have secretly exulted. After all, greater gratification would come from divulging the secret of his imitation to someone else, from sharing a private joke. But that was not his way, his last wife declaring that during their seventeen years together he never talked about his work with anyone, even herself.[16]

Hemingway must also have stopped competing with the "dead" because he realized the inferiority of his efforts. None of these last three novels stands up well when compared with the genre they compete in or the predecessor they compete against. And even if he did not accept that, then surely he realized that each time he competed with the dead he risked getting caught in his surreptitious efforts. Once caught his three novels would be compared and found wanting. And critics would quickly conclude that all of his works must derive from some predecessor's model—as, I confess, I concluded at an early stage in studying him. That conclusion would deny Hemingway all originality.

The ultimate reason Hemingway stopped competing with his

predecessors was, I think, that his experiments did not give him the psychotherapy that, among other things, he sought in writing them. To the extent that his writing was prompted by his need to please, exorcize, or relate to his father, he had to get some deep gratification from the displacements that his imagination and unconscious created. Though I may have discerned some of those displacements, I think that they were so opaque to himself, so screened by transformation, so overwrought by the modes and models he was working from, that he was not getting the gratification that simpler narrative constructs could give him. His own subtlety was repressing, rather than releasing, his deeper wishes and anxieties, defeating a primary motive for writing in the first place. The work of the fifties better serves those wishes and anxieties, deeply flawed though it is.

THE ANTITHETICAL PHASE

5

Foreword

The four works of this phase, products of Hemingway's last decade, are deeply flawed. Their intended meanings and designs are at odds with repressed but discoverable wishes and anxieties, causing me to read each work antithetically. My readings intend to show, then, that Hemingway loses artistic control of his materials during this decade, that the effects he seeks clash against the effects he causes. But my readings also intend to show that the works are richer documents because of their esthetic defects than had they been more artistic, for they let us glimpse more clearly the fixations and obsessions, the daimon, that made Hemingway a writer who speaks deeply to us. Because each work's antithetical reading is quickly discoverable in the process of analyzing it, I suspend my use of afterwords and incorporate in each chapter the psychological interpretations that I have been reserving for those sections.

A Not-So-Strange Old Man:
The Old Man and the Sea

Of *The Old Man and the Sea* Hemingway said, "I tried to make a real old man, a real boy, a real sea and a real fish and real sharks."[1] Try though he did, no critic commends this novella for its realistic writing, subject, or hero.[2] And understandably so, for especially when the sharks mutilate his gigantic marlin, Santiago's philosophic resignation is not realistic. It is certainly not when set next to the behavior of the anonymous man in the anecdote that grew into the novella: "He was crying in the boat when the fishermen picked him up, half crazy from his loss, and the sharks were still circling the boat" (*By-Line*, 240).

A symbolic character, Santiago embodies only virtues that ask for moral approval of him as an idealized Papa. He is selfless, thoughtful, courageous, durable, reliable, and, above all else, gentle. Ever thoughtful of his "brother" the marlin, at one point he wishes he "could feed the fish" (59), at another is "sorry for the fish that had nothing to eat" (75), and still later deeply grieves when the first shark mutilates the fish's beautiful body (103). He shows no anger toward the fishermen who make fun of him (11). And he respects Manolin's father's decision that the boy fish with someone else after forty fishless days with Santiago. Even his dreams are innocuous, filled with mating porpoises and frolicsome, not fierce, lions. He is violent only when killing the attacking sharks. But such actions, in defense of his "brother," sanctify hostility. Finally, Manolin's adoration shows the absence of any punitiveness in Santiago's role as his substitute father.

To do other than approve and admire the old man would be unseemly, if not blasphemous. Yet Hemingway is excessively protective of his "saint," does everything artistically possible to immunize the "strange old man" against adverse criticism. Even Santiago's "sin" of "going out too far" we are to hallow for its noble effort and the moral truths the old fisherman learns from it. But I keep hearing Santiago's refrain: " 'I wish I had the boy. . . . I wish I had the boy. . . . I wish the boy was here. . . . I wish I had the boy. . . . I wish the boy were here' " (45, 48, 50, 51, 56). Santiago utters these wishes, of course, because he needs help with the huge marlin. And Hemingway asks us to hear them as prayers. With one ear I do. But with the other I hear their resentment and anger: that the boy, Manolin, is not with him, that Manolin obeyed his parents' orders to fish in another boat, that Manolin has not vowed discipleship to Santiago. The malice in Santiago's wishes makes me ask, is he truly a "strange old man" (14), as he calls himself; or is he quite ordinary, as much a hypocrite as the next person, as deficient in self-awareness as the rest of us? And do Santiago's actions, like ours, harbor unconscious wishes that are incongruent with the phosphorescent nimbus that circles, like a halo, his skiff? Can he be read antithetically?

If Santiago loves the marlin as much as he declares, must he kill it? An ordinary fisherman would, of course. But neither hunger, poverty, his identity as fisherman, his reputation of being "salao," nor the marlin's condition requires him to kill it. A truly "strange old man" or even an extraordinary fisherman might have released the marlin once it rolled over on its side next to the skiff, for that would have proved the fisherman's domination of it. Santiago's killing it questions the sincerity of his declared love and his benevolence. And it shows a sizeable lack of intelligence. Surely a wise, old, experienced fisherman would know that he would have to harpoon the huge marlin, that he would not be able to boat the fish but would have to lash it to the side of his skiff, that, consequently, the blood from the wound would quickly lure hungry sharks, and that he would have to fight them off or let them feed.

Must Santiago return with the mutilated carcass? If he genuinely loves the marlin, he should be loath to let it suffer the ignominy of becoming either "garbage waiting to go out with the tide" (126) or a spectacle to stupid tourists: " 'I didn't know sharks had such handsome, beautifully formed tails' " (127). Were Santiago really selfless, strange, he would have unleashed the marlin at sea, for a saint has no need to vaunt his achievement before his fellow men. Or does he stand to gain something by bringing home the carcass? Naturally he regains community regard. But he also gains what he has wished for in five of the nineteen wishes that flood the novella—Manolin: " 'I told the boy I was a strange old man. . . . Now is when I must prove it' " (66). Unquestionably the boy can best continue to learn the skills of fishing from Santiago. So Santiago's wish merely extends Manolin's. But two other men have legitimate claim to Manolin—his father and the fisherman he has been fishing with the past forty-odd days. Santiago brings home the mutilated carcass, then, because without proof of his exploit he can not show his superiority to such lesser men. Nor can he wrest Manolin from their parental authority without confronting them. Nor can he compel Manolin's pledge of discipleship: " 'We will fish together now for I still have much to learn' " (125).

I also question why *brother* dominates Santiago's word-hoard. He confers brotherly status on the marlin (59), on porposes and flying fishes (48), even on the stars (77). His fraternity should also enroll the man-of-war bird, the lions on the beaches of his dreams, the "negro of Cienfuegos," and bone-spurred Joe DiMaggio. Although Manolin is a boy, Santiago treats him as a brother, an equal, and acknowledges their interdependency. In contrast, the other fisherman whom Manolin's parents ordered him to fish with treats him as an "inferior" (24) and " 'never wants anyone to carry anything' " (27). Manolin's concern for Santiago portrays him as a good brother, too: "I must have water here for him, the boy thought, and soap and a good towel. Why am I so thoughtless? I must get him another shirt and a jacket for the winter and some sort of shoes and another blanket" (21). Indeed, despite some local fishermen who laugh at Santiago, brotherhood is the dominant chord of the novella, reiterated in the generosity of Martin, the proprietor of the Terrace, and of Pedrico, who cares for Santiago's skiff after his return. The story's very emphasis upon Santiago's two hands—in contrast to his one-armed predecessor, Harry Morgan—underlines with synecdoche the importance of brotherhood: "There are three things that are brothers," thinks Santiago, "the fish and my two hands" (64). This implies that Santiago's wishes for Manolin to be with him are wishes for a brother, since a *mano*(lin) is literally a little hand, figuratively a small brother.[3]

By taking Santiago at his word, we should see brotherhood in its ideal form, agape, and should realize that the archetype that Hemingway assigns him is brother's keeper.[4] Santiago's attitude toward Manolin, the marlin, and *la mar* vouches for his wish to be brother's keeper to virtually all creation.

An antithetical reading of Santiago's fraternal ethic finds it self-serving. It grants Santiago and any who embrace that brotherly ideal a measure of irresponsibility not available to people who must fulfill the role of parent, spouse, or child. Quite simply, a brother's responsibilities have only the force of religious commandment; psychologically self-imposed, they are not obligatory. A brother can honor fraternal responsibilities and bask, modestly or immodestly, in the self-satisfaction of his supererogation. Or a brother can ignore those responsibilities without feeling guilty. But children and spouses lay legitimate claims and responsibilities at parents' and mates' feet; and guilt pursues them, frequently whether they honor or dishonor those claims. Children feel guilt too. They are plagued by the compulsion to measure up to parental values and by the virtual impossibility of doing so—because of the contradictions in those values, of the tortuous ways of their own experiences, and of the rebelliousness of their own impulses.

These considerations explain why Santiago is a widower, has begotten no children, and in neither dream, memory, nor statement traces his lineage to father or mother. The absence of parents, wife, and children eliminates filial, conjugal, or parental obligations. That absence also frees Santiago from compulsory duties to his fellow man. And that absence tells me that self-serving ingredients foul the air of his apparent altruism and show that he is "one of us," someone who wants to be thought better of than he deserves. He is our ordinary, not our strange, brother, even though we indulge ourselves in Hemingway's fantasy of Santiago's nobleness.

Far below the conscious surface of the novella, like the marlin beneath Santiago's skiff, are other proofs of an antithetical reading of Santiago as not so strange, as a man with normal, sublimated, aggressive, and erotic drives. For example, Santiago acts out, and so shares, parricidal wishes.[5] Notwithstanding his age or his scars, "as old as erosions in a fishless desert" (10), Santiago is an interesting version of the parricidal son. By defeating at arm wrestling "the great negro from Cienfuegos who was the strongest man on the docks" and whose "shadow was huge" (64), Santiago defines early the parricidal nature and purpose of his actions. His deep regard for the marlin before and after he kills him, his lack of aggression toward him, and his failure to show delight in conquering him, though, all reveal a sympathy and concern uncommon in the Oedipal clash. But parricide is parricide. Santiago obliquely admits this when he equates hooking the marlin with "treachery" (50) and when he recalls the time he bereft a male marlin of his mate by catching and killing her, calling it "the saddest thing I ever saw" (50). The love and respect Santiago professes for the marlin, then, are insidious because he disguises them with piety. Like the pretense of the cast net and the pot of yellow rice with fish (16), Santiago's regard for the marlin is also a pretense that conceals antithetical feelings of filial hostility. Similarly the ordeal, the suffering, and the wounds he must endure conceal his motives for killing it.

Santiago seems without a motive for killing the marlin, merely trying to survive as a Gulf Stream fisherman. His ordeal and suffering, as the story's chronology of events indicates, are simple results of catching such a large fish. But psychologically the ordeal antedates hooking the marlin, as Santiago's old, "deep-creased scars" (10) indicate. One motive for catching and killing this surrogate father, then, is to avenge the suffering it has previously inflicted upon him. And any prospect of reconciliation with it is nullified by what happens to (what Santiago wishes to happen to?) that once-noble marlin. Repeatedly mutilated, when beached it is a mere skeleton, making highly visible to Santiago's community his literal—and to a psychoanalytic community his symbolic—achievement. And his exaggerated defense of the marlin's carcass, just one of many instances of reaction formation, makes evident his guilt and the wish underlying that guilt. The sham of Santiago's brotherliness, then, is again confirmed when he kills the marlin. That act shows that his exaggerated fraternal feelings screen an unconscious fratricidal wish. And since such a wish displaces more primary father-son hostilities, it partly represents parricide. Moreover, by slaying the gigantic marlin Santiago figuratively executes the fathers who have demanded Manolin's obedience and who have impugned his own abilities. Another version of Saint George's dragon, Jack and the Beanstalk's giant, or Tom Thumb's ogre, Santiago's marlin shows once again that whether heroically defeated, fiercely slaughtered, gruesomely butchered, or piously slain, a dead father is a dead father.

One thing that dignifies Hemingway's novella is its refusal to celebrate the victory with a happy ending. And one thing that secures its identity as adult literature is that parricide is not its only wish. Because Santiago performs his deed in full view of the third person expected in all Oedipal triangles—in this case *la mar*—an erotic fantasy accompanies its aggressive one. In its simplest, if perhaps crudest, form, the erotic wish is for an epic sexual orgy. Whereas the giant marlin is the father in the parricidal fantasy, in an incestuous one it is the phallus. Once hooked, the huge marlin's sustained underwater voyage disguises an episode of gigantic penetration in those warm currents of *la mar*, "which is what people call her in Spanish when they love her. Sometimes those who love her say bad things of her but they are always said as though she were a woman. . . . The old man always thought of her as feminine and as something that gave or withheld great favours, and if she did wild or wicked things it was because she could not help them" (29–30). In the parricidal fantasy Santiago's esteem for the marlin is reaction formation that conceals hostility. In the erotic fantasy it is self-admiration: "Never have I seen a greater, or more beautiful, or a calmer or more noble thing than you, brother" (92), Santiago immodestly admits. Climaxing the erotic fantasy, Santiago drives in the harpoon, "leaned on it and drove it further and then pushed all his weight after it" (94), whereupon the marlin "came alive," "rose high out of the water showing all his great length and width and all his power and his beauty," then "sent spray over the old man and over all of the skiff" (94).

Such gargantuan, libidinous pleasures belong to a god. Half-gods and mortals who seize them must pay, be they Prometheus, Adam, or Santiago. When the son, however disguised, desecrates the "mother" and the taboo forbidding sexual knowledge of her, he sets into motion the inevitable anxiety that accompanies the Oedipal complex: castration. The first to react to the desecration should be the father who, tyrannical and vindictive by nature, can mutilate the son in the name of justice. True to form, the first to hit the marlin is the mako shark, "the biggest *dentuso* that I have ever seen" (103), says Santiago. And it strikes "in the meat just above [i.e., forward of] the tail" (101), the marlin's genital area. Its inward-slanted, eight rows of teeth are "shaped like a man's fingers when they are crisped like claws" (100–101), Santiago tells, vivifying the mako's castrating instruments in imagery reminiscent of the sharp talons of that eagle that fed, circumspectly, upon Prometheus's liver. As the mako approaches Santiago's now-quiescent marlin, properly lashed in place alongside his skiff, Santiago thinks, "I cannot keep him from hitting *me* but maybe I can get him" (101). I italicize the pronoun because it unequivocally identifies the marlin as a part of Santiago. So does Santiago's subsequent thought that "when the fish had been hit it was as though he himself were hit" (103). Consistent with the castration fantasy are the later attacks by the various *galanos*. If the father is unable or unwilling to avenge fully the sexual outrage, then the brothers assume the task, also punishing under the aegis of justice the brother who has performed the very act they themselves only dreamed of doing.

Whether father or brother figures, the mutilating sharks avenge the wrongs committed in both the parricidal and incestuous fantasies. But the sharks disguise another principal who directs their castrating forays.[6] *La mar*'s agents, they act on her behalf to deny her willing participation in incest. Killing the second *galano*, Santiago tells it, " 'slide down a mile deep. Go see your friend, or maybe it's your mother' " (109). Just as the superego, seeking to preserve the mother's immaculate image, denies the id's hunger for incest with her carnal image, these ambivalent attitudes toward the mother as angel and whore, as gratifying lover and castrating bitch, also show up in the incestuous fantasy. The vision of a three-day orgy with mother is, to the fantasizing unconscious, beatific, especially when it glorifies the huge organ whose strength contributes to such colossal delights. But the reality is brutal. Santiago hopes for a quick conquest: "Eat it so that the point of the hook goes into your heart and kills you, he thought. Come up easy and let me put the harpoon into you" (44). But he gets a grueling ordeal, not a suppliant female but a fierce antagonist. Just as Santiago asks whether he has hooked the marlin or it him, the narrative asks whether Santiago's antagonist is the marlin or a female power that uses the marlin to disguise her sadistic designs; for once coupled, Santiago must submit to her dominance, to his partner's ruthless impulses. In the dark of the first night she makes a lurch "that pulled him down on his face and made a cut below his eye" (52). Her second lurch, cued at the moment he calls her "a friend," nearly pulls him overboard and cuts the flesh of his hand (55–57). She enjoys humiliating him by making his hand cramp: "A cramp, he thought of it as a *calambre*, humiliates oneself . . . " (62). She even delights in trying to nauseate him: with her third lurch and nocturnal leaps "he had been pulled down tight onto the bow and his face was in the cut slice of dolphin and he could not move" (82). Back bent in agony, hands lacerated to mush, body exhausted so that he grows faint and sees "black spots before his eyes" (87), Santiago's orgy is a sadomasochistic nightmare. And his only escape from it and from subsequent sexual torture is self-mutilation. This he inflicts with his harpoon. Wrathful at his act, the *dentuso*'s subsequent mutilation represents the male dread that a women's genital orifice conceals castrating teeth: the vagina dentata. I truly hope that "the old man looked carefully in the glimpse of vision that he had" (94)!

Unlike Santiago, tenaciously holding one taut line, my reading must seem to dart to and fro, like the sucking fish that lash about, eel-fashion, around the great fish (90). One moment I hold onto a father figure, the next to a phallus, then to *la belle dame sans merci*. One moment I see the mako as father and the *galanos* as brothers. And then I see both kinds of sharks as finny versions of the Erinyes, those avenging Furies who sprang into being when, as goddesses of guilt, the blood of Ouranos, castrated by his son Kronos, fell upon Gaia-earth. But in fiction and dreams, of course, identities and relationships are neither static nor single. Dynamic and multiple, they not only tolerate but invite interchangeable readings. To do less is to shortchange the complexity of a writer's psyche and creative imagination. Call it condensation, Freud's term for a dream's superimposition of different, even contrary, components or ideas onto one composite structure or image. Or call it ambiguity, New Criticism's derivative catchword for a literary work's multiple meanings, a symbol's several referents. Either way, the critic's and analyst's task is to see things in both-and ways, to find what is latent in what is manifest, to trust the tale and not the teller.

Despite what may seem like psychoanalytic prestidigitation in my reading, then, it follows the Oedipal constellation of parricide, incest, and castration and so is internally consistent. And by arguing repeatedly that Santiago is not strange, I intend for my antithetical reading to enrich Hemingway's novella, not to impoverish it. After all, Santiago is a richer character for having complex motives, however much his simplicity appeals to us.[7]

My reading does impoverish Hemingway, though, for there is psychological imbalance in *Old Man*. Hemingway reveals it partly by sentimentalizing Santiago. Spurred by his own affiliative wish, Hemingway insists that his old fisherman be acknowledged as strange, be well liked, and be seen as brother to all creation. And contrary to Hemingway's usual technique of letting readers infer their own conclusions on the basis of what he shows or dramatizes, here Hemingway pushes his conclusions by telling, by assertions. He tells us that Santiago has "confident loving eyes" (13) that are "cheerful and undefeated" (10). He tells us that Santiago had "attained humility" even though "he was too simple to wonder when he had" done so (13). He tells us that Santiago has "strange shoulders" (18), that his cramped "left hand was still as tight as the gripped claws of an eagle" (63), and that he looks "carefully into the glimpse of vision that he had" (94). And he tells us that the novel should tell us something about going "too far out." This lack of subtlety, this excess of statement, unusual in Hemingway, exposes Hemingway's imbalance because it shows him struggling to repress anxieties that conflict with his wishes.

Among the reasons for Hemingway's excess here is a wish to idealize himself. Long accustomed to the role of "Papa"—as all intimates, regardless of age, sex, race, or blood, called him—he seeks through Santiago to portray his best self. And the novella's insistence upon fraternal relationships expresses Hemingway's affiliative wish and his wish to escape the guilts that plague, as I mentioned, fathers, husbands, and sons. Of course, Jake Barnes, Frederic Henry, Harry Morgan, and Robert Jordan are men whose actions are well flanked with fraternal motives. But Santiago is archetype to their prototypes. And since Santiago's fraternal ethic is self-serving, then Hemingway's valuation of it is too. Confident that his creation of Santiago is without irony, I also suspect that Hemingway identifies with Santiago's sense of mission because it lets him again dodge, Christ-fashion, any familial wrongs he is culpable of. I allude to Jesus' response when told that his mother and brothers are waiting to speak with him: "Who is my mother? Who are my brothers? . . . Whoever does the will of my heavenly Father is my brother, my sister, my mother." Surely Hemingway would identify with Santiago, able to justify any conduct by invoking his life's mission, declaring, "Now is the time to think of only one thing. That which I was born for" (40). Santiago's statement may be nobly appropriate to the occasion, but it also insinuates that he—and an author whose primary allegiance is to the Muse—be pardoned for any domestic neglects.

The neglect that ignites Hemingway's anxiety is his neglect of his own three sons. He can be deservedly proud of his resourcefulness and devotion during both Patrick's concussion and recovery in the spring of 1947 and Gregory's emergency appendectomy in June of 1949.[8] But a father is more than handyman in a medical crisis. More typical of Hemingway's relationship to his sons is the Christmas of 1950 at the Finca, just before he began writing *Old*

Man: "Patrick was there with his new wife Henny; Gigi appeared with a girl whom Ernest did not like. There was a constant stream of visitors, including Winston Guest, Tom Shevlin, Gary Cooper, and Patricia Neal. . . . "[9] There is nothing unusual about this instance of Hemingway domesticity. Filial visits crowded by notables and intimates was the perennial pattern for the Hemingway sons. And so their relationship with him was seldom more than a holiday one.

Although Hemingway's guilt for neglecting his sons is partly shown in his creation of a man whose excessively fraternal duties excuse his irresponsibilities, it is also shown by his preoccupation in the other two works he composed during the winter and spring months of 1950–51.[10] Like the second and third sections of *Islands in the Stream*, drafted on either side of the novella, *Old Man* is deeply preoccupied with the loss of a son.[11] That preoccupation stems partly from Hemingway's loss of influence over his three sons at precisely the time he was writing these three works. His oldest son, John, was still soldiering, "the only trade he knows."[12] His middle son, Patrick, had just married and was preparing to leave the States for Kenya. His youngest, Gregory, was growing more difficult and rebellious than before. Only he was bold or naive enough to challenge his father's parental and marital behavior. And the death of his mother, Pauline, in October of 1951 gave him the occasion to bear a long grudge against his father's treatment of her—and of himself.[13]

It takes no large leap of imagination to see that Manolin's separation from Santiago after forty fishless days expresses Hemingway's anxiety over his loss of influence on his departing or defecting sons, whatever his neglect of them had been. That anxiety also explains Santiago's perseverance with the marlin and his willingness to go "out too far" for it. Both behaviors are projections of Hemingway's wishes: to compensate for his shortcomings, his "salao" as a father, and to believe that he would go far out to regain his sons or his influence over them. Indeed, as Wylder notes, Santiago's conflict is with Manolin's "parents for control of the life of the boy," partly showing that Santiago's motives are aimed at regaining Manolin's discipleship.[14] Hemingway heightens this parental conflict by having Santiago wrest Manolin from two fathers, his legitimate one and the fisherman he had been "ordered" to fish with.[15]

Finally, because excessive behavior always signals antithetical wishes, Santiago's excessive benevolence reveals the most repressed wish in *Old Man*, the wish common to all the work of Hemingway's last decade, filicide, the wish to kill or have killed his sons. The marlin is brother, father, and phallus. But it is also son, as the fish and the boy's nearly identical names suggest. Manolin's forced separation from Santiago is mirrored in the marlin's attempted separation from Santiago's skiff, line, hook, and harpoon. The fish, then, is Manolin's virile double, and Santiago's ordeal, killing and returning home with its mutilated carcass, reveals his perseverance in acting out his filicidal wish.

Old though he is, through "trickery" (14, 23, 99), intelligence, and experience Santiago can subjugate any male, regardless of strength or disguise, who challenges his supremacy. And what of a son who entertains thoughts either of freeing himself of his father's infuence or of finding a replacement for his father? Since both thoughts are latent in Manolin's departure after forty days of luckless fishing, that son would be well advised, if fiction were prophetic, to recognize the alternatives of acting out such thoughts of defection. He must escape altogether or return, vowing discipleship. Otherwise, he may end up dead, a skeleton "among the empty beer cans," "garbage waiting to go out with the tide" (126). Santiago's act of killing the marlin, then, is ultimately an act of fratricide, parricide, and now, filicide. And Santiago should stand revealed as a not-so-strange old man, one who expresses in sublimated ways those deeply submerged wishes all humans share but suppress.

Perhaps I present the idea of filicide too abruptly and assign to Hemingway an utterly alien wish. But it is felt in his hostility toward his youngest son, the complications and difficulties of whose person were, and continued to be, a problem to Hemingway, according to his wife.[16] And it is invariably present in the makeup of the human psyche. As dramatized in that "most meaningful synthesis of the essential conflicts of the human condition," Sophocles' *Oedipus Rex*, filicide is a central, precipitating factor in the character and destiny of Oedipus and so of all humans.[17] Responding to the dire prophecy that their child would slay his father and commit incest with his mother, Laius and Jocasta pierce their child's feet and order him to be killed or abandoned when only three days old. Oedipus's subsequent parricidal and incestuous acts, then, issue directly from his parents' attempted filicide and his unconscious wish to avenge their wrong to him. The circular blame of this situation acknowledges reciprocal anxieties that all parents and children have of being rejected, harmed, or abandoned. And it follows that every family situation of a father, mother, and child will contain the repressed wishes of filicide, incest, and either matricide or patricide or both. There is nothing intrinsically hideous or abnormal about filicidal wishes in Santiago, Hemingway, or anyone else. They become abnormal only when they are strongly denied or when there is an undue if not compulsive need to express only benevolent wishes, as Santiago's case nearly shows.

Although I emphasize that Hemingway's filicidal wishes are unconsciously aimed at his three sons, they are also self-directed. More precisely, as the works of the fifties will show, Hemingway feels increasingly responsible—and so increasingly guilty—for his father's suicide. Because suicides always act out upon themselves the homicidal feelings they have for others, Dr. Hemingway's suicide expresses a filicidal wish toward his neglectful son. And Hemingway unconsciously owns that his father's wish is just. For as I mentioned in the previous afterword, Hemingway was absent during the ordeals of his father's last years. In one formulation Hemingway's guilt for his absence issues in the fantasy that Santiago-as-father—old, luckless, alone, and struggling against great odds—can overcome vicissitudes, be they of *la mar*, the sea as terrible mother, or of life with Grace Hemingway. In a second formulation Hemingway's guilt for his absence issues in Santiago's indictment of Manolin: " 'I missed you' " (124). A bland indictment? I think not. After all, the tears and grief of Manolin-as-Hemingway already show the mental mutilation caused by his guilt for having been absent during Santiago's ordeal. The old man's words will surely reverberate deeply in Manolin's conscience. And should Santiago die because of his ordeal? The already lachrymose Manolin will flagellate himself for not having vowed discipleship earlier to Santiago. All his life he will feel responsible for Santiago's death and will feel remorse for not having responded to the old man's affiliative needs.[18]

A Guilt-Ridden Father: *Islands in the Stream*

Because it was composed and revised at different periods in Hemingway's life, was unfinished, and was left with several unresolved problems, *Islands in the Stream* can never be discussed with certainty.[1] But its focus upon Thomas Hudson's relationship with his three sons just before and after they prematurely die portrays a father so preoccupied with his children that his premonitions of, and subsequent grief over, their deaths unify the novel. A man whose remorse is as curious as his transformation from withdrawn artist to obsessive warrior,[2] Hudson invites antithetical conclusions: he is either an exemplary or a guilt-ridden, filicidal father, a man who will get from us garlands or ashes.

"Bimini" sets the domestic context for the novel's three sections. Its basic event, the five-week visit of Hudson's sons, is framed on either side by the evening before their arrival and then by Hudson's initial reactions to news of the two younger sons' deaths. Their visit has five episodes: Tommy's reminiscences of life with Hudson in Paris, David's near-fatal attack by the hammerhead shark, his ordeal with the swordfish, Andrew's rummy scene in Mr. Bobby's bar, and, finally, the three boys' crush on Audrey Bruce. Although Hemingway omits the homecoming scene and treats abruptly the sons' departure, the five episodes lavish considerable detail upon the boys and Hudson's relationship with them.

Tommy, born when Hudson was a struggling artist in Paris after World War I, is the weakest of the boys. A young man who wants his father's approval, he gets it by reminiscing about things that show what a good father Hudson was. Astute enough to know that his father likes to bask in memories of his famous artist friends, Tommy also knows that he dislikes being reminded of his first wife, Tommy's mother. Cued by Hudson's recitaton of the route *he* took when pushing Tommy around Paris in a baby carriage, Tommy selectively recalls Hudson's biparental qualities. It was Tommy and Hudson who would bring home pigeons for dinner, Tommy remembers, Hudson killing them with a slingshot and Tommy cuddling them beneath the carriage blankets so they could sneak them home. It was when Tommy and Hudson were together that they would go to the circus and see "the crocodiles of Le Capitaine Wahl" (62), or sit with Joyce in a corner of a cafe with a brazier warming them, or visit with Pascin while he drew pictures of Tommy on napkins. Tommy tells Audrey Bruce that he went often with Hudson to the racetracks, walked the Seine so often with him that he remembers all of the bridges over the river between Suresnes and Charenton (188), even visited with him one of Audrey's stepfathers, Dick Raeburn, while he had been very ill. Roger Davis, Hudson's longtime friend, joins in the tribute, telling the boys that their father made up young Tom's bottles every morning and marketed, buying cheap but good vegetables (65). When David tells how Tommy exquisitely rebuffed a homosexual, he adds further testimony of Hudson's paternal virtues, for Tommy's fine manners resulted from life in France with Hudson (180). Tommy, the solicitous son, is perfectly typecast in the rummy scene as the worrying, responsible child, "patient and long-suffering" (167).

Tommy's equally limited counterpart is brother Andrew, innocent and *enfant terrible*. He enviously punctures Tommy's nostalgia, quizzing him about *braziers, poireaux,* and *arrondissements*. And he taunts both father and brother by resolving to become Roger Davis's protégé, planning to make up "vicious stories" like Tommy's (72). To Tommy's boast that he was Joyce's " 'youngest friend,' " Andrew mocks, " 'I'll bet he misses you a lot' " (64). Tactless, Andrew calls Eddy, the hero of the shark episode, a rummy. And he's skeptical when David declares his love for the swordfish, saying that he is unable to understand it (142). Tommy cannot "keep his mouth off" David's fish, but it is Andrew's questions and statements—" 'Nobody in our family's ever caught a broadbill' "—that make Hudson scold them for the bad luck that their statements implicitly wish David. Whatever Tommy's faults may be, he is superior to Andrew, for Hudson has not spent the time with this son that he had with the other two (53). That is, he has obviously been a better parent to Tommy than Andrew's mother has been to him.

Unlike his brothers, David does not vouch for Hudson's superior parenthood. Nor does he share Tommy's supposed intelligence but actual fatuousness or Andrew's precocious athletic talent and "dark side." He wants to be self-sufficient, asking for no successful or famous adult to inflate his identity.

To this boy Hemingway gives special status. In the midst of his ordeal with the swordfish Tommy pronounces David " 'a saint and a martyr,' " adding that such a wonderful brother as David— " 'the best of us' "—is unknown to other boys. And after the swordfish gets away, Hudson tells David that he battled the fish better than any man ever did (141). This may sound like exaggerated parental consolation. But David's conduct, because dramatized, compels respect. He gets it from Roger, who reproaches himself for endangering David's life a second time, and from Eddy, who gets into countless brawls that night by boasting of David's bravery and perseverance.

David's life-endangering episodes with shark and swordfish— the biggest ones ever seen by Hudson (86, 137)—suggest that David is a young Santiago.[3] Like the old fisherman, David admits his goggle-fishing error with the hammerhead: " 'I just went too far out' " (90). And he expresses the same ambiguity and love for the swordfish that Santiago has for his marlin, saying that when he was most tired he could not differentiate the fish from himself, that he " 'began to love him more than anything on earth,' " that he is happy the swordfish is all right and that they are not enemies (142–43). Another echo of Santiago is in Tommy's comment, " 'He's a strange boy' " (127). David's biblical namesake, his welted back, and his injured hands and feet do not damage his claim to special status.

Hemingway seems to have intended David to represent a heroic youth whose death significantly impoverishes the world. If Santiago's virtues inspire emulation, David's approximation of them should too. But his potential is cut short. And when to the death of this " 'king of underwater,' " as Tommy calls him, Hemingway adds that of horseman Andrew and aviator Tommy, their collective deaths seem to lament man's loss of control over three of the classical elements. Hemingway gets the fourth element by having Hudson die "by fire."

I would not push an allegorical reading were it not for the novel's apocalyptic motif. Hudson's personal losses animate the novel as a whole, but they are part of a general lament for cosmic losses, as a chorus of events and allusions imply. And Hudson seems an appropriate figure to mourn the forthcoming doom. Intimate with great artists and unheralded guerrillas, with princesses and movie stars, with cats and the archipelago of small islands off Cuba's coast, his cosmopolitanism and experience in the double roles of creative artist and destructive warrior let him express the collective grief mankind will feel for the forthcoming loss of its world, portended in the loss of its sons. Coupled to the bizarre crew he captains in "At Sea," his pursuit of an invisible German submarine crew has a haunting anxiety that exceeds fear of personal annihilation. And "Cuba's" nostalgic, erotic, therapeutic, and horrific images emerge from a cold, windswept, intoxicated winter landscape that prophesies bleakness.

These two sections, however, are less overtly apocalyptic than "Bimini." The most conspicuous of its allusions are the canvases that Mr. Bobby verbally sketches. Reading like some colloquial addendum to the Book of Revelations, the pictures he asks Hudson to paint expand from a canvas with one waterspout to one with three of them, to a full hurricane, to the disaster of the *Titanic*, to a combined Breughel-Bosch canvas of "The End of the World." Even though Hudson completes only the waterspouts, " 'a small subject' " in Mr. Bobby's view, it suggests *Dies Irae*.

The narrator's mention of the hazards of night swimming and hurricanes in the beginning chapter of "Bimini" seems irrelevant until Hudson's houseboy, Joseph, startlingly compares the forthcoming visit of Hudson's three sons to a big fire in the past, a memorable event that Joseph ranks " 'along with the Second Coming' " (11). Other events on the eve of the boys' arrival have equally destructive implications. On Hudson's way to Mr. Bobby's, the little Negro boy, Louis, tells him of the " 'Big man from up north' " who's been throwing " 'anything [in the hotel] he can get his hands on' " (13), whose havoc contributes to Mr. Bobby's visions of catastrophic canvases. Even the banter that evening among Hudson, Johnny Goodner, and Roger Davis includes Johnny's mock reproach that after dark it is unwise to talk of God slightingly. " 'He's liable to be right behind you with his bat poised' " (27).

The "two worthless sporting characters," Fred Wilson and Frank Hart, add to the apocalyptic mood. Frank shoots flares at Mr. Bobby's place, at Brown's dock with its drums of gasoline, and, encouraged by the natives, at the commissioner's house, repeatedly conjuring the image of a conflagration like the one Joseph had mentioned earlier in the day. Roger's fight with Mr. Bobby's havoc-causing yachtsman interestingly ends the judgment-day violence. Both the yachtsman and Frank Hart, troublemakers, deserve comeuppance. But rather than set them against each other, Hemingway has the yachtsman, for unknown reasons, abuse Roger. Roger's excessively brutal beating of him indicates that the yachtsman ignites some malaise in Roger, some guilt and vengefulness that originate in other causes.

Tommy's reminiscences of Paris in chapter 3 seem to militate against the apocalyptic motif, but they underscore the doomsday atmosphere, for Hemingway ends the chapter of reminiscences with Hudson's mention of Pascin's suicide and begins the next with Roger's recall of his younger brother's drowning while canoeing with him. Roger's memory of that accident and his feeling of guilt is not the only thing that portends a comparable fate to the Hudson son who shares Roger's brother's name, David. Numerous references to suicides, deaths, and near disasters collect as a refrain in "Bimini." Mr. Bobby's " 'old Suicides,' " a man who had suffered from " 'Mechanic's Depressive,' " (158) is only the more conspicuous example of corpses. Others are one of Roger's sadomasochistic lovers, one of Audrey's stepfathers—killed by a runaway bobsled—and, of course, David, Andrew, and their mother. This panorama of disorder also includes the comic images of Ezra Pound and Ford Madox Ford, both rumored mad and pictured in Tommy's eyes as having " 'that awful lather dripping down' " their jaws (64). Even the death of the hammerhead shark makes an image of horror that Eddy cannot shake. "His belly was shining an obscene white, his yard-wide mouth like a turned-up grin, the great horns of his head with the eyes on end" (86). Eddy insists that for the rest of his life he will " 'see that old evil son of a bitch' " (89).

The rummy scene at Mr. Bobby's is intended to frighten tourists with a glimpse of a perverted world. And David's ordeal with the swordfish presumably contains something that frightened Hudson. But whether they effectively contribute to the apocalyptic motif is questionable. Still, Hemingway reiterates it in "Bimini's" coda: "The end of a man's world does not come as it does in one of the great paintings Mr. Bobby had outlined. It comes with one of the island boys bringing a radio message up the road from the local post office and saying, 'Please sign on the detachable part of the envelope. We're sorry, Mr. Tom' " (194–95).

Had Hemingway sufficiently amplified David's character, had he given him Santiago's mythic dimensions, the youth might have resonated the apocalyptic strings tied to him. But as "Bimini" stands, it appears that Hemingway decided against making David a world-redeeming hero or a demigod whose premature death, like Adonis's, blights the surrounding world. In his struggle with the swordfish David invokes a mythical hero trying to slay the dragon and thereby release "the vital energies that will feed the universe."[4] But Hemingway denies David victory over the huge fish. He diminishes David's role as hero to spotlight the mourning parent. The apocalyptic imagery, then, bears on Hudson's grief, partly to imply, I think, that since disaster and havoc are rampant, a good father can do little to protect his sons from premature death.

Hudson appears to offer his three sons simply a five-week vacation on a lovely island. But he actually exhibits himself as an ideal parent. Though once involved in the affairs of the world, he has now retired to an outpost. And his renunciation of women, minimal contamination by the sweep of modern life, and disciplined work routine show how responsibly he husbands esthetic values and the gift of his talent. The stability and orderliness of his island home and his loyal and dependent friends show also his domestic reliability. He bears no resemblance to Bimini's "bad fathers": "dignified" Uncle Edward, satirized by an unseen child because his gifts are rotten candy; the anonymous yachtsman at Mr. Bobby's who abuses his wife and children; the authority-defiant adult pranksters, Fred Wilson and Frank Hart; the self-indulgent, chili-pepper-eating Johnny Goodner; and the flesh-seeking stepfathers of Audrey Bruce. Least of all is he the father who corrupts his offspring by letting them drink alcohol, as the rummy-child joke at Mr. Bobby's presumes to prove.

As ideal parent, Hudson also provides his sons with a pair of substitute fathers who, along with himself, give them a range of adult models to fashion themselves upon. Unlike Hudson, contemplative and passive artist, Eddy is the fanatic father, the man of action who responds violently to events. Although Hudson, for example, deliberately aims but ineffectively fires his rifle at the hammerhead, it is Eddy who impulsively grabs the submachine gun and extravagantly sprays bullets that save David. An intensely emotional "father," it is Eddy who is so distraught over the near calamity that he pours down drink upon drink after it is over. It is he who futilely dives after the swordfish, gaff in hand, having coached and cared for David during the six-hour ordeal. And it is he who carries out the role of the proud father, boasting David's feat and fighting any scoffers.

Between the famous and the fanatic father Hemingway puts Roger Davis. The prostitution of his talent with Hollywood writing, affairs with faithless or sadistic women, and a lack of discipline have made him an artist manqué who cares more for people than for art. He becomes the Hudson boys' companion, swimming, deep-sea and goggle-fishing, and rehearsing practical jokes with them. Susceptibility to erotic and aggressive temptations, Audrey Bruce and the anonymous yachtsman, shows another facet of his humanness. Another is his deep sense of remorse: for his younger brother who died, for the two men his fists have bludgeoned, for his self-assigned irresponsibility in David's near disasters, for the women he's been stupid about.

These two outflanking "fathers" help show Hudson's unpossessiveness. He lets his sons emulate any combination of himself, Eddy, and Roger. He is not jealous when Andrew says he intends to claim Roger as his good friend, imitating Tommy's appropriation of Joyce as his. Nor does Hudson interfere with Eddy and Roger as they coach David during his ordeal. Just as he stands confidently aloof on the flying bridge during this episode, so too does he keep to his porch, painting, while Roger teaches the boys how to relate with women during the Audrey Bruce episode.

A broad-minded father, Hudson of "Bimini" does not square with the deeply grief-stricken Hudson of the "Cuba" and "At Sea" sections of the novel. Hemingway never accounts for Hudson's remarriage, recommitment to the world, and patriotic role in the war as captain of a Q-boat. But Hemingway has developed David's special status, "a well-loved mystery" (143), so that I accept that his death could significantly alter his father's life. After all, David's and Andrew's deaths obliquely indict him for not being a normal father. His virtue of unpossessiveness indirectly causes their deaths and—as "Cuba" slowly reveals—Tommy's death, too. Other factors may explain Hudson's drastic change of character in the years that separate "Bimini" from "Cuba," but Hemingway's refusal to suggest them isolates the cause in Hudson's remorse over the deaths of Andrew and David. Consistent with that is the remorse that Tommy's death causes. Hudson tries to repress it in "Cuba" and, as "At Sea" indicates, still grieves morosely some fifty days later.[5]

In "Cuba" Hemingway withholds the cause of Hudson's grief, divulging it only indirectly. Hudson's relationship with the cat,

Boise, whom he talks to and treats as though it were a child, reflects the cause, for if Boise were to die, Hudson "did not know what he would do" (208). Like a son, Boise is distressed whenever Hudson is gone for any length of time. After one sea stint Mario tells Hudson that Boise suffered more than ever before (233). This relationship seems uncanny until Hudson remembers Boise's origin: the son about whom he thought no more, presumably David, had asked that they take home the orphaned kitten as a "Christmas gift" (210). The cat's role as substitute son is clear from Hudson's abbreviated name for him, "Boy."

Hemingway also uses different landmarks to convey the cause for the sorrowful cast of Hudson's mind. En route to the Floridita bar Hudson sees a bridge that recalls a girl dismembered by her policeman lover; a hill that recalls the execution of Col. Crittenden and one hundred twenty-two American volunteers (246); an old barque that recalls Chinese victims of a submarine shelling; a lean-to by the railway tracks that recalls the old Negro couple who, with money Hudson's third wife gave them, bought a white dog, now dead. The landmarks culminate at the waterfront. The old Pacific and Orient docks recall the French ship that returned all of the whores of this part of Havana to Europe: though a lot of people regarded it as a source of amusement, to him it was sad (251).

The characters in "Cuba" uniformly reflect Hudson's sorrow. His chauffeur, Pedro, is unhappy because of the scarcity of food, Marine Warrant Officer Hollins because of shore duty, Lt. Commander Fred Archer for unspecified reasons: his healthy looks did not betray his unhappiness (255). Ignacio Natera Ravello is unhappy because of the ambassador's rudeness, huge Henry Wood because of his unrequited desire for a small girl, Willie because of much suffering (275). The *Alcade Peor* is unhappy because of political corruption, Honest Lil because of her waning beauty and waxing weight, and Tommy's mother because of his death. When placed beside Hudson, however, none of these characters has as significant a reason as Hudson to be unhappy. Not even Tommy's mother. Still " 'the most beautiful woman in the world' " (310), she has her career and a man in love with her who can assuage her sorrow. And, as "Bimini" had indicated, she had not been much of a mother to Tommy anyway.

To alleviate Hudson's sorrow, Honest Lil keeps asking him to tell her happy stories. Hudson never tells her that the death of Tommy, whom she fondly regards as though he were her grandson, is the specific cause of his sorrow. But she eventually intuits that only one thing could cause such grief to him. He tells her that although he has been " 'desperately,' " " 'unbearably happy,' " with women, never has he been " 'as happy as with my children when we were all happy together' " (286).

Honest Lil's mothering, Boise's childlike anxiety and jealousy, the erotic visit of Hudson's first wife, and his reminiscences of erotic pleasures with princesses and exotic women—neither can these domestic comforters nor countless drinks anesthetize Hudson's woe. Its depth shows how a truly devoted father regards his children. He will not affront their memory by wanting more. He will find consolation in patriotic duty curiously free from vindictiveness toward the nation responsible for Tommy's death or, later, the representative of his enemy, the German commanding the submarine crew Hudson pursues. Obedient to his role as exemplary father, Hudson commands a Q-boat to capture as many Germans as possible for interrogation purposes, hoping to help end a war that brings death to other men's sons.

"At Sea" fittingly concludes Hudson's relationship with his sons. That is, his crew is more a family than a military patrol. There are responsible men like Antonio, cook and chief mate, and Ara, a reliable, strong Basque, as well as inconspicuously obedient men like Gil, George, and Juan. But its most conspicuous members are Henry Wood, Peters, and Willie. Henry Wood is the diffident, questioning child who defers to Hudson's authority. To his request that he be forgiven should he ever behave stupidly, Hudson paternally replies, " 'You were forgiven when you were born. . . . You are a very brave boy, Henry, and I am fond of you and trust you' " (341). Peters is the refractory, rebellious son. A radio man on loan from the Marines, he is the ship's rummy, a possible traitor, and the only crewman to be killed. Hudson's "other problem child" (401) is Willie, an ex-Marine. His marginal recovery from a mental breakdown, undefined but severe sufferings and aggressive traits make him the unpredictable, violent child. Though there is bad blood among him, Peters, and Henry, Hudson keeps sibling rivalries from breaking out, showing his parental expertise.

Hudson's parental role in "At Sea" is also see in the mission he must carry out. He must hunt down the remains of a submarine crew, tracking and second-guessing their movements through the hazardous archipelago of islands along Cuba's shallow north coast. This is certainly not as heroic as sinking or capturing a

German submarine. But Hudson's enemies commit domestic crimes. After they destroy a small island village and kill its inhabitants to pirate boats, they execute an apparently treacherous crew member. " 'Family trouble' " (339), Hudson calls it. They abandon a young sailor dying of gangrenous legs. And they leave a wounded third sailor aboard their grounded turtle boat, presumably to ambush Hudson and his crew. Although, for some unexplained reason, this wounded sailor does not fire upon Hudson, Willie, and Peters when they board the turtle boat, later he does kill Peters with a short burst from his machine pistol. It clatters "like a child's rattle" (425)—the most incongruous simile in the novel.

The fate of these three German sailors indicates why this section of the novel offers more than impressive "descriptions of physical action" or "pure childhood fantasy, a modern Huck Finn or Tom Sawyer adventure."[6] Their deaths indirectly condemn Hudson's antagonist, the German commanding the fleeing submarine crew. In domestic terms his execution and abandonment of the sailors show him to be a filicidal father, Hudson's antithesis. So to pursue him and to die in the act of exterminating him completes Hudson's characterization as the self-sacrificing good father. By administering this retribution, Hudson also avenges the deaths of three other young men: Andrew, David, and Tommy.

The crimes of Hudson's German counterpart are tailor-made to show Hudson to advantage, but they also allow an antithetical reading that sees Hudson and him as doubles—as filicidal fathers.

Whether indebted to Conrad or not,[7] "At Sea" is about Hudson's relationship with his "secret sharer." Hudson decides early that his adversary is a "methodical bastard" (339), a trait that also applies to Hudson, a careful tracker. He realizes that although his adversary's acts against the three sailors appear ruthless, in each case the German leader has shown considerateness. He cruelly shot the treacherous young sailor at the base of his spine. But, Hudson notes, " 'Afterwards whoever did it was kind and shot him in the neck' " (339). For the abandoned second sailor Ara tells Hudson that he had been left in a shelter with a good bed, water, a crock of food, and a ditch in the sand for drainage (364). Of the wounded third sailor, apparently abandoned on the grounded turtle boat, Willie concludes that his crewmates must have been fond of him. Hudson agrees: " 'Probably. Or they wouldn't have let him

take up space' " (442). Kindness toward, and admiration of, subordinates characterize Hudson as well as his adversary. And
Hudson's compliment of his adversary's intelligence and naviga-
tional skill—" 'They must really be sailors' " (412)—does not go
unanswered, Willie later congratulating him, " ' . . . you chased
pretty' " (451).

The nearer Hudson gets to the fleeing German crew the more
intense grows his "feeling that this had happened before in a bad
dream" (414), "that it had all happened before" (416). He senses
that the experience "was happening with such an intensification
that he felt both in command and at the same time the prisoner of
it" (414). To this recurrent-dream motif, common in Conrad, Hemingway also adds the slow pursuit, island by island, of Hudson's
quarry. Such Conradian prolongation adds to suspense but even
more to the impression that the journey is as much internal as
external. So when Hudson's and his adversary's crews turn out to
be the same size, there can be little doubt that the elusive man
Hudson chases is his shadow self, that "the repugnance that I feel
toward meeting [the Germans]" (376) mirrors his repugnance for
his own dark side. And the parallel between the deaths of Hudson's three sons and the three sailors, two of whom are young, is
not a coincidence, objectionable in realistic fiction, but a convention, obligatory in psychological fiction. A man responsible for
the deaths of three young men, Hudson's adversary objectifies the
repressed guilts that Hudson must annihilate. At the least Hudson wishes to deny that he had been a bad father to his sons, that
any irresponsibility of his contributed to their deaths. At the most
he wishes to deny that he had filicidal feelings toward them. But
events expose him. He repeatedly tells his crew, for instance, that
they must capture some portion of the German crew for interrogation purposes. But they recognize the gap between what he says
and what he wishes and make sure that no Germans survive.

Unlike his Conradian counterparts, either the anonymous
young captain of "The Secret Sharer" or Marlow, Hudson is not
preoccupied exclusively with his secret sharer. Nor does Hemingway ever let Hudson see his double, denying the recognition scene
so common to literature of "the double."[8] But like Conrad and
Dostoevsky, Hemingway populates the novel with a phalanx of
doubles, be they contemporaries, children, or adversaries. Some of
them, of course, are conventional, like David's swordfish, evoking
as it does his hatred and his love, or Hudson's ship, a Q-boat that
passes for a scientifically equipped pleasure craft. But others are

psychological doubles who fulfill their role of enacting repressed wishes and so reveal Hudson as a father who unconsciously wants his three sons dead.

Besides the German captain, Hudson's most conspicuous double is Roger Davis.[9] Their lives have intersected in Paris, Cap d'Antibes, and now on Bimini. Artists, boxers, and deep-sea fishermen, they are also "stupid with women." Virtual brothers, almost interchangeable, they both easily attract the love of Audrey Bruce and the admiration of Hudson's sons. And Mr. Bobby's question of whether they are kin points to their visual likeness. An even stronger similarity, which has precipitated Mr. Bobby's question, is their affliction with remorse. Hudson has done nothing that we know of for him to feel guilt like that which Roger feels over the accidental death of his younger brother, David Davis. But Hemingway rests Roger's recall of that event and David Hudson's near disaster next to Roger's awareness that he is responsible for the near repetition of the childhood calamity with this second David. And that, in turn, suggests the deeper cause of his guilt. He feels responsible for his brother's death because it gratified his unconscious wish to kill his brother or see him killed. The recurrence of Roger's brooding guilt after David's struggle with the huge swordfish confirms the strength of his fratricidal wish.

The two fishing episodes also show that Hudson shares Roger's repressed wish, modified in him to filicide. He knows, for instance, that Roger is a failure, that he is cruel to women, that he had nearly killed two men with his fists recently, and that he may well be envious and hostile because of Hudson's success. Yet when to these traits that incriminate him as dangerous Roger also adds his fratricidal guilt, Hudson seems oddly deficient in parental precaution. Before letting his boys goggle-fish with Roger, he merely asks that David be careful (79). Not only does Hudson leave David under Roger's surveillance, but his lack of paternal diligence alarms another double, Eddy. Eddy insists that they anchor closer to where the boys are fishing; he urges Hudson to take his rifle topside and look for sharks; and he sprays the bullets that save David. Once the danger is over, Eddy tries to obliterate the event with drink while Roger broods over it in morose silence. Their repressive and obsessive responses suggest an unconscious reason Hudson values the presence of these two violent men during the fishing episodes. They are accomplices to his filicidal wish. After all, Eddy's beatings the night after the swordfish episode partly reflect a desire to be punished for having such a wish and for having failed to execute it. And the agony of David's ordeal, like all initiation ceremonies, exposes the sadistic, filicidal wish beneath his father's benign motive of assisting his initiation into adulthood.

Hudson tries to safeguard his own image by standing passively upon the flying bridge all during David's ordeal. He lets his two doubles, Roger and Eddy, coach David, fail him by letting the fish escape, and permit his injuries—"bloody hands and lacquered-looking oozing feet and . . . welts the harness had made across his back" (136). Andrew appears to be the only one who wishes David ill, for David construes his inability to "keep his mouth off" the swordfish as secretly wishing him bad luck. But when Tommy declares, " 'I don't want any damned fish to kill him,' " and Hudson responds, " 'Neither do I and neither does Roger and neither does Eddy' " (114), it is clear that no one "keeps his mouth off" David's fish, that all secretly wish him ill.

If proof that Hudson is a hypocritical, filicidal father depends wholly upon his doubles, my antithetical reading may be tenuous. But Hudson himself verifies it. For all of his artistic success, he is a domestic failure, as his broken marriages confirm. He compensates for his failure by gathering to him other failures and rejects, Roger and Eddy here, motley crews later. And though the novel's apocalyptic imagery may suggest that his failures merely coincide with impending cosmic disaster, it is as easy to conclude the reverse, that the imagery externalizes his wish to see others fail, to see disaster strike them. We can grace his premonitions of disaster by calling them an artist's sixth sense or uncanny intuition. But they are, quite simply, a masked wish whose extreme form is filicide.

The clearest indication of Hudson's wish for his sons' deaths follows David's swordfish ordeal: sitting in his chair and trying to read, Hudson thinks about the day, "from the beginning until the end and it seemed as though all of his children except Tom had gone a long way away from him or he had gone away from them" (143). The thoughts of this sentence would not occur unless Hudson wished that David and Andrew would indeed go "a long way away from him." The motives for such a wish are not hard to find. In part Hudson knows that he exerts little influence on his sons, and he fears their rejection of him. Of course he asserts that he wants David to get as much as he can from Roger and that he is happy the two so well understand each other (143). But his sense that "something about today frightened me" (144) has several translations. To the reading that he was frightened that something *would* harm David can be easily added the reading that he was frightened by his wish *that* something harm David. He is also frightened by the prospect of David's rapid coming-of-age and his own obsolescence, for never once during the six-hour ordeal does David ask for Hudson's help. And because the huge swordfish symbolizes the father, Hudson would be most frightened by the parricidal wish latent in David's action. Andrew's and especially David's deaths, then, are propitious. They relieve Hudson from being frightened by them ever again. Tommy is spared, for the time being. He pays proper court to his father and does not frighten him.

In "Cuba" Hudson withholds the fact of Tommy's death. That seems to indicate his dislike of pity. And as the fact becomes known to Ignacio, Willie, and Honest Lil, his dislike is justified. Formal, tough, or lachrymose, their pity is inadequate to Hudson's needs, if not Tommy's memory, only magnifying the discrepancy between a man bereft of his children and those who had none to begin with. But Hudson's behavior actually indicates his repressive traits. Even more than pity, he dislikes unpleasant facts, preferring the pleasures of various narcotics: double frozen daiquiris, erotic fantasies, or the maternal consolations of Honest Lil, who continually asks to hear his happy stories. Hudson even gives narcotics to Tommy's mother. He tells her that a flak ship shot Tommy down in a routine firing off Abbeville. But when she asks whether his parachute burned, he tells her that it did not, deliberately lying because he is sure he has told her enough for one day (332). His lie may be justifed as trying to protect Tommy's mother. But when aligned with other repressive traits, it makes Hudson vulnerable to the suspicion that his grief over Tommy's death is also a lie. Although the lengthy Floridita Bar episode seems intended to show Hudson's ability to contain his grief, it also has a celebratory air, exuded by the number of relatively carefree characters who populate the bar. They collectively merge into yet another of Hudson's doubles and mirror his repressed wish to rejoice in Tommy's death. Ultimately even duty serves Hudson as a narcotic. It lets him flee Tommy's self-pitying mother and fill his mind with the pleasurable vision of discharging his murderous impulses, sanctified as they are by war.

It is tempting to say that Hudson's depression, so prevalent in "At Sea," simply conceals his pleasure in having his filicidal wishes gratified. But his depression is more complicated than that. Forebodings of his own death figure in it. When he acknowledges that the grounding of his ship "had come to him as a personal wound," his immediate remark about "the feeling of reprieve that a wound brings" (416) also expresses relief at a temporary delay of his death sentence. And his strategy in finally confronting the enemy shows strong suicidal impulses. Ara, anxious that Hudson's behavior jeopardizes their lives and mission, had earlier exhorted him, " 'Now that you have ceased to be careful of yourself I must ask you to be, please' " (358). But Hudson, ignoring his repeated worry of being ambushed, does not anchor at the head of the fatal island and disperse his crew. Instead he sails headlong down "the narrow brush river of the channel" (454) and conspicuously invites the "three chickenshit bullets" that cut him down. His decisions to attack a second time, to have Willie and Ara look for survivors, and then to go back to detrap the turtle boat are suspicious delays that lessen his chances of getting the medical attention his wounds require. Rather than praise his self-abnegation, we must suspect neurosis.

His depression, minimal desire to cling to life, self-reproaches, sleeplessness, unwillingness to interest himself in anything but duty, and even his refusal to accept his standard source of nourishment, alcohol, mark Hudson a melancholiac disguised as a mourner.[10] After all, like Roger's remorse, Hudson's mourning for Tommy exceeds its ostensible cause. Neither Tommy's character nor his relationship with Hudson justifies the duration or intensity of Hudson's grief. Little more than a worrying bundle of reminiscences, except in his earliest Paris years Tommy was left to mama, nurse, and boarding school as were his two brothers. So Hudson's grief must entail more than a guilty admission of his deficient fatherhood. Indeed its genuine cause is not whom he has lost but what he has lost in Tommy. Hudson's tendency to remember Tommy only as an infant, a physical extension of himself, shows Hudson's narcissism. And though Tommy's reminiscences supposedly vouched for Hudson's love of Tommy, they also reflect, narcissus-fashion, Hudson's self-love. Just as Hudson's earlier grief over David's death mourned the image of himself as hero, here then he mourns the image of himself that Tommy best recalls, the artist.

Mourning what he loves about himself also gives Hudson, as any melancholiac, opportunity to punish himself for desiring the deaths of his sons. Proof of this is not only in his suicidal wish but also in the pleasure he gets from pursuing and punishing his filicidal counterpart, the German pilot. Hudson insists that he does not desire the pilot's death (419). But clearly he does. Why else is he so careless about his own safety? He knows that any injury he gets will inflame his crew to vindictiveness, as Ara shows by shooting "a man walking toward them out of the smoke with his hands clasped over his head" (460). And Hudson can be certain that the pilot will be killed when he sends the murderous Willie on the island " 'to have a look' " (460).

Since suicides inflict upon themselves the homicidal feelings they have against others, it is propitious for Hudson to be able to obscure his suicidal wish by chasing a German pilot at whom he can obliquely aim his murderous impulses. Even more propitious is the final exoneration of his filicidal wishes, for he aims them at those who deserve them. After all, his assailant is not his German double. Rather his assailant is plural. The three bullets that fatally wound Hudson are fired by the men Willie identifies as the "three deads" of the first fight (465). The novel asks us to wonder whether Hudson will survive his wounds. But his conduct after his wounding leaves little question about his chances of survival. And there is even less question that three men who liked underwater diving in "Bimini" surface as part of a submarine crew in "At Sea," or that doubles of Andrew, David, and Tommy avenge their deaths and succeed in parricidal ambush, even though they pay with their lives and are assisted by the suicidal wish of the man they slay.

Santiago and Hudson's shared need to be exemplary men and their equally shared unconscious hostility toward their "sons" partly corroborate my antithetical reading of *Islands*. So does the fact that the books were composed within the same period, Hemingway having conceived of *Old Man* as an epilogue or fourth book of *Islands*.[11] Biographical information also supports my reading, even though it already props too much of the criticism on the novel.[12] Scarcely veiled are the parallels between Hudson and Hemingway; between Hudson's and Hemingway's sons, John, Patrick, and Gregory; between the car accident that kills the younger Hudson boys and one that occurred in April 1947 injuring Gregory's knee and giving Patrick a delayed, serious concussion.[13] But let me add that the three German sailors are heavily veiled portraits of the same three sons, both Hudson's and Hemingway's. The son deserving execution is the malicious, treacherous Andrew-Gregory, the son whose complications and difficult behavior always bothered his father.[14] The abandoned son who stoically resists interrogation and asserts that "nothing is important" (362) earns Hudson's admiration (363). His attitude would mirror both Hemingway's and Hudson's feelings toward David-Patrick, the favorite son. The third sailor had been made a mess by Willie's grenade and a short burst from Hudson's submachine gun. But Hudson examines the body and finds that the sailor had suffered from two wounds, one "in the fleshy part of his left shoulder" (426). This so closely corresponds to John Hemingway's World War II injury, "in the right arm and shoulder by grenade fragments and six rounds from a high velocity carbine,"[15] that equating them seems reasonable. Hudson's refusal to give Tommy's mother the precise details of Tommy's death suggests some hideous or disfiguring wounds that would be as gruesome a sight as the "mess" beneath the "blasted forward hatch" of the turtle boat (429, 434).

To explain why filicidal wishes surfaced in 1947, when Hemingway began composing "Bimini," requires looking at some biographical details that seem to refute such wishes in Hemingway. In May 1945 Hemingway was informed that his oldest son—who had been missing in action, badly wounded, and then moved from one POW camp to another—had been liberated.[16] It is likely that this news would heighten Hemingway's thoughts about his relationship with that son and with his other two sons as well. But a more serious event in mid-August of 1946 stimulates the question that *Islands* literally addresses: How should a man conduct himself when he loses those he is closest to? I refer to Mary Hemingway's near death. She and Hemingway were driving to Sun Valley to resume the annual autumn vacations he had begun in 1939, to meet the three boys, and to give Mary a "lying-in" period. Her pregnancy turned out to be tubular, and when it ruptured in Casper, Wyoming, had it not been for Hemingway's resourcefulness, reports Baker, she would surely have died.[17] Both of these near losses, along with the aforementioned April 1947 car accident, could have precipitated the narrative Hemingway began composing.

If we also ask why Hemingway places "Bimini" back in the thirties, makes his main character a painter, and provides him with a companion who strongly resembles John Dos Passos, then still other factors seem to have coalesced in Hemingway's mind. Childless, Dos Passos had an especial fondness for two boys with the same first name, Patricks Hemingway and Murphy.[18] Patrick

Murphy was the second son of well-known expatriates, his father, Gerald, being a painter with some talent.[19] More importantly, both of his sons, Boath and Patrick, died young. While fishing with Dos Passos in March 1935, Hemingway learned of Boath Murphy's death, and both men wrote letters of condolence to the Murphys.[20] Two years later Patrick Murphy finally died of tuberculosis, Dos Passos having posted Hemingway on Patrick's condition in four of the six letters he wrote Hemingway between May 1935 and July 1937.[37] Though Hemingway was not particularly fond of Gerald Murphy, a father with three sons could easily empathize with Murphy's situation.

These biographical matters would seem to argue only the existence of Hemingway's fear for his sons, only his anxiety that some unforeseen harm would assail them. And it also seems likely that his sons' growing independence of him during 1950–51 would increase his guilt rather than spur filicidal wishes. Like any parent he would feel remorse for things he had done and not done for them. And he would feel especially culpable for having been only a part-time father to them. Yet their independence would also breed parental resentment to accompany the guilt, for their independence, their rebelliousness, or their acquisition of values different from his would be tantamount to rejecting or abandoning him. And though the normal way a father deals with his maturing sons' rejection is by accepting it, he does so with a measure of hostility.[22]

Hemingway's hostility would be fueled by the uncanny feeling that he assigns Hudson, the "feeling that this had happened before in a bad dream" (414), "that it had all happened before" (416). Hemingway's sons' abandonment of him had indeed "all happened before": it had happened when *he* had abandoned *his* father. And because Hemingway's affiliative wish, his need for male companionship, was so strong, his maturing sons' departures would be a repudiation of his needs. So, like his father before him, Hemingway reacts, albeit unconsciously and fictitiously, by committing suicide (himself-as-Hudson), directing upon himself the filicidal wishes he has against his sons.

Hemingway corroborates this inference in his letter of 13 June 1951 to his old World War I friend Gen. E. E. "Chink" Dorman-O'Gowan. Writing about "At Sea," he says: "I had to write a long part of the book that I hoped I would never need to write and which I dreaded writing. But I wrote it, liveing in it, and I hope you will like it because there is one good fight . . . except that in this fight the other people, the enemy, are being pursued and they out-class those who pursue them" (*Letters*, 730). Hemingway's sense of compulsion ("I had to write a long part") and of dread ("I hoped I would never need to write" that part) expresses here a fear that none of his available letters elsewhere expresses. That fear has no external cause—no fear of libel, no fear of being caught imitating some dead master, no fear of governmental reproach for revealing top-secret information about his World War II activities on the *Pilar*. So the cause of that fear must be internal, must reveal neurotic or moral anxiety that signals to him that he was writing about forbidden wishes.[23] Were Hudson genuinely resolved to bring the Germans back alive, his behavior would have fewer neurotic symptoms than it has. But those symptoms indicate that he hunts down his adversaries to kill them and so to kill those doubles they represent. Hemingway's anxiety, his dread, then, was due to his uncanny sense that in Hudson were his own filicidal wishes.

A final reason for these wishes is Hemingway's fixation on his father. The strong return of Hemingway's repressed guilt for having abandoned his father and for being partly responsible for his suicide demands that he compensate for it. And so through Hudson he wishes for the death of his sons, hoping that his disaffiliation from them will somehow affiliate him again with his father. And he agrees through Hudson to abandon also his interest in art and women, both of which lured Hemingway from his father early on. Surely that will prove Hemingway's rededication to his father. For by making Hudson a patriot, a man who endangers and loses his life for the land of his father, Hemingway asserts the primacy of his love for his own father.

An Obsessed Onlooker:
The Dangerous Summer

The last work published during Hemingway's life, *The Dangerous Summer* presents one of the more complicated textual problems in the Hemingway canon. According to Hotchner, Hemingway could not meet *Life* magazine's deadlines nor keep the contracted-for, 10,000-word account of the 1959 rivalry between matadors Antonio Ordóñez and Luis Miguel Dominguín from swelling to nearly 109,000 words.[1] For three solid weeks in June of 1960 Hemingway tried to prune the manuscript but managed to cut only 278 words (240). He finally called upon Hotchner for help. With Hemingway's approval Hotchner cut some 55,000 words in nine days (242). This done, Hemingway still felt compelled to return to Spain for photographs to accompany the text. While there, he continued to tinker away at text and galleys, never eliminating all the loose ends.[2]

Because the manuscripts have only recently become available to scholars, it may be some time before we can answer whether the half-text that *Life* published resembles the overall design of the completed draft, whether Hemingway's intention is still visible.[3] Though contracted to report the Ordóñez-Dominguín rivalry, Hemingway presumably told Hotchner that he changed his mind and wanted "to make a real story which would be valuable in itself and worth publishing after there had been no deaths or dramatic endings to the season" (237). But he also confessed to Hotchner that "it started to be one thing and then became another and then another and I boxed myself into a corner" (245). To his fellow author and Spanish friend Jose Luis Castillo-Puche, Hemingway allegedly admitted, "very seriously," that he was " 'writing a bunch of crap' " (63). Not the least of the factors that complicate the text of *Summer*, of course, was the state of Hemingway's health.

Notwithstanding these complications, the half-text published in *Life* is at least as solid a skeleton as Santiago's marlin. And from this piece of quasi history we can reconstruct its father-son dynamics, its affiliative and filicidal obsessions, and Hemingway's preoccupation with his guilt for neglecting his three sons and his father.

Even a quick reading of *Dangerous Summer* finds Hemingway deifying Antonio Ordóñez. The first time he sees him perform in the bullring is a vision of perfection: "I could tell he was great from the first slow pass he made with the cape. It was like seeing all the great cape handlers, and there were many, alive and fighting again except that he was better. Then, with the muleta, he was perfect. He killed well and without difficulty. Watching him closely and critically I knew he would be a very great matador if nothing happened to him. I did not know then he would be great no matter what happened to him and increase in courage and passion after every grave wound."[4] So able is Ordóñez that the second time Hemingway watches him he "invents" a bull, transforming a worthless bull "into a fighting bull before your eyes" (1:94). And when an aspirant bullfighter vaults the barrera to show his own skill with Ordóñez's second bull at Aranjuez, he endangers Ordóñez by giving the bull time to learn quickly what he needs to know to gore the man with the deceptive cape. But Ordóñez, neither alarmed nor angered, "ran over to him with the cape, said something to him very quickly and put his arm around him and hugged him" (1:106). Turning to the bull, he proceeded to make the "most complete and classic faena with him that I had ever seen," writes Hemingway, until Ordóñez began a series of trick passes and "the bull's right hind foot slipped and he lurched and his right horn drove into Antonio's left buttock" (1:109). Severely gored, Ordóñez operatically refused to leave the ring before killing the bull: "his brother, his manager and his sword handler grabbed him and tried to hold him and make him go to the infirmary. Antonio shook them all off in a rage saying to [his brother] Pepe, 'And you call yourself an Ordóñez' " (1:109). Ordóñez is so good that Hemingway does not even have to have been present to declare that "Antonio fought twice in Mont-de-Marsan in France where he was wonderful" (2:75).

The second and third installments in *Life*, each covering three "duels" between Ordóñez and Dominguín, climax with Ordóñez performing great faenas. But Hemingway reserves Ordóñez's greatest achievement for the last installment, writing of his killing of the last bull at Bilbao *recibiendo*, on the third *cite*. Not only is this the rarest way to kill, receiving the bull's charge rather than charging him, but it is the riskiest way too: "No one in our time cites twice recibiendo. That belongs to the times of Pedro Romero, that other great torero of Rondo [Ordóñez's birthplace] who lived two hundred years ago" (3:90).

Outside the ring Ordóñez is equally superb. Only a week after his severe goring at Aranjuez he takes an early morning walk, without his cane, with Hemingway. And he ignores a slight goring during an *encierro* at Pamplona. But he is also fun-loving, helping Hemingway "kidnap" a pair of American beauties. And during the birthday festivities for Hemingway and Ordóñez's wife, seven times he recklessly lets marksman Hemingway shoot the ashes from the cigarette in his mouth: "Finally he said, 'Ernesto, we've gone about as far as we can go. The last one just brushed my lips' " (2:76). The embodiment of agility, this heroic merrymaker catches a tennis ball in each hand while diving into a swimming pool. And for a lark he even risks grave penalties by going along with the "absolutely illegal" ruse of letting his "double," Hotchner, enter the Ciudad Real bullring as his substitute matador. Watching "El Pecas" Hotchner and Ordóñez don their outfits, Hemingway writes, "it was the most carefree preparation for a bullfight I have ever seen" (3:81).

What demonstrates Ordóñez's genuine heroic qualities is his "duel" with Dominguín, his brother-in-law and chief competitor, to determine which of them is Spain's best matador. Hemingway implies that Dominguín comes out of retirement to show his superiority to Ordóñez and to hush the clamor for Ordóñez. But the older matador fails. Ordóñez outperforms him in all but one of their joint engagements and that, Hemingway implies, was because Dominguín "had two ideal and perfect bulls" while Ordóñez "had two worthless bulls" (2:73).

Despite Hemingway's obvious bias, he tries to show that he is impartial, that he has genuine regard for Dominguín. He helps him to the infirmary after his goring at Valencia (but gets back to the ring in time to see Ordóñez perform another superlative faena). And Hemingway ends *Summer* with his solicitous visit to Dominguín, recovering from a goring at Bilbao. The telegram-cable epilogue in *Life*, updating the rivalry in 1960, duly praises

Dominguín for having "fought himself into shape" and for "improving in confidence with each fight" after "a generally disastrous fair in early August" in Malaga. But compared with Ordóñez, his achievements are negligible. For even with a crippled right arm Ordóñez "made one of the finest and most truly valiant faenas I have ever seen" (3:96).

As Hemingway presents him, Ordóñez is too good to be true. And many discrepancies between fact and *Summer* show this to be the case. For one, the rivalry is more imagined than real, more a publicity stunt than "the duel of the century" that Hemingway makes it out to be. Castillo-Puche contends that Hemingway "was half convinced he was witnessing a genuine 'civil war' in the bullfight world, though I for my part thought the whole affair was a big laugh, and almost everyone else did too" (321–22, 82, 246).[5] Reporting on Ordóñez and Dominguín's first meeting in the ring at Zaragoza, Hemingway implies that Ordóñez gets higher marks. But Hotchner says that Hemingway told him unequivocally that "Miguel [Dominguín] had turned in the best performance that afternoon" (210). *Summer* ascribes no mundane or ignoble motives to Ordóñez. But Hemingway told Hotchner, "Antonio considers it an insult that Miguel does not treat him as an equal" (211), implying resentment. And Castillo-Puche suspects that Ordóñez's regard for Hemingway has a root in self-advertisement (140, 247, 360). Hemingway ends *Summer* with his visit to, and conversation with, Dominguín just after his goring at Bilbao. But Hotchner reports that there was no exchange between the matador and the author: "Ernest talked to him for a short while in a low voice, and Dominguín nodded and smiled a little" (228). For the Spanish, Hemingway's largest deviation from fact is his utter disregard for Manolete as matador. Dominguín's predecessor as Spain's number one matador, Manolete was widely acclaimed as the best among modern matadors. For Hemingway to dismiss him cavalierly as a practitioner of tricks, having seen him but once, and then on a windy day, and in Mexico, and with "the two worst bulls" (1:85), was outrageous.[6]

The question that *Dangerous Summer* invites is why Hemingway sought to mythify Ordóñez, why, in Castillo-Puche's words, "Ernesto looked upon him as the resurrection of a *torero* god, the living image of all the mythical matadors who had ever lived" (157). To answer this question requires asking another: Why is Hemingway so concerned about Ordóñez? Is this just one more instance of Hemingway's affiliative needs? He is at Ordóñez's bedside after the severe Aranjuez goring, he oversees his convalescence and changes the dressing on his wound, he visits him before almost every fight, and he takes care of the wound Ordóñez gets in the calf from an *encierro* at Pamplona. His commitment to follow Ordóñez tirelessly across Spain from bullfight to bullfight is not simply to ensure the authenticity and accuracy of his report on the Ordóñez-Dominguín rivalry. To do that he did not need to go to even a half-dozen bullfights before Dominguín was severely gored at Bilbao.

Castillo-Puche amplifies the conclusion that Hemingway's relationship with Ordóñez was excessive: "There was something almost religious about Ernesto's devotion to his idol. He not only prayed for him; he made promises and vows whenever he thought Antonio was in particular danger. Before a *corrida* he would tiptoe into his room very quietly, as though overcome with awe. If he allowed himself to crack a joke, he made sure that it was a really funny one that would cheer Antonio up, and never one that would remind him that he was about to enter the ring for yet another fearful and dangerous *corrida*" (158). Recalling Hemingway's behavior while Ordóñez was being operated upon after the Aranjuez goring, Castillo-Puche adds:

> He was absolutely crushed, and kept wandering in and out of the operating room and pacing up and down, unable to sit still. It wasn't simply nervousness, it was more like a very peculiar sort of hysteria. As we waited there for news of how the operation was going, I saw an Ernesto I had never seen before: a hesitant, terrified, almost desperate man. . . . Ernesto kept asking [Dr. Tamames, the surgeon] over and over: 'What about his femoral artery? Is his femoral artery okay?' Ernesto was so paternal he seemed childish. He would exaggerate the danger to Antonio's life one minute and play it down the next. . . . Ernest was so concerned about the wound in Antonio's leg you would have thought he was watiing outside a delivery room for news that he was the father of a bouncing baby boy. [164–65]

Such exaggerated behavior easily leads to Castillo-Puche's conclusion that Hemingway found in Ordóñez great material for fiction, the "perfect protagonist," "the hero of an epic he would write" that would "crown not only Ernesto's work of art, but the legend, the myth of Antonio" (204, 205). Hemingway's exaggerated behavior also leads to the conclusion that, as no previous matador had done, Ordóñez incarnated the values Hemingway had first identified with as far back as 1922, when he first saw a bullfight. Ordóñez, then, represented Hemingway's idealized vision of himself as valor-artist and enabled him to conceal his narcissism with paternalism. Yet another conclusion is that in his exaggerated regard for Ordóñez Hemingway expresses the awe and admiration he had for youth in general, epitomized as it is in this son of sons. An embodiment of beauty, courage, intelligence, and artistry, Ordóñez is Santiago writ young, the representative son whom all fathers can idolize, the son deserving of every man's affiliative—if not homerotic—wish. Castillo-Puche records that Hemingway declared, " 'I'm so fond of him—he means more to me than a son' " (154).

Beneath Hemingway's regard for Ordóñez, marked as it is by inordinate paternalism, is still another conclusion, that Hemingway mythifies him partly to assuage his guilt for having shortchanged his own three sons. His behavior toward Ordóñez shows how paternal he can indeed be when he chooses. The nasty edge to this, of course, is that he reserves such fatherly fondness for only a deserving son. Likewise, because his uncritical acceptance of everything Ordóñez does is out of character, Hemingway permits a glimpse of his wish that his sons (and readers) will be as tolerant of him as he is of their exemplar.

Hemingway's excessive protectiveness toward Ordóñez intends to show that he feels no hostility for him nor, by extension, for his own sons. But because every exaggerated behavior signals the presence of a repressed, antithetical wish, his protectiveness reveals several counterintentions. Half consciously Hemingway wishes that his solicitude will protect himself from filial discontent and aggression, that neither Ordóñez nor his own sons will try to harm him. And unconsciously he wishes that harm will strike them. For different reasons, Castillo-Puche shares this conclusion, saying that it was

> the exhausting struggle between his needs as an artist and his feelings about his beloved friend that in the end finally unbalanced Ernesto's mind. He dreamed of writing a great epic about his idol, but would he be capable of writing it? Such a work almost demanded that Antonio die in the ring, and Ernesto had a premonition and a very great fear that that was how Antonio would die (what part did Ernesto's unconscious, unavowable wishes play in this fear that came close to being abject terror?). . . .
>
> I do not believe it would be straying too far from the truth to maintain that this strange psychic ambivalence was the cause of the guilt complex that so clouded his mind in the last months of his life. I am sure that Ernesto had already unconsciously imagined Antonio's death in the ring a thousand times in his tortured mind, and could almost have set it down on paper. And that was why he was obliged to

take such scrupulous care of his friend, to pray so often for him, to indulge his every whim. [204–5]

Hemingway's "psychic ambivalence" is stronger and wider than Castillo-Puche senses; for the unconscious wish beneath the paternal devotion, pride, and protectiveness in *Summer* is the same one beneath the previous two novels of this phase—filicide.[7]

Foremost among my reasons for this conclusion is the fact that Ordóñez's father was the matador Hemingway had idolized and then heaped abuse upon. In *Death in the Afternoon* Hemingway owns that Cayetano Ordóñez inspired his creation of Pedro Romero, the hero of *The Sun Also Rises* (89). As Niño de la Palma, Cayetano had begun his career brilliantly, performing great faenas that enamored Hemingway esthetically and Hadley personally (*Afternoon*, 270). But after a severe goring at the end of his first season, Cayetano spoiled. The next year, according to Hemingway, he turned in "the most shameful season any matador had ever had up until that year in bullfighting" (*Afternoon*, 89–90). As if that were not defamatory enough, Hemingway pronounced that "if you see Niño de la Palma the chances are you will see cowardice in its least attractive form; its fat-rumped, prematurely bald from using hair fixatives, prematurely senile form" (*Afternoon*, 87–88).

Even if Ordóñez disliked his own father and shared Hemingway's criticism of his bullfighting, it is hard to imagine that he would have grown up with any fondness for a man who, with impunity, had publicly assailed his father. As fellow-Spaniard Castillo-Puche asks—properly alluding to a Spaniard's fierce pride of family, which Hemingway was not ignorant of—"How could Antonio have forgiven Ernesto for writing such harsh words about his father?" (165). It is even harder to imagine Hemingway not regarding Ordóñez a genuine threat. After all, Hemingway was superstitious and believed in omens. Even a facial resemblance could "spook" him. (One of the better instances of this was when, still legally married to Pauline Pfeiffer, he arrived in Sun Valley with Martha Gellhorn in 1939. The first woman he met, Tillie Arnold, all but unmanned him because she was Pauline's look-alike.)[8] There is no mention in *Summer* that Hemingway was apprehensive about his first meeting with Ordóñez in 1953. (Perhaps it was cut from the manuscript?) But surely he felt some anxiety when, having seen Ordóñez in the bullring and having then found out who he was, Hemingway was told that Ordóñez would like him "to come up to the hotel Yoldi to see him" (1:86).

And surely Ordóñez must have seemed to Hemingway like an apparition rising out of the past, a son fit to avenge the treachery and mortification his father and his own pride had suffered by Hemingway's criticism. Although Hemingway declares only that Ordóñez "had everything his father had in his great days" (1:86), then, his solicitousness overtly shows that he does everything he can to please Ordóñez, trying to placate whatever hostility Ordóñez may have for Hemingway. Covertly his solicitousness shows his wish that Ordóñez be killed before he takes vengeance on his old foe. Indeed, the persecutory mania that afflicted Hemingway's last year reflects his fear of vindictive sons, genetic or surrogate.

Hemingway's fascination with the rivalry of the *mano a mano* also shows his unconscious wish for his sons' deaths. The term, literally meaning hand to hand, refers to a bullfight in which only two matadors, rather than the customary three, kill the six bulls of the fight. The ostensible purpose is to let the spectators decide who is the superior matador, as determined by which of them harvests more bulls' tails or ears. But as Santiago's young helper's name, *Mano*lin, suggests, a *mano* is also a hand, a brother. *Mano a mano*, then, figuratively means brother against brother, a translation particularly apt in this case because Ordóñez and Dominguín are brothers-in-law. That the *mano a mano* is fratricidal may seem farfetched. But recall the biblical patriarchs. Anxious about their dwindling power and jealous of the threat of their potent sons, Adam, Abraham, Isaac, and Jacob—behind a mask of innocence—shrewdly engineered or unconsciously created situations that pitted son against son, usually to the death of one and the disgrace of the other. The strife between Abel and Cain, Isaac and Ishmael, Jacob and Esau, and Joseph and his brothers recurs too predictably to conclude otherwise. And it nearly recurred at the end of the 1959 season, Dominguín severely gored in Bilbao and Ordóñez "debarred for a month after a dispute with bullfight officials" over improper use of his picadors.[9] Admittedly, though Ordóñez and Dominguín stayed briefly with the Hemingways en route to "winter engagements in Central and South America" in 1955,[10] nothing indicates that Hemingway either masterminded or encouraged their 1959 *mano a mano*. But neither does anything show that he tried to keep them from such fratricidal competition.

Adding to the view that the *mano a mano* pits son against son is Hemingway's paternal regard for Dominguín. Familiarity with *Death in the Afternoon* or even with Hemingway's remarks upon

Manolete, Chicuelo II, and other matadors in *Summer* teaches that Hemingway never balks at criticising a deficient matador. But he holds back on Dominguín. Repeatedly he tries to find something to applaud him for, whether for his disciplined training (1:87), his hospitality (1:88), his work with the banderillos (2:66), or his quiet valor after being gored (2:82). And though he faults Dominguín's abilities, he quickly offers reparation by comparing him to the great Joselito (2:68), by praising his mastery of tricks (2:76), and by commending his domination of the fifth bull at Malaga after it had tossed him (3:76). So anxious is Hemingway to treat Dominguín fairly that when the second installment of *Summer* was issued, he was horrified at the picture of Dominguín executing a *pase ayudado*, telling Hotchner, " 'hell, that's the kind of picture photographers use to blackmail bullfighters. . . . that picture is malicious' " (253). Not even Ordóñez's reassurances were enough, reports Hotchner, to convince Hemingway that Dominguín would not resent the picture as a treacherous act (261).

Setting aside their six-year-old friendship, Hemingway's solicitude for Dominguín is unusual, especially given his judgment that at Bilbao Dominguín "had been eliminated in a stupid way" (3:87). An obvious explanation for his regard is that he knows he must have in *Summer* that ingredient vital to all fiction, conflict. Hemingway establishes the relative equality of the matadors, then, to ensure that the rivalry is neither hoax nor melodrama. And he compounds conflict by insisting upon the internal conflict caused him because of his regard for both matadors. But this internal conflict exposes also his ambivalence about the fratricidal struggle between these surrogate sons: he dreads but desires it. An irrational persecution mania may explain Hemingway's anxiety over the photograph of Dominguín, but so does genuine guilt. Consciously or not, Hemingway sent the photograph so that its "malicious" intent would show Dominguín's inferiority to Ordóñez.[11]

Hemingway's repressed filicidal wish is also evident in his endorsement of the prank of letting "El Pecas" Hotchner be Ordóñez's *sobresaliente*, his substitute matador, in the Ciudad Real *mano a mano*. Hotchner's book hopes to convey the impression of his favored status among Hemingway intimates. But he was just another of the many surrogate sons Hemingway liked to gather about himself. As surrogate son and Ordóñez's stand-in, then, Hotchner would have had to enter the ring with the remaining bull or bulls had both Ordóñez and Dominguín been injured at

Ciudad Real. The outcome would surely have spelled disaster. Short of that, exposure of the prank could have levied upon Ordóñez heavy penalities and accompanying disgrace. For a writer who let the narrator of his first novel about bullfighting express anxiety over possibly ruining a young matador, who castigated the decadence of modern bullfighting, who criticized even a matador's looks if they detracted from the integral esthetic experience of the *corrida*, it is strange that Hemingway would approve of the travesty of permitting the pock-scarred, unhandsome Hotchner to enter the sacrosanct bullring—unless there were an ulterior motive or unconscious wish, such as displaced filicide.

That same lethal wish, drawing Hemingway to the *mano a mano*, also surfaces in the father-son relationship between Dominguín and Ordóñez. Hemingway—or, more correctly, the text of *Summer* that *Life* was given to publish—does not tell that when only twenty, Dominguín had engaged in a *mano a mano* with the aging, Spanish-acclaimed but Hemingway-defamed Manolete. Nor does Hemingway tell, but Hotchner does, that "in that punishing duel the veteran Manolete, no longer as quick as he once was, was pushed by the young, reckless Dominguín beyond where he should have gone, and in one such moment he was severely gored and died before dawn the next day" (208).[12] But we do not need to be told that, legendized though that rivalry has been, the scenario of the young Dominguín driving his older rival to death is Oedipal, casting Dominguín into the role of the parricide. Nor do we need to be told that by the time Hemingway first sees Ordóñez fight in 1951, Dominguín is now cast as father. Two years away from his first retirement, he has already become sufficiently legendary to allure the likes of Ava Gardner and has a "bronze life-size statue of [himself], a rare thing for a man to have around his own finca in his own lifetime" (1:87). When we also consider that Ordóñez had taken on Dominguín's father, Domingo, as his manager and had married Dominguín's younger sister, Carmen, it is hard not to see that the *mano a mano* between Dominguín and Ordóñez fascinated Hemingway because it acted out the parricidal-filicidal contest that he was now obsessed with. Actually Dominguín was only a half-dozen years older than Ordóñez. But by the time of the 1959 rivalry, Dominguín had to play the father to Ordóñez the son. And to side with the son would manifestly deny any filicidal wishes in Hemingway. At least it would have, if Hemingway's solicitousness and protectiveness of the son had been less exaggerated.

Near the beginning of *The Dangerous Summer*, Hemingway states that he "had resolved never to have a bullfighter for a friend again because I suffered too much for them and with them when they could not cope with the bull from fear or the incapacity that fear brings" (1:85). Hemingway's irrepressible affiliative wish would be one reason to cancel that resolution. Another would be that in his paternal relationship to Ordóñez, Hemingway could portray the role he wishes his own father had taken during the twenties, when Hemingway was competing against his rivals to establish himself as *numero uno*. Still another reason to cancel that resolution would be that his behavior would give the lie to what Hemingway felt was his father's strongest accusation, the charge that haunted Hemingway all his life, that he was irresponsible.[13] But among the reasons would also be that the rivalry between these brothers-in-law allowed him, like a biblical patriarch, to be an interested, involved, but innocent observer of the fratricidal struggle of his "sons," a struggle that invariably reveals those sons' hostility against their fathers, that conceals from them the onlooker's filicidal obsession.[14]

A Self-Justifying Son: *A Moveable Feast*

Mary Hemingway's *How It Was* and the "Sources and Notes" to Carlos Baker's *Life Story* make it clear that Mary Hemingway kept accurate, regular entries in her diary. So there is little reason to doubt her report of the December 1957 exchange between her and her husband after she had read a group of the Paris sketches that were later incorporated in *A Moveable Feast*:

> "It's not much about you," I once objected. "I thought it was going to be autobiography."
> "It's biography by *remate*," Ernest said.[1]

Baker explains that though Hemingway used the jai alai term *remate*, he probably "meant to say *rebote*, the back wall or a rebound off it. . . . The evidence that he was writing autobiography by showing himself rebounding from the personalities of others is everywhere in the book."[2] I grant that Hemingway worked on the sketches for at least four years, and during that time he may have changed his intention.[3] But there is no reason to gloss his term. *Remate* means a "kill-shot." A jai alai player makes such a shot by hurling the ball so low and hard against the playing wall that his opponent cannot return it—as any handball or racketball player also knows. The malice and vindictiveness in *Feast*, then, is intentionally lethal. Outliving most of his victims, Hemingway serves kill-shots they are literally unable to return.

The success of Hemingway's verbal assassinations partly depends on whether we share his values. If the discovery of Miss Stein's lesbianism deeply shocks us, then she is among the first casualties of Hemingway's siege of Paris. If we find opium addicts offensive, then Ralph Cheever Dunning lies on the battleground too, near the three milk bottles and one cracked cold cream jar of opium he had thrown at Hemingway. If foppish pride annoys us, then the "cut" that Ford Madox Ford gives Hillaire Belloc gets, in turn, Hemingway's more effective parries, and he too expires.

Hemingway's success as assassin also depends on our limited knowledge of his victims. A profligate adolescent unmanned by a predatory wife, F. Scott Fitzgerald would be as dead as he is to Georges, bar chief of the Ritz, were it not for Fitzgerald's elsewhere-documented generosity to an aspiring young Hemingway; and so he limps with some honor from the field.[4] And the unmasking of Ernest Walsh, a literary poseur, would be fatal were it not offset by his early death from consumption in October 1926, his publishing in *This Quarter* both "Big Two-Hearted River" and "The Undefeated," his poem about Hemingway, and his favorable review of Hemingway's writing.[5] Even John Dos Passos, gaffed as a treacherous "pilot fish," squirms free if we see him used as a scapegoat.

Successful or not, Hemingway is a skillful, though rarely aggressive, assassin. At his most aggressive in "New School," he insults the intruding Hal and justifies himself with military diction, saying that it was not good to let someone drive him out of the Closerie des Lilas, that he would have to "make a stand or move" (92). But he usually slays his victims by letting them die of self-exposure. Hemingway ironically writes that it is as "soothing as the noise of a plank being violated in the sawmill" to hear the Robert Cohn/Harold Loeb–like complaints of this same, self-pitying, sentimental Hal, who accuses him of thoughtlessness toward other people and their problems, of disregard for life and other people's sufferings, of cruelty to fellow human beings (93–94). Gertrude Stein's dogmatic lectures on a *sujet inaccrochable*, homosexuality, and on *une génération perdue* allow her the same verbal rope to hang herself with that Fitzgerald's anxiety about the size of his penis allows him. Even the proprietor of the bookstall along the quai condemns herself by declaring that a book's pictures and binding determine its value. On occasion a snapshot is as lethal as these "tape recordings." The ad hominem cameo of Wyndham Lewis, frog-faced, with the eyes of an "unsuccessful rapist," intends him as much harm as the one of Zelda Fitzgerald, whose hawk's eyes sum up her predatory nature. Sometimes insinuation is Hemingway's weapon. In the minimemoir of T. S. Eliot, Hemingway's reference to horses that race while influenced by stimulants (112) insinuates the comparison to poets whose poems are spiked with other writers' "juice"—as a favorite Hemingway metaphor would call it. And the small Greek temple in Miss Natalie Barney's garden? A fit place to entomb Eliot, Hemingway implies.

Hemingway is no messy killer. He usually executes his victim in a single episode. It takes one scene to slay the pompous, petty Ford; one car trip from Lyon to strip the feckless Fitzgerald of dignity; one whispered secret from Zelda about Al Jolson's superiority to Jesus (186) to show her lunacy or Machiavellianism or both. On the same day that Hemingway walks through the little Luxembourg garden, sees wood pigeons perching in the trees and hears others that he cannot see, he also hears at Miss Stein's voices of women he can not see either. One of them, proof to Hemingway of lesbianism, pleads, " 'Don't, pussy. Don't. Don't, please don't' " (118). A tally of Hemingway's victims might find him as effective as the Arlberg avalanche that buried a party of thirteen imprudent German skiers, nine of whom died (204).

The apparent reason for Hemingway's vindictiveness is that against each of his victims he has some long-standing grudge. Whether the grudges are just is a matter for literary historians and friends of his victims to decide.[6] But just or not, Hemingway gives ample scope to destructive impulses that, overtly, are noticeably subdued in most of the work of his last decade.[7] By setting aside the topical interest of the actual or imagined wrongs his victims had done him, and by turning instead to his victims' common wrong, I find a major motive for these murderous memoirs. Hemingway believes his victims are, quite simply, irresponsible—every last one.

In his gallery the most irresponsible are Stein and Fitzgerald. At the end of a day with either, Hemingway feels contaminated by their wastefulness and self-indulgence. Walking home from 27 rue de Fleurus, where Miss Stein has just instructed him about sex, he writes that he would need to work hard the next day: "Work could cure almost anything, I believed then, and I believe now" (21). Near the end of the car trip with Fitzgerald he misses not working and feels "the death loneliness that comes at the end of every day that is wasted in your life" (165–66). In Hemingway's eyes Miss Stein answers for little. She bandies about "dirty, easy labels" that show her "mental laziness." To her court she welcomes only notables, disciples, claquers, and flunkies who will type her manuscripts and read her proof. The responsibilities common to all writers, the labor of revision and the duty to make writing coherent (17), are beneath her. And Hemingway implies that her advice, that he expunge from his writing *inaccrochable* matter, is a reprehensible instance of artistic compromise, for she ignores whether such matter is essential to his artistic vision.

Fitzgerald flunks his accountability test too. Confessing that he changed good stories, knowing precisely the "twists" to convert them into "salable magazine stories" (155), he too lacks artistic integrity. The Lyon episode italicizes his fecklessness, Hemingway declaring that until then he had never known a grown man who missed a train (157). And he shares, unlike Fitzgerald, the Lyon garage owner's feelings that owning a vehicle imposes an obligation upon oneself (162). In Hemingway's eyes, then, Fitzgerald pays no heed to his low tolerance of alcohol, he ignorantly assumes he has congestion of the lungs, he is blind to the obvious fact that his mate is a vampire, and he stupidly worries about the size of his penis. These all reflect an intellectual negligence that Hemingway spots even in his diction. Had Hemingway's father, Fitzgerald tells him, been a doctor in New York rather than in Chicago, he would have learned a "different gamut of diseases. He used the word gamut" (163)! Even the eloquent epigraph to the three Fitzgerald sketches actually faults him for having abused a talent that others, were they lucky, might never acquire, even after considerable labor.[8]

Hemingway's memoirs, then, become a literary morgue. On its slabs he lays his irresponsible acquaintances: a "pilot fish" who enters and exits from others' lives without being caught himself but leaving them to be "caught and killed" (207–8); a well-read tutor who has never read Russian writers (134); a poet who relies upon friends or benefactresses to free him from working; a magazine editor who deceives a writer with the lure of a writing award, only to leave him with the task of seeing his magazine through printers who read no English (128); a thwarted writer who interrupts the habits of a working writer; and a wheezing, mustache-stained has-been who makes someone else drink a brandy he denies having ordered.[9] If not fit for a morgue, such acquaintances can be sent to the Café des Amateurs, the opening setting of *Feast*. All who have abandoned responsibility and purpose drain into it—a "cesspool."

But *Feast* is also a shrine. The antithesis to such irresponsible people is one self-disciplined, diligent apprentice whose commitment to exacting standards of artistic excellence—read responsibility, please—enables him to become a major writer. No raven-haired beauty lures him from his duty of writing "Three-Day Blow" in the Good Café. Of his trips as correspondent, Miss Stein is interested only in "amusing details," "funny parts," "gallows-humor stories," "the gay part of how the world was going," "strange and comic things that happened in the worst time." Not Hemingway. For him "the real, . . . the bad" were more worth knowing (25). To travel writers the men who fished the Seine were supposedly crazy and caught nothing; but Hemingway knows better and reports that "it was serious and productive fishing" (44). Only to him will Pound entrust Dunning's jar of opium. Only to him will Walsh entrust the publication of an issue of *This Quarter*. Only to him will Stein entrust the typing and proofreading of the early serialized sections of *The Making of Americans*. Hemingway can even rise above his antipathy to several of Ezra Pound's friends. Magnanimous, he campaigns actively for Bel Esprit and Eliot. He tries liking and befriending Wyndham Lewis (110). And he tries remembering that he must never be rude to Ford, that only when very tired did Ford lie, that Ford was a fine writer who had just come through "very bad domestic troubles" (85–86). Jean, a waiter at the Closerie des Lilas, serves Evan Shipman and Hemingway large, brimful glasses of whiskey on ten-franc saucers to protest the new management's orders that he shave off the dragoon's mustache he has worn all his life. Evan rejoices in Jean's defiant act. But Hemingway, concerned that Jean will lose his job, pleads with him not to do it, not to risk being fired (139).

Hemingway even makes his apparent self-indulgences in food and sport read like responsible behavior. He will dine only to compensate for being conned, to satisfy an appetite from rigorous exercise in the Vorarlberg, or to celebrate either winning at the track at Enghien or getting six hundred francs for his published writing. He temporarily succumbs to the allure of gambling on horses. But alert to the need to show his responsible profile, he justifies it. It gave him the material for "My Old Man." And, emphasizing the terms he uses unstintingly for all his activities, to gamble profitably, as he knew he must, was a "full-time job," "took full-time work," was "hard work" (61–62). He also justifies his later addiction to bicycle racing. He carefully enumerates different kinds of racing (65) and pledges that he "will get"—in fiction, presumably—the bike racing at the Velodrome d'Hiver and "the magic of the *demi-fond*" (64). Lest the Vorarlberg winters of reading and winter sport be thought a lark, Hemingway early indicates that he found it "necessary" to follow a day of writing with reading and exercise (25). Besides, for the great glacier skiing at the end of the winters he needed to build the strength to climb the slopes and carry the heavy rucksacks, refusing the self-indulgence of buying a ride to the top. To have that strength was "the end we *worked* for all winter and all the winter built to make it possible" (207; italics added).

Hemingway also differs significantly from most of his Paris contemporaries by being a family man. He refuses to appreciate Miss Stein and her friend's condescending forgiveness for his being in love and married (14). He prides himself on his and Hadley's democratic household. They make joint decisions whether they go to the races, bet on the horses, or select a restaurant. The considerate husband, Hemingway offers his spouse an economical trip south for the winter when the bad weather comes to Paris. And after Bumby's birth he accepts his parental role. He sees that Paris winters are too cold for Bumby and so defers to the duty of taking his family to Schruns in the Vorarlberg from Thanksgiving until Easter (200). Hemingway does not forget to mention that in the spring mornings he would rise early to work while Hadley slept (49). Implying that it was quite normal, he also admits that he rose early every morning, fixed and fed Bumby his bottle of milk, and proceeded to work at the dining room table before Hadley awoke (96). Testimony that Hemingway is no chauvinist is reflected in Hadley's statement that Chink and he included her in conversation: " 'It wasn't like being a wife at Miss Stein's' " (54). Nor, until the invasion by the rich, was he unfaithful to his *légitime*, as his refusal of Pascin's generous offer "to bang" the dark sister" intends to prove.[10]

Hemingway's responsible image might have been shown to even better advantage had the published text been faithful to his own ordering of the sketches.[11] Had the last chapter on Schruns been placed, as he intended, between the Dunning sketch and the Lyon episode with Fitzgerald, then the coda of *Feast*, "A Matter of Measurements," would underscore Hemingway's role as protective father to the prodigal Fitzgerald. This sequence would also nicely telescope Paris into the near present, and *Feast* would end in the fifties with Hemingway and Georges conversing at the Ritz bar. Moreover, *Feast* would end with a tentative answer to the question that the book invokes time and again: Why did Hemingway write it? For "A Matter of Measurements" gives Hemingway's motives. *Feast* fulfills his long-standing promise to himself to "write about the early days in Paris" (193), and it honors Georges's immediate request to be told something about Fitzgerald so that he can include him in his memoirs (192).

Neither of these reasons, of course, satisfactorily answers the question of why Hemingway wrote *Feast*. Nor does the notion that his irresponsible victims deserved flailing adequately answer it. Because exaggerated behavior reveals repressed wishes and anxieties, as I have argued previously, Hemingway's reason for writing this exaggerated portrait of himself as the responsible artist must have been to conceal irresponsibilities he was deeply anxious about. Surely he would have little need to show so aggressively how responsible he had been, unless he felt vulnerable to the charge that he had not. So onto his rebuked fellow artists he defensively heaps his own irresponsibility. And the questions in *Feast*, then, are, What irresponsibility is he reluctant to own up to, and Who did he feel he had to justify himself to when he wrote *Feast*?

The obvious answer to both questions points to the first Mrs. Ernest Hemingway, Hadley, the betrayed wife. A good part of his guilty debt to her seems well repaid in *Feast*'s memorialization of her as an ideal wife, her desires and pleasures harmonizing well with her husband's. Had she any fault that contributed to his abandoning her, it was a defect of her virtue: unsuspecting innocence. But his apology to her hedges. She too is irresponsible. Her neglect had, after all, cost him a suitcase full of early work, an event he will not strike from the record. The trauma of that loss was so severe that thirty-five years later he still cannot divulge the horrible things he did when he found that all of his work was lost. He will only write cryptically, "I remember what I did in the night after I let myself into the flat and found it was true" (74).[12] Hemingway's insidious hostility toward Hadley also comes through in his neglect to write much about what she did while he worked. He commends her acceptance of the lack of domestic amenities and her not complaining about there being no heat where she went "to work at the piano" (197).[13] But he gives the impression that he and "Marie, the *femme de ménage*," took care of the majority of the domestic chores. And Hadley's conversation is banal, full of trite phases and naive sentiments. So although Hemingway may write *Feast* to confess his wrong to her, the day-to-day tally minimizes his guilt. And the book's closing pages disingenuously plead that he and she were innocent victims, further minimizing his betrayal.

A more immediate reason for writing *Feast* would have been to deny any irresponsibility to his sons. Since his relationship with all three of them was not ideal, he could deflect the implied accusation that he was guilty of child neglect with his self-portrait as the most responsible artist-father in Paris.[14] An omitted sketch that might have borne this out is an eight-page holograph beginning, "My first son, Bumby," which Hemingway planned to follow chapter 17, the car trip with Fitzgerald. A tribute to his oldest son, its references to "the Rohrbacks, Marie and Ton-Ton, who had often taken care of the child while his parents were traveling," would show that despite frequent absences, Hemingway made sure that Bumby had been well cared for.[15] Coming before the chapter "Hawks Never Share," the tribute would also contrast Hemingway's responsible fatherhood to Fitzgerald's frivolous ways, providing his daughter, for example, with "an English nanny'" so that when she grew up she would talk "like Lady Diana Manners" (180).

An instance of Hemingway's pride in his sons might suggest that he felt no obligation to justify himself to them. Baker notes that in the fall of 1955 "he said that he was luckier in fatherhood than James Joyce, citing the undistinguished career of Joyce's son Giorgio as proof."[16] Yet scarcely a year earlier in "The Christmas Gift," though grateful for Patrick's hasty monetary help after the two African airplane crashes, Hemingway added a disparaging parenthetical remark: "This is the first time any son of mine has ever arrived without being broke or, if you did not hear from him, asking you to either get him back into the Army or get him out of jail" (*By-Line*, 455).[17] Even making allowance for the bravado in this essay, I cannot ignore Hemingway's feeling, justified or not, that his sons were not as responsible as they should have been. Some of the aggression in *Feast*, then, displaces hostility he feels toward them and defensively argues his responsibility.

Rejecting Hadley and his sons, I must conclude that Hemingway wrote *Feast* to deny that he was irresponsible to his father, to justify himself to Dr. Hemingway.

Dr. Hemingway, however disguised, hovers over *Feast*. His presence explains some of Hemingway's more puzzling attacks. What precipitates Hemingway's hostility toward Hal in "New School," for example, is the paternal rebuke of Hal, who questions what Hemingway can be doing by trying to work at a cafe table (91). To a father, a cafe is an improper place for a young man to work. Dr. Hemingway's censure is also in Hal's rebuke that Hemingway thinks about nobody else or about the problems that others may have (93).[18] Similarly, in his encounter with Ford, Hemingway's hostility aims less at Ford's personal than at his parental shortcomings. A repressive, egocentric father, he repeats things he has told Hemingway earlier, he disregards Hemingway's insistence about already knowing where the Bal Musette is, he reproaches him for drinking brandy, and, most, he refuses to regard him as a gentleman.

Dr. Hemingway even lurks behind one of the oddest passages in *Feast*. Criticizing Pound for liking his friends' work, in this instance Wyndham Lewis's paintings, Hemingway says it "is beautiful as loyalty but can be disastrous as judgment" (107). He might have credited Pound for an act of fatherly benevolence, from which he frequently benefited too. Instead Hemingway erupts with a bitter comparison:

> If a man liked his friends' painting or writing, I thought it was probably like those people who like their families, and it was not polite to criticize them. Sometimes you can go quite a long time before you criticize families, your own or those by marriage, but it is easier with bad painters because they do not do terrible things and make intimate harm as families can do. With bad painters all you need to do is not look at them. But even when you have learned not to look at families nor listen to them and have learned not to answer letters, families have many ways of being dangerous. [107–8]

This cuts a wide swath. It indicts former wives who stood up to him, Pauline Pfeiffer and Martha Gellhorn; a rebellious son, Gregory; a censorious sister-in-law, Jinny Pfeiffer; a domineering mother and stern father; and the older sister who was "a bitch complete with handles," Marcelline.[19] But it is particularly odd that the diatribe occurs in this chapter. It would be more appropriate in the Stein or Fitzgerald material. For family harms would show to best advantage among the tyrannizing and castrating ways of Stein and Zelda Fitzgerald, women who embody the two qualities Hemingway disliked in his own mother.[20] That the passage occurs in the chapter on Pound indicates Hemingway's need to fault his father's irresponsibilities and treacheries.

Family problems, abundant in *Feast*, hark back to Oak Park. To Miss Stein's Grace Hemingway, Ezra Pound plays Dr. Hemingway. The clash between the two American artists recalls Marcelline's comment, "surely no two young people could have been more opposite than my father and mother."[21] And Hemingway's remark, "The studio where [Pound] lived . . . was as poor as Gertrude Stein's was rich" (107), recalls the economic disparity between his parents. Not only had it existed before their marriage, but after Grace Hall and Clarence Hemingway were wed, her fifty-odd voice pupils were earning her "as much as a thousand dollars a month" while his income "was sometimes as little as fifty dollars a month."[22] Even the alleged cause of the rift between Pound and Stein sounds like the result of a marital spat: Pound cracked or broke a fragile chair by sitting down too quickly on it (28).

Hemingway's relationship to Pound is distinctly son to father. He will not argue wtih Pound over things he does not like (107), he tries making him look good while boxing in front of Lewis (108), he tries to be friendly to almost all of Ezra's friends (110), and he dutifully defers to Pound's advice: " 'Keep to the French. . . . You've plenty to learn there' " (135). Together with his defense of Pound against Stein, Hemingway's attitudes here express a son's submissive reverence. But Hemingway also satirizes Pound, for his noisy bassoon and inability to learn how "to throw a left hook" (108), for his eccentric taste in Japanese art and bizarre efforts on Eliot's behalf. Even Hemingway's account of the faux pas that lost Pound Miss Stein's regard makes Pound look like a vaudeville character taking a pratfall.

Hemingway's alternation of filial deference and satiric rebellion reflects a son's normal ambivalence toward his father, actual or substitute. And it appears in Hemingway's early, quixotic tribute, "Homage to Ezra." Hemingway's catalogue suggests that Ezra's indefatigable efforts on others' behalf are laudatory and laughable:

> So far we have Pound the major poet devoting, say, one fifth of his time to poetry. With the rest of his time he tries to advance the fortunes, both material and artistic, of his friends. He defends them when they are attacked, he gets them into magazines and out of jail. He loans them money. He sells their pictures. He arranges concerts for them. He writes articles about them. He introduces them to wealthy women. He gets publishers to take their books. He sits up all night with them when they claim to be dying and he witnesses their wills. He advances them hospital expenses and dissuades them from suicide.[23]

However ambivalent Hemingway felt toward Pound, when the Hemingways returned to Paris after Bumby's birth, they made home just up the hill from Ezra and Dorothy Pound, the Hemingways at 113, the Pounds at 70, rue Notre-Dame-des-Paris.

That Pound and Dr. Hemingway merged in Hemingway's mind seems variously evident. Their Vandyke beards, acquiline noses, thin-lipped, taut mouths, and penetrating eyes show a pronounced facial resemblance. Hemingway commends Pound for helping anyone in trouble, whether he valued them or not (110).

228 / The Antithetical Phase

Dr. Hemingway was similarly charitable. He taught "nature lore to boys' clubs," cared for many patients without charge, gave his services to an Oak Park orphanage, even did free plastic surgery on "several babies born with facial deformities."[24] Pound's and the doctor's altruism would make a jealous son resentful that they squandered their attention and abilities upon the less deserving. But that same son would seek them out since both men were broadly knowledgeable and were disciplinarians when it came to applying the techniques and craft of that knowledge. The doctor's sternness has its analogue in Pound's insistence upon the Flaubertian mot juste, and the doctor's moral absoluteness matches Pounds' esthetic and economic absoluteness. Both were also noteworthy as cooks, and though the doctor neither drank nor smoked at all, Pound was distinctive among expatriates as "an abstemious drinker, bordering on teetotalism, and an infrequent smoker."[25] The poet's love of energetic activities would surely have endeared him to Hemingway because that was a quality of the doctor too. And Pound's well-known irascibility would not be strange to Hemingway. His father's mercurial moodiness was a household institution. Hemingway's ear might even hear in Pound's noisy bassoon an echo of the doctor's cornet. Marcelline's remark that her father's "ear was never reliable" is true too of Pound, notwithstanding his composition of an opera and other musical works.[26]

That Pound was more to Hemingway than a tutor is, of course, confirmed by his long-standing regard for Pound and by his repeated efforts on Pound's behalf. In 1943 he was corresponding with Archibald MacLeish and Allen Tate, trying to suggest ways to keep Pound from being tried as a traitor for his pro-Fascist speeches.[27] He sent money to Dorothy Pound after the poet's 1946 incarceration in St. Elizabeth's. He used the Nobel Prize award as an opportunity to announce that "this would be a good year to release poets." He wrote a tribute to be used for advocating Pound's release. And when Pound was freed he sent him a check for $1,500, a check Pound framed in plastic as a souvenir of friendship.[28]

The resemblance between Pound and Dr. Hemingway suggests to me that Hemingway's disenchantment with Pound in *Feast* actually displaces Hemingway's disenchantment with his own father. Pound's advice about Ford, for example, is meant to help Hemingway be tolerant of him. But like much fatherly advice it curdles. So Hemingway gets imposed upon by a repressive bore.

Worse, he is made to feel like a fool, for his mistaken identification of Aleister Crowley gets a "great friend's" scornful, " 'Don't be a silly ass' " (88). Hemingway esteems Pound's learning, but when Pound confesses that he has never read Russian writers, the formula of Hemingway's lengthy sentence registers the classic shock of recognition that accompanies every young man's discovery that his father is not all-knowing: "I felt very bad because here was the man I liked and trusted the most . . . , the man who believed in . . . the man who had taught me to . . . ; and I wanted his opinion on . . . " (134). A son also values his father's friends and associates—until he sees that their defects highlight his father's infirmities. And so Hemingway's apparent attempts to be friends with Wyndham Lewis, T. S. Eliot, Ernest Walsh, and Ralph Cheever Dunning mirror a filial wish to like a father's friends. But he comes to resent them, partly because they exploit Pound's generosity as did, in Hemingway's mind, Dr. Hemingway's wife and the many recipients of his generosity.

Hemingway's final reference to Pound in *Feast* criticizes his unreliability, the last thing a son expects in a good father. In "An Agent of Evil" Pound asks Hemingway to substitute for him by medically assisting Dunning. Since this poet "lived in the same courtyard where Ezra had his studio" (143), proximity should have guaranteed that Pound knew him well. But Dunning turns out to be an ungrateful patient whose retaliatory acts jeopardize Hemingway. However comic the episode, it exposes the trusted father's unreliability, and it justifies Hemingway's earlier outburst against Pound's fatherly benevolence toward his friends' work: indeed, it "can be disastrous as judgment."

Hemingway's disenchantment with Pound as Dr. Hemingway's proxy is defensive. It tries to conceal Hemingway's sense that he had been irresponsible to his father. One proof of this is in Hemingway's use of the standard defense mechanism of reaction formation. The exaggeration and compulsiveness of his portrayals of others' irresponsibilities unwittingly expose his anxiety over his own irresponsibility. Another proof of this is in the repressive quality of these memoirs. That is, Hemingway halts them at the point of his impending breakup with Hadley. Perennially desirous of his father's approval, as my afterwords have argued, and aware that his divorce from Hadley and marriage to Pauline Pfeiffer had severely strained his relationship with his father,[29] Hemingway is reluctant to let his memoirs carry on into the events of the "murderous summer" of 1926. Unwilling to face the figure who would judge his conduct most harshly, he tries to acquit himself of moral irresponsibility by stressing how responsible he had been during the Paris years before his infidelity and by disingenuously claiming that the rich had victimized him and Hadley.

Another proof of Hemingway's wish to conceal his filial irresponsibility is in the regressive quality of the memoirs. Hemingway uses here a two-column bookkeeping system. One column is for Responsible Ernest and one is for Irresponsible Others. Childishly oversimplified, this glaringly resembles the system young Ernest used in the account book that he had to present each week to his father. Marcelline tells that "we had to keep track of how we spent our allowances and show our account books to Daddy once a week. I remember overhearing Father say to Uncle Tyley: 'B.T., Ernest's system is unique. He puts down five cents for Sunday School and all the rest under Miscellaneous.' "[30]

The irresponsibility Hemingway resists owning up to is, as I have mentioned before, his betrayal of his father. Unless he can show his long-dead but long-internalized father that he was responsible, then he is susceptible to the charge and guilt of filial abandonment. And his feeling of the justness of that charge makes his abandonment loom larger and larger as a contributing cause of his father's suicide in 1928. Admittedly, a series of depressing facts preceded the doctor's suicide. His own father died in the fall of 1926; he discovered in 1927 that he was diabetic, later that he had angina pectoris; and in 1928 he found that his heavy investments in Florida real estate were failing.[31] But he also suffered because of his estrangement from his expatriated son, evidenced in what Marcelline saw as his "almost possessive love for his youngest child, my brother Leicester. Daddy clung to Les even more than he had before. Les had meant almost everything to Daddy *ever since Ernest left home*."[32]

Of course Hemingway strongly reacted to his father's suicide. Part of his reaction concealed his pleasure in having his unconscious parricidal wish realized. But the larger part of his reaction registered pain, for his father had abandoned him most unforgivably. He tried to ignore it, dismissing it from his mind so that he could finish revising *A Farewell to Arms*, then parading his affected indifference to it in *Death in the Afternoon*. Discussing there violent death as one of "certain simple things," he offhandedly regrets never having "been able to study them as a man might, for instance, study the death of his father" (*Afternoon*, 3). But he obsessively returned to his father's suicide, as my afterwords to the two preceding phases have explained. His fixation on it in this phase helps to explain why his preoccupation with father-son relationships is so pronounced.

As Hemingway's own sons came of age he would construe their departures as a rejection, an abandonment, of him and his affiliative needs. Awakening his earliest acquired anxiety, separation anxiety, their abandonment, in turn, would likely stir up the trauma of the earlier abandonment he had suffered because of his father's suicide. But he would now feel that it might have been *his* abandonment of his father that triggered the suicide. And since suicides act out upon themselves the hostilities they feel toward others, it is also likely that Hemingway would feel that much of the doctor's hostility was directed at him.

To demonstrate, then, that his father had little reason for such filicidal hostility partly accounts for Hemingway's creation of the exemplary fathers in the work of his last decade. Projections of himself, they even fault his father by comparison. And to deny Dr. Hemingway reason for filicidal feelings against his son ultimately explains Hemingway's exaggerated self-image in *Feast*. The Paris years would prove, he hoped, that he was not an irresponsible son who deserved that strongest of paternal reproaches, the filicidal wish. During his last months, Clarence Hemingway "lived almost as though he defied anyone to get close to him, or understand or help him."[33] Had he called upon his son, *Feast* implies, Ernest Hemingway would not have failed him.

Epilogue

Like any writer who compels long-standing attention, Ernest Hemingway was blessed and cursed by an obsession that empowered all of his writing. His lifelong obsession with his father, what the Greeks would have called his daimon, was the inspiriting and tormenting genius behind his art. Its presence is in his comment about Lillian Ross, who is driven—as he admits he is too—by "the real devil of work." "I always thought it," he goes on to say, "my trustee or Liege Lord that I had sworn to serve and would serve always until I die. . . . My master does not interfere nor ever change a decision that I make. He is dead, as a matter of fact, but I have not told anyone and I serve him as though he were alive."[1] Appropriately, the recipient of this was Bernard Berenson, born the same decade as Hemingway's father, a man Hemingway had never met. Nevertheless, during the fifties Hemingway's frequent letters to him are filial; he refers to him as brother and father, offers himself as a son, and asks forgiveness for writing, admitting that he does so, "my only existing father," "only because I am lonely."[2]

Hemingway's regard for Berenson is matched only by his regard for another "father," Charles Scribner, whose death deeply grieved him, whose close friendship and correspondence Hemingway would sorely miss.[3] Indeed, during Scribner's last year, Hemingway's behavior toward his publisher was what he wished it had been during his own father's last year. He acknowledges that they wrote each other when they felt bad, hoping to cheer each other up. And after Scribner visited him in Cuba during late February 1951 and Hemingway realized that his publisher was ill, not inefficient, "I knew I must never hurt him nor worry him if I could help it. I wish to Christ I could have done something for him. . . . I loved Charlie very much and I understood him and appreciated him I hope and I feel like hell that he is dead."[4]

Hemingway's filial regard for Berenson and Scribner reflects his obsession with his father, and its accompanying affiliative wish plangently echoes throughout his letters, early and late. He tells Howell Jenkins that he misses him "like hell and am lonely for the men." He asks Sylvia Beach, "Please write us a letter. We miss you a lot." To John Dos Passos he begs, "For god's sake come down. . . . Come on down. . . . Come on down and we will go to Tortugas. . . . Come on down kid." He writes Henry Strater, "I wish I could talk to you." Of Maxwell Perkins he tells Scribner, "I wish he would come down though. I never see the bastard any more. Why can't he take an interest in me like he took in Tom Wolfe?" He wishes that Evan Shipman would write, that Archibald MacLeish could come and talk over lots of things. "It probably sounds wet but I was, and am, absolutely homesick for the regiment and I miss you very badly," he admits to "Buck" Lanham, exhorting him for news and to keep writing. He scolds "Chink" Dorman-O'Gowan for not visiting, respects his decision, and confesses, "Seeing you again was all I gave a damn about." He tries to console Vera Scribner by writing, "Now my dear and good friend is gone and there is no one to confide in nor trust nor make rough jokes with and I feel so terribly about Charlie being gone that I can't write any more." He tells Dorothy Connable, "I was very moved to hear from you. More than I thought I ever could be about almost anything." And saying that it has been too long since Berenson's last letter, he beseeches him to write "and let me know you are well." To Adriana Ivancich he says, "I am not as good a companion as I should be because I have a death lonesomeness for you."[5]

Although none of these appeals was made to Dr. Clarence Hemingway, his ears were meant to hear them. His ears were also meant to hear Hemingway's last mortal act, for it originates in Hemingway's grievance against, and sympathy for, him. And Dr. Hemingway's ears were meant to hear his son's "oral strategy":

> . . . What it says, early and late, is always this—"This is what I see with my clean keen equipment. Work to see it after me." What it does not say but implies is more important—"For you I have narrowed and filtered my gaze. I am screening my vision so you will not see all. Why?—because you must enact this story for yourelf; cast it, dress it, set it. Notice the chances I've left for you: no noun or verb is colored by me. I require your senses." What is most important of all—and what I think is the central motive—is this, which is concealed and of which

the voice itself may be unconscious: "I tell you this, in this voice, because you must share—*must* because I require your presence, your company in my vision. I beg you to certify my knowledge and experience, my goodness and worthiness. I mostly speak as *I*. What I need from you is not empathy, identity, but patient approving witness—loving. License my life. Believe me."[6]

I think we now ought to know whose presence, company, certification, "patient approving witness," and belief Hemingway needed. And we ought to know to whom the voice in Hemingway's work continuously spoke.

Notes

INTRODUCTION

1. See especially Charles A. Fenton, *The Apprenticeship of Ernest Hemingway: The Early Years* (New York: Farrar, Straus & Cudahy, 1954); Nicholas Joost, *Ernest Hemingway and the Little Magazines: The Paris Years* (Barre, Mass.: Barre Publishers, 1968); and Richard Bridgman, "Ernest Hemingway," in his *The Colloquial Style in America* (New York: Oxford University Press, 1966), pp. 195–230, rpt. in *Ernest Hemingway: Five Decades of Criticism*, ed. Linda Welshimer Wagner (East Lansing: Michigan State University Press, 1974), pp. 160–88 (hereafter cited as *Five Decades*). For a cogent analysis of Hemingway's parody of Sherwood Anderson, see Delbert E. Wylder, *Hemingway's Heroes* (Albuquerque: University of New Mexico Press, 1969), pp. 11–30.

2. Frederick L. Gwynn and Joseph L. Blotner, eds., *Faulkner in the University* (New York: Vintage Books, 1959), p. 149.

3. The essays that push such monocular views are legion. A recent monograph that does is Lawrence J. Broer's *Hemingway's Spanish Tragedy* (Tuscaloosa: University of Alabama Press, 1973). The best corrective to the notion that Hemingway's style petrified is Richard K. Peterson's *Hemingway: Direct and Oblique* (The Hague and Paris: Mouton, 1969) (hereafter cited as *Direct and Oblique*).

4. Peyton E. Richter, ed., *Perspectives in Aesthetics: Plato to Camus* (New York: Odyssey Press, 1967), p. 57.

5. See Carlos Baker's summary in *Ernest Hemingway: A Life Story* (New York: Scribers, 1969), pp. 454–55 (hereafter cited as *Life Story*); and Aaron Latham's "A Farewell to Machismo," *New York Times Magazine*, 16 October 1977, pp. 52–53, 55, 80, 82, 90 ff.

6. My chapters on the antithetical phase address what Carlos Baker writes was "a touchy subject," Hemingway's relationship with his sons (CB to GB, 24 November 1975). Baker's biography glosses over the parent-child problems. He mentions in passing the difficulties between Hemingway and his youngest son, Gregory, intimating that they surfaced during the Christmas of 1950, came to a head with Pauline Pfeiffer's death in October 1951, continued by correspondence for three years, but were finally patched up during 1954 (*Life Story*, pp. 489, 506, 526). But Arthur Waldhorn, *A Reader's Guide to Ernest Hemingway* (New York: Farrar, Straus & Giroux, 1972) (hereafter cited as *Reader's Guide*), notes that Hemingway's twenty-year correspondence with General Charles Trueman "Buck" Lanham reveals that in the mid and late fifties Hemingway's "references to Gregory (Gigi), his youngest son, who was then under psychiatric care, are gratuitously

238 / Notes to Pages 6–10

harsh and explicitly brutal. At the same time he writes tolerantly but with mild condescension about his eldest son, John (Bumby), who had entered a brokerage, and enthusiastically about Patrick (Mouse), who had become a successful professional hunter in Africa" (p. 255). For Gregory's account of his difficulties with his father during the fifties, see *Papa: A Personal Memoir* (Boston: Houghton Mifflin, 1976), pp. 6–16.

7. See David J. Gordon, *Literary Art and the Unconscious* (Baton Rouge: Louisiana State University Press, 1976), especially the introduction, pp. xiii–xxx, and "The Unconscious in Literary Criticism," pp. 1–51. As my afterwords and chapters on the antithetical phase will demonstrate, I attend to what Gordon defines as "problematic effects," any "false note or irrational component which prompts the reader to frame an interpretation that cannot have been intended by the writer." Such problematic effects, he goes on to explain, "may fit together into a counter-intended meaning if we presume the agency of a specific unconscious process of distortion. What we perceive are imbalances that might plausibly be accounted for according to a hypothesis of unconscious influence" (p. xvi). Gordon would probably disapprove of my use of *antithetical* to describe Hemingway's last phase, for to him the term implies, I think, a conscious program that is artistically developed or designed in some "qualifying relation to the rest of [a] work" (p. xvii). But I choose to use it rather than his preferred phrase *problematic effects* because outside the context of his book the phrase is critically flaccid.

8. For a learned discussion of the relationship between a writer and his precursors and a poetic theory that derives from Freud's concept of the "family romance," see Harold Bloom, *The Anxiety of Influence* (New York: Oxford University Press, 1973).

9. The most recent lip service paid Hemingway's complexity is Scott Donaldson's *By Force of Will: The Life and Art of Ernest Hemingway* (New York: Penguin Books, 1978), p. xiii.

10. Introduction to *The Short Stories of Ernest Hemingway: Critical Essays*, edited, with an overview and checklist, by Jackson J. Benson (Durham, N.C.: Duke University Press, 1975), p. xii (hereafter cited as *Short Stories*).

11. See Sydney J. Krause's unduly ignored "Hemingway's 'My Old Man,' " *Explicator* 20 (1962), item 39, to which my reading is indebted.

12. Carlos Baker reprints the text in *Hemingway: The Writer as Artist*, 4th ed. (Princeton: Princeton University Press, 1972), p. 339 (hereafter cited as *Artist*). While revising my manuscript for publication, I was strongly taken with the idea of adding to this list a second statement. Michael S. Reynolds unearthed it from the manuscripts in the Hemingway Collection, housed in Boston's John F. Kennedy Library, and used it as the epigraph to his introductory essay, "Hemingway's Bones," in his *Hemingway's Reading, 1910–1940: An Inventory* (Princeton: Princeton University Press, 1981), p. 3: "Education consists in finding sources obscure enough to imitate so that they will be perfectly safe." An ink note penned on the back of an envelope dated New Year's Eve 1927, this item seems to have been made to order for my purposes as well as Reynolds's. For surely it indicates that Hemingway sought obscure sources that he could then safely imitate. But there is that vague pronoun referent, "they." Who or what will be perfectly safe? Surely the obscure sources, the apparent referent of "they," have no need to be perfectly safe. Hemingway must mean, then, that the works he has written or will write, by imitating obscure sources, will be perfectly safe from detection. Or does this excerpt omit a context that identifies the referent of "they?" In *Catalog of the Ernest Hemingway Collection at the John F. Kennedy Library*, comp. Jo August (Boston: G. K. Hall & Co., 1982), 1:77 (hereafter cited as *Catalog of Hemingway Collection*), item 489 records that the inked notes mention Eliot, "The Waste Land," and Pound. Perhaps, then, this provocative quotation refers not to Hemingway's practices—at least in 1927—but, sarcastically, to those of Eliot and Pound, the "they" of the quotation?

13. For a different discussion of Hemingway's reasons for being secretive about what he had learned from artists, see Emily Stipes Watts, *Ernest Hemingway and the Arts* (Urbana: University of Illinois Press, 1971), pp. 171–72.

14. Philip Young, *Ernest Hemingway: A Reconsideration* (New York: Harcourt Brace & World, 1966), pp. 43–48 (hereafter cited as *Reconsideration*).

15. I am convinced of Uncle George's paternity in "Indian Camp," for it accounts for that story's otherwise two basic flaws: why George is in the story at all, and the sensationalism of having an injured Indian commit suicide while "his" child is being delivered. George's paternity explains why he gives cigars to the two Indians who row him, Nick, and Dr. Adams across the lake; why the younger Indian laughs without reserve when the Indian woman bites George and later smiles "reminiscently" when George looks at his bitten arm; why George sarcastically responds to his brother's boasts about having performed the cesarean with primitive equipment; and, finally, why he does not return with his brother(-in law?) and nephew. George's paternity also satisfactorily explains the Indian husband's suicide. His act can be that of a distraught cuckold who, knowing that his wife is giving birth to a white man's child, surrenders his life in an act of futility, as testimony of his feelings of utter impotence. I prefer to see him as an Indian "brave." His suicide aims to inflict a strong sense of guilt on Uncle George, becomes a dignified act that affirms the need to live with dignity or not at all, and lays at the feet of another treacherous white man the death of yet one more of the countless, dispossessed native Americans. I lay no claim to originality by calling George the father, for earlier critics have dealt with the issue. Nevertheless, both G. Thomas Tansell, "Hemingway's 'Indian Camp,' " *Explicator* 20 (1962), item 53, and Kenneth Bernard, "Hemingway's 'Indian Camp,' " *Studies in Short Fiction* 2 (1965): 291, assign such a heavy symbolic value to the question that they deserve Philip Young's riposte, *Studies in Short Fiction* 3 (1966): ii–iii, in which he confesses that *he* fathered the child.

16. Compare Sheldon Norman Grebstein's analysis of "The Mother of a Queen" in *Hemingway's Craft* (Carbondale: Southern Illinois University Press, 1973), pp. 56–58. To his reading I would remark that "Hemingway's scorn for homosexuals [which] resounds throughout his work" (p. 113) is not as evident here or elsewhere as Grebstein believes it to be.

17. *Straw for the Fire: From the Notebooks of Theodore Roethke, 1943–63*, ed. David Wagoner (Garden City, N.Y.: Doubleday, 1974), p. 170.

18. *Life Story*, p. vii.

19. Ibid., pp. 5, 554–57. See also A. E. Hotchner, *Papa Hemingway: A Personal Memoir* (New York: Random House, 1966), pp. 266–74, 280–81, 284; and Mary Welsh Hemingway, *How It Was* (New York: Knopf, 1976), pp. 481, 492–96, 502.

20. The extent of Hemingway's reading and the size of his library have been measured in Richard Layman's "Hemingway's Library Cards at Shakespeare and Company," *Fitzgerald/Hemingway Annual 1975*, pp. 191–207; Noel Fitch's "Ernest Hemingway—c/o Shakespeare and Company," *Fitzgerald/Hemingway Annual 1977*, pp. 157–81; Reynolds's *Hemingway's Reading*; and James D. Brasch and Joseph Sigman's *Hemingway's Library: A Composite Record* (New York & London: Garland Publishing, 1981).

21. Robert O. Stephens, "Hemingway and Stendhal: The Matrix of *A Farewell to Arms*," *PMLA* 88 (1973): 271–80, also argues Hemingway's debt to source materials, namely *The Charterhouse of Parma*; for the oversight in his reading see Stirling Haig, "Forum," *PMLA* 88 (1973): 1192–93.

22. Marcelline Hemingway Sanford, *At the Hemingways: A Family Portrait* (Boston: Little, Brown & Co., 1961), pp. 61–62, 109. (In this chapter I parenthesize subsequent references to her book in the text.) Madelaine Hemingway Miller, in *Ernie: Hemingway's Sister "Sunny" Remembers* (New York: Crown Publishers, 1975) (hereafter cited as "*Sunny*" *Remembers*), protests this notion: "I wish Mother

were here now to set a lot of people straight on the many untruths and exaggerations that have been written regarding members of our family. But the many family pictures that Mother kept for each of the children in the baby books refute the idea that got started about Mother dressing Ernest as a girl, and that he and Marcelline were dressed as twins" (p. 98). Not only does the generous swarm of photographs Miller includes give the lie to her protest—see pp. 10, 13, 14, 17, 20, 21, 24—but the fact that Marcelline and Ernest were six and five years old when "Sunny" was born also casts some doubt upon her protest. I recognize that Marcelline's recall of her childhood emphasizes different events and impressions than Hemingway's would. But her recall of affect-laden events of their childhood provides an external viewpoint that would differ from his and that would minimize the falsification and distortion that he, like all of us, would color those events with. Her version of those events and of the domestic milieu they shared allows a measure of reliability upon which to attempt to reconstruct some of the forces that shaped his psychic makeup.

23. Miller, *"Sunny" Remembers*, pp. 9–15.

24. For a wider collection of Hemingway's nicknames, see Baker, *Letters*, e.g., 29, 58, 66, 74, 89, 183, 201, 300, 433, 497, 563, 584, 844, 861, 908.

25. Sigmund Freud, "The Ego and the Super-Ego (Ego Ideals)," in *The Ego and the Id*, trans. Joan Riviere, rev. James Strachey (New York: Norton, 1960), p. 27.

26. The customary practice among neo-Freudians who analyze Hemingway's personality is to oversimplify it and to base their analyses upon Hemingway's public behavior, ignoring how his works qualify and even contradict that behavior. One definition of generic personality traits that seems tailor-made to fit the better-known features of Hemingway's personality is Karen Horney's *Neurosis and Human Growth* (New York: Norton, 1950), particularly her chapter "The Expansive Solutions: The Appeal of Mastery," pp. 187–213. Two subsequent Horneyan analyses are Jacqueline Tavernier-Courbin, "Striving for Power: Hemingway's Neurosis," *Journal of General Education* 30 (1978): 137–53; and Irvin D. Yalom and Marilyn Yalom, "Ernest Hemingway—A Psychiatric View," *Archives of General Psychiatry* 24 (1971): 485–94. In the former, Professor Tavernier-Courbin presents sound evidence of Hemingway's competitiveness. But she proves neither that his competitiveness was neurotic nor that the competitiveness—much less his "striving for power"—dominates his fiction. Indeed, she altogether fails to consider whether Hemingway's characters strive for power as much as they strive for achievement and, even more, affiliation. In the latter, the Yaloms persuade me that it is accurate to define Hemingway's ego ideals as ones that "crystallized around a search for mastery," that exalted masculine traits and subdued "the softer feminine side." But to most boys' formulation of ego ideals that definition applies with equal validity. Consequently, their conclusion not only oversimplifies Hemingway's ego ideals and implies that they must be one-dimensional but also rests heavily upon the public, adult image Hemingway projected. Subscribers though they are to Karen Horney's personality theory, they appear derelict in failing to examine the childhood factors that contributed to Hemingway's ego ideals. Surprisingly, they write off or ignore the best account of the household in which Hemingway grew up, the only account we have that can claim firsthand knowledge and experience of those important early years of Hemingway's life, Marcelline's *At the Hemingways*. Equally surprising, the Yaloms claim that "all available evidence suggests that the public and private Hemingways are merged: the Hemingway of private conversations, of letters, and of notebooks is identical with the Hemingway who careened across the pages of newspapers and journals and the many Hemingways who fought, loved and challenged death in his novels and stories" (p. 487). Overlooking such dust-jacket rhetoric, I fail to understand why conversations, letters, and notebooks classify as "private documents," particularly Hemingway's twenty-year correspondence with General C. T. "Buck" Lan-

ham, upon which the Yaloms draw so heavily. Admittedly such documents are less public than Hemingway's fiction or his *Esquire* "letters." Nevertheless, letters and conversations are "public" inasmuch as they are shared with others; and notebooks, the product of a verbalizing process, become "public" as soon as they become written. Given Hemingway's "anal-retentive" habits, testified to by the mountain of material he saved—drafts, typescripts, fragments, and so forth—virtually everything he wrote was conceived to be, eventually, public. My point is that all of Hemingway's written material is "public," none of it "private." However much his writing is a screen between his private and public selves, it also reveals his private self.

27. Miller, *"Sunny" Remembers*, p. 82.

28. For other studies of the father-son theme in Hemingway's fiction, see William White, "Father and Son: Comments on Hemingway's Psychology," *Dalhousie Review* 31 (1952): 276–84, and David Gordon, "The Son and the Father: Responses to Conflict in Hemingway's Fiction," in his *Literary Art and the Unconscious*, pp. 171–94.

29. Baker, *Life Story*, p. 184. The psychological significance of this story has been best analyzed by Richard B. Hovey, *Hemingway: The Inward Terrain* (Seattle: University of Washington Press, 1968), pp. 47–53 (hereafter cited as *Inward Terrain*). I would remark, however, that he stresses unduly the castrative power of the destructive mother and overlooks what I take to be the more crucial issue, Nick's shock at his father's response to Mrs. Adam's deed.

30. My reason for using the term *homoerotic* rather than *homosexual* is not squeamishness. Rather it is that *homosexual* denotes genital sexuality, whereas *homoerotic* denotes a wider range of erotic displacements and sublimations, a range appropriate for my discussion. For an earlier discussion of Hemingway's homoerotic tendencies, see Richard Drinnon, "In the American Heartland: Hemingway and Death," *Psychoanalytic Review* 52 (1965): 5–31.

31. Baker, *Life Story*, pp. 5, 6.

32. Ibid., p. 5.

33. Ibid.

34. Sigmund Freud, *The Ego and the Id*, pp. 21–24; see also Otto Fenichel, *The Psychoanalytic Theory of Neurosis* (New York: Norton, 1945), p. 88.

35. By using the term *feminine* I intend no sexist sterotyping. Rather I use it and its companion, *masculine*, as Freud does, to differentiate between active and passive (assertive and submissive) behavior, between male and female biological functions, and between observable sociological differences in individual men and women. As Freud is careful to point out in *Three Contributions to the Theory of Sex*, trans. A. A. Brill (New York: Dutton, 1962), due to our bisexuality all individuals show a mixture of their "own biological sex characteristics with the biological traits of the other sex and a union of activity and passivity" (p. 77).

36. I do not mean that Hemingway simply fictionalizes his experiences or replicates himself in his protagonists. That idea oversimplifies the man and the individuality of the works he created, as Wylder argues in *Hemingway's Heroes*, pp. 3–9, 223–25. But like all writers Hemingway cannot circumvent the repetition compulsion to project onto his protagonists the anxieties, wishes, and obsessions that reveal his most private self, his deepest fixation, and the dominant patterns that unify his work.

37. The classic study of paranoia is Freud's "Psycho-Analytic Notes on an Autobiographical Account of a Case of Paranoia (Dementia Paranoides)," better known as "The Case of Schreber" (1911), in *The Standard Edition of the Complete Psychological Works of Sigmund Freud*, trans. and ed. James Strachey (London: Hogarth Press, 1958), 12: 3–82 (hereafter cited as *Standard Edition*); see also Fenichel, *The Psychoanalytic Theory of Neurosis*, pp. 427–35.

38. Among the reasons for Hemingway's latent homoeroticism would have been castration anxiety. Antipathy for his mother directed his sexual energy toward his father. But fear of his father's castrating power would have passively steered him that way, too. (Indeed, Hemingway's often-remarked misogyny is partly a defense against the threat of castration by his father.) In his fiction, "God Rest You Merry, Gentlemen" explicitly acknowledges castration anxiety. But it also occurs, interestingly, in the Nick Adams "war" stories. Like many Hemingway critics, I too am indebted to Philip Young's "wound theory." But I regret that he did not probe the etiology of the wound and failed to see that Hemingway's war wounding was so traumatic because it was preconditioned: the shelling at Fossalta remobilized repressed castration anxieties. As Fenichel states, "What is most characteristic in the reaction to a trauma is that associative connections are immediately established between the trauma and the infantile conflicts that become activated" (p. 124). One specific association that connects infantile castration anxiety to Hemingway's late-adolescent wounding is a river, the recurrent setting in "A Way You'll Never Be," "Now I Lay Me," and "Big Two-Hearted River." In the first story Hemingway projects onto Nick the "emotional spells" he himself undoubtedly suffered, one of which compulsively focuses upon the stretch of river where his wounding occurred. In the second, Nick tries to assuage his "insomnia" by refishing a stream. In the last, of course, he "concentrates all of his available mental energy" upon fishing a stretch of river. (Emotional spells, insomnia and "concentration of all mental energy on one task" are three of the basic symptoms of traumatic neuroses, notes Fenichel, pp. 118–21.) It seems clear that fishing the rivers of the second and third stories is therapeutic, the second one requiring a mental and the third a physical reconfrontation of a place analogous to the setting where he was wounded. Given the well-known specifics of the actual wounding itself—227 bits of shrapnel in the legs and groin—and Hemingway's fears of amputation, it takes little imagination to link the wounding to castration anxiety. And the source of that anxiety? I think we need look no further than to a young boy's fishing experiences with his father. Their only deeply disturbing event would be the moments the father takes his knife to the fish and cleans them. When coupled to those "jars of snakes and other specimens that [his] father had collected as a boy and preserved in alcohol" (*Stories*, 365), the terror of that riverbank or lakeshore scene would have forcefully imprinted such a dread of castration that when shelled at Fossalta on the Piave River Hemingway's repressed anxiety resurfaced with explosive force.

39. See David C. McClelland, *The Roots of Consciousness* (Princeton: D. Van Nostrand Co., 1964), pp. 18–19.

40. A fine corrective to esthetic purists is Robert Rogers, *Metaphor: A Psychoanalytic View* (Berkeley: University of California Press, 1978), especially chapters 1 and 2, "Modes of Mentation" and "Modal Ambiguity," pp. 13–76. See also David Gordon, *Literary Art and the Unconscious*, pp. 16–29; and C. Barry Chabot, *Freud on Schreber: Psychoanalytic Theory and the Critical Act* (Amherst: University of Massachusetts Press, 1982), especially chapter 3, "Psychoanalysis as Literary Critcism/Literary Criticism as Psychoanalysis," pp. 49–75.

A FAREWELL TO ARMS

1. Baker, *Life Story*, p. 44; Michael S. Reynolds's *Hemingway's First War: The Making of "A Farewell to Arms"* (Princeton: Princeton University Press, 1976) definitively refutes the notion that personal experience dictated the specifics of the novel.

2. The motif of irrationality has been variously dealt with, nowhere more succinctly than in Frederick H. Marcus, "*A Farewell to Arms*: The Impact of Irony and the Irrational," *English Journal* 51 (1962): 527–35. The basic difference be-

tween our views of the thesis is that he believes that Frederic can escape irrational forces by retreating to the world of appetite—sex, drinking, and eating. I do not.

3. For discussions of the relationship between Peele's poem and Hemingway's novel, see Jerome L. Mazzaro, "George Peele and *A Farewell to Arms*: A Thematic Tie," *Modern Language Notes* 75 (1960): 118–19; Clinton Keeler, "*A Farewell to Arms*: Hemingway and Peele," *Modern Language Notes* 76 (1961): 622–25; and Bernard Oldsey, "Of Hemingway's *Arms* and the Man," *College Literature* 1 (1974): 174–89.

4. Respectively, Ray B. West, Jr., "*A Farewell to Arms*," in *The Art of Modern Fiction*, ed. Ray B. West, Jr., and Robert W. Stallman (New York: Holt, Rinehart & Winston, 1949), p. 633; Young, *Reconsideration*, p. 94; Earl Rovit, *Ernest Hemingway* (New York: Twayne Publishers, 1963), pp. 105–6; Robert W. Lewis, Jr., *Hemingway on Love* (Austin: University of Texas Press, 1965), pp. 49–52; and Dewey Ganzel, "*A Farewell to Arms*: The Danger of Imagination," *Sewanee Review* 79 (1971): 576–97. The first four of these are reprinted in Jay Gellens, ed., *Twentieth Century Interpretations of "A Farewell to Arms": A Collection of Critical Essays* (Englewood Cliffs, N.J.: Prentice-Hall, 1970), pp. 27, 32, 39–40, and 48–51, respectively.

5. Carlos Baker reprints "The Original Conclusion to *A Farewell to Arms*" in *Ernest Hemingway: Critiques of Four Major Novels* (New York: Scribners, 1962), p. 75 (hereafter cited as *Critiques*). But see Bernard Oldsey, *Hemingway's Hidden Craft: The Writing of A Farewell to Arms* (University Park: Pennsylvania State University Press, 1979). He not only explains why the version Baker reprinted should more precisely be referred to as "The Original *Scribner's Magazine* Conclusion" (pp. 71–72) but also analyzes the forty-one variants of Hemingway's conclusions to the novel. Among them, only variant 41, in his listing among "Miscellaneous Endings," expressly "entertains possibility of suicide" (p. 107). That will prove to many readers that Hemingway saw Frederic's suicide as less probable than the other kinds of endings that Oldsey groups under eight headings. And I am taken with Oldsey's idea that Hemingwy's final ending subsumes, iceberg-fashion, those other kinds of endings: the *Nada*, Fitzgerald, Religious, Live-Baby, Morning-After, Funeral, and Combination (i.e., epilogue) endings. Yet not only is the final ending nihilistic, like the *Nada* endings. But even Oldsey concludes that it was "conceived . . . in the spirit of rejection" and is "a compressed exemplification of the process of rejection and negation" (p. 82). What action would better express that "spirit" and "process" than suicide? Moreover, though Hemingway was uncertain about how to end his novel, the variant endings show that his final version flatly rejected the affirmative variants. Most important to note, Hemingway also discovered that his final ending was so congruent with the novel's character, thesis, and atmosphere that the rest of his text did not require serious modification, extensive revision. Readers who must salvage something positive from the novel, who nurse the illusion that the novel affirms selfless love, will, of course, opt for Frederic's growth or "initiation" and the therapeutic motive behind his storytelling. Like any great novel, this one bears both that reading and mine.

6. Grebstein, *Hemingway's Craft*, p. 73; and Oldsey, *Hemingway's Hidden Craft*, p. 91. My following three sentences present, I hope fairly, the proofs upon which Professor Grebstein bases his conclusion, pp. 73–76; Oldsey, in contrast, offers no support for his assertion, one that he makes in several places.

7. E. M. Halliday, "Hemingway's Narrative Perspective," *Sewanee Review* 60 (1952): 210; rpt. in Baker, *Critiques*, p. 178.

8. Julian Smith, in "Hemingway and the Thing Left Out," *Journal of Modern Literature* 1 (1970–71): 163–82 (rpt. in Benson, *Short Stories*, pp. 135–47), offers a different but interesting reading of the narrators of both stories.

9. Walker Gibson, "Tough Talk: The Rhetoric of Frederic Henry," in his *Tough,*

Sweet, and Stuff: An Essay on Modern Prose Styles (Bloomington: Indiana University Press, 1966), p. 40. The following questions I raise in the text are based upon Gibson's conclusions about Frederic, pp. 34–41. In fairness to him, he acknowledges that he bases them upon a small sample, the novel's first two paragraphs. But that neither subdues his dogmatism nor causes him to consider the inadequacy of his tidy, triadic format. If, for instance, the speaker of Marvell's "Coy Mistress," a speech by Winston Churchill, and the story told by Frederic Henry all employ "tough" styles, then wherein lies the value of a classification that groups together a lover, a patriot, and a disoriented storyteller? Gibson's case for defining Frederic as "tough" is one of the more explicit discussions of the "Hemingway style." But also see Walter J. Ong, S.J., "The Writer's Audience Is Always a Fiction," *PMLA* 90 (1976): 9–21, who follows Gibson to conclude that Hemingway's style serves the purpose of casting the reader "in the role of a close companion of the writer" (p. 13). Ong, too, fails to consider that disoriented and neurotic people use language, particularly demonstrative pronouns, "that," and definite articles, in much the same way as Frederic does.

10. Gibson, "Tough Talk," pp. 36–37.

11. John Edward Hardy, "*A Farewell to Arms*: The Death of Tragedy," in his *Man in the Modern Novel* (Seattle: University of Washington Press, 1964), p. 136.

12. Philip Young and Charles W. Mann, *The Hemingway Manuscripts: An Inventory* (University Park: Pennsylvania State University Press, 1969), item 18. See also Philip Young and Charles W. Mann, "Fitzgerald's *Sun Also Rises*: Notes and Comments," *Fitzgerald/Hemingway Annual 1970*, pp. 1–9.

13. Recent scholarship should disabuse me of this view. Professors Reynolds (*Hemingway's First War*, p. 56), Oldsey (*Hemingway's Hidden Craft*, p. 64), and Wirt Williams (*The Tragic Art of Ernest Hemingway* [Baton Rouge: Louisiana State University Press, 1981], pp. 71, 72–74) remark on the poetic quality of the opening. The first two arrange it as a piece of free verse, overlooking the fact that the cadences of a disoriented narrator, an emotionally disturbed person, even a normal person under emotional stress, form rhythmic patterns that could be similarly scanned. Indeed, Oldsey argues that the opening is a poetic and evocative overture to the novel (pp. 62–68). Interesting though this idea is, it reads like an exercise in New Criticism, one that has no basis in the manuscripts that presumably underpin his study.

14. Sheridan Baker, *Ernest Hemingway: An Introduction and Interpretation* (New York: Holt, Rinehart & Winston, 1967), p. 67 (hereafter cited as *An Introduction*). I cite Baker not to pillory him for his misreading here but to note that he too recognizes a "strange confusion" in the narrative voice of the opening chapters; his conclusions, however, differ considerably from mine.

15. Grebstein, *Hemingway's Craft*, p. 212; italics added.

16. I wonder if Hemingway ever ruefully felt about *A Farewell to Arms* what he wryly acknowledged about "Out of Season": that he omitted the end of the story, the old man's hanging himself, basing the omission on his theory

> that you could omit anything if you knew that you omitted and the omitted part would strengthen the story and make people feel something more than they understood.
>
> Well, I thought, now I have them so they do not understand them. There cannot be much doubt about that. (*Feast*, 75)

17. Daniel J. Schneider, in "Hemingway's *A Farewell to Arms*: The Novel as Pure Poetry," *Modern Fiction Studies* 14 (1968): 283–92, also argues that Hemingway did not intend to create a rich, complex character in Catherine; his argument, however, rests on the idea that Hemingway uses her, as he uses action, only to reflect the lyric consciousness of a narrator concerned with conveying image clusters that reveal his mood of bitterness, despair, and so on. Williams, in *The Tragic Art*, argues a similar reading, pp. 66–67, 70–85.

18. See, for example, Chaman Nahal, *The Narrative Pattern in Ernest Hemingway's Fiction* (Rutherford, N.J.: Fairleigh Dickinson University Press, 1971), p. 62 (hereafter cited as *Narrative Pattern*); and Wylder, *Hemingway's Heroes*, p. 86.

19. For a different reading of Catherine's "craziness," see George Dekker and Joseph Harris, "Supernaturalism and the Vernacular Style," *PMLA* 94 (1979): 311–18.

20. See Grebstein, *Hemingway's Craft*, pp. 212–15.

21. Sigmund Freud, *Civilization and Its Discontents*, trans. and ed. James Strachey (New York: Norton, 1962), p. 29.

THE SUN ALSO RISES

1. Respectively, Edwin Berry Burgum, "Ernest Hemingway and the Psychology of the Lost Generation," in his *The Novel and the World's Dilemma* (New York: Oxford University Press, 1947), rpt. in *Ernest Hemingway: The Man and His Work*, ed. John K. M. McCaffery (New York: Avon, 1950), pp. 281–85 (hereafter cited as *The Man and His Work*); Richard P. Adams, "Sunrise out of the Waste Land," *Tulane Studies in English* 9 (1959): 119–31; Mark Spilka, "The Death of Love in *The Sun Also Rises*," in *Twelve Original Essays on Great American Novels*, ed. Charles Shapiro (Detroit: Wayne State University Press, 1958), rpt. in *Hemingway: A Collection of Critical Essays*, ed. Robert P. Weeks (Englewood Cliffs, N.J.: Prentice-Hall, 1962), pp. 127–38 (hereafter cited as *Critical Essays*); Jackson J. Benson, *Hemingway: The Writer's Art of Self-Defense* (Minneapolis: University of Minnesota Press, 1969), pp. 28–46 (hereafter cited as *Self-Defense*); Dewey Ganzel, "*Cabestro* and *Vaquilla*: The Symbolic Structure of *The Sun Also Rises*," *Sewanee Review* 76 (1968): 26–48; and Young, *Reconsideration*, pp. 82–85.

2. For a different reading of the same paragraph, see Terrence Doody, "Hemingway's Style and Jake's Narration," *Journal of Narrative Technique* 4 (1974): 216–17.

3. See Claire Sprague, "*The Sun Also Rises*: Its 'Clear Financial Basis,'" *American Quarterly* 21 (1969): 259–66.

4. William L. Vance, "Implications of Form in *The Sun Also Rises*," in *The Twenties, Poetry and Prose: Twenty Critical Essays*, ed. Richard E. Landford and William E. Taylor (Deland, Fla.: Everett Edwards Press, 1966), pp. 87–91.

5. In contrasting Lady Brett and Count Mippipopolous, Hemingway seems to be juggling the late-Victorian hedonisms of *The Rubaiyat of Omar Khyyam* and Walter Pater. Both the poem and the esthetician value sensory experience and debunk intellectualization. Unable to gain any rational understanding of the "whithers and thithers" of the universe, the poem urges seizing the day and its triumvirate of bread, wine, and woman. Pater likewise confirms life's inconstancy and impenetrability, rejects abstract theorizing, and urges collecting sensory impressions. Omar, like Brett, asks for no discriminations among pleasure-seeking activity (and Brett shares bread, wine, and bed with nearly all comers). But like the count, Pater demands a discerning mind both to intensify and expand each moment and to achieve a "quickened, multiplied consciousness." To be sure, Pater's esthetic is more epicurean and cultured than the count's. Yet the count's common level of experience domesticates Pater's hedonism, broadens its applicability, and defines the species of hedonistic conduct that the novel advocates.

6. "Bull Fighting as Tragedy," *By-Line*, 95.

7. Admittedly, Hemingway does not endorse all Spanish traditions. And so Jake's attempts to worship in church note that belief in institutionalized religion is defunct, is incapable of revival. And Jake is also careful to observe that even the vital traditions of the bullfight can be corrupted by innovations and phony matadors. I also acknowledge that "traditionalism" is but a different form of hedonism

insofar as it sublimates a hedonist's more elementary means of gratification. Still, the dichotomy helps us see the differences between immediately gratified sensations and displaced or sublimated ones.

8. See, for instance, Wylder, *Hemingway's Heroes*, pp. 39–49.

9. Other critics who find in Jake limited vision are Rovit, *Hemingway*, who calls Jake "a particularly opaque first-person narrator" (p. 148), and Hovey, *Inward Terrain*, who sees the ambiguity of Jake's relationship to Hemingway due to Jake's psychological unreliability (pp. 62–67). Like me, they affirm Jake's success as narrator, but for reasons that differ from mine. For a provocative essay on this issue, see Doody, "Hemingway's Style and Jake's Narration." Doody assumes that Hemingway is incapable of characterizing Jake ironically and that "there is nothing else in Hemingway's work or career to support such a reading" that he could create "a portrait of the artist as a middle-aged loser" (p. 221). And so he concludes that the novel is flawed, that Hemingway does not know what he is doing with Jake, "has not thought out the first person novel and its demands with care." Not only does Doody overlook Hemingway's "portrait of the artist as a middle-aged loser," Richard Gordon of *To Have and Have Not*, but he also asserts that a novelist must finally give some clear idea of when, where, why, and to whom a narrator tells his story, some "formal recognition of the motive or the occasion of Jake's retrospect," some "indications of his imaginative agency in producing the narrative, if even only for the purpose of his own self-discovery" (p. 220). As I would argue about both this novel and *Farewell*, such a prejudicial expectation violates an author's right to defy any expectation or convention. It also insists that narrators always be so integrated that they can address openly such expectations or that their creators allow us some clear signal of distance between themselves and their narrators. Shades of Wayne Booth's prescriptive categories!

10. Delmore Schwartz, "Ernest Hemingway's Literary Situation," *Southern Review* 3 (1938), rpt. in McCaffery, *The Man and His Work*, pp. 100, 107.

AFTERWORD TO THE THESIS PHASE

1. See, e.g., Grebstein, *Hemingway's Craft*, p. 212.

2. Much less, of course, does Hemingway violate the entire novel with the kind of optimism Paramount furnished the ending of its 1932 filming of the novel. Returning to the bedside of Helen "Catherine" Hayes, Gary "Frederic" Cooper lifts her sheet-draped, dead body from the hospital bed and carries her to the threshold of her room's balcony. A breeze ruffles the gauze curtains of the open door and sunlight pours in, accompanied by the orchestral sounds of Armistice bells. Overhead fly innumerable doves, symbols, I think. My Hemingway teacher, Harry Burns, enjoyed repeating what Hemingway told him in response to that ending: " 'Why the Hell didn't they have her give birth to the American Flag!' "

3. Sanford, *At the Hemingways*, p. 129.

4. *Life Story*, pp. 144–45, 148–51, 155–57.

5. For the record, Hemingway did not extensively revise the Madrid episode. In fact, his ambivalent treatment of Brett was not affected by his subsequent adultery with Pauline Pfeiffer. Nevertheless, in the same notebook in which he drafted the ending to *The Sun Also Rises* (item 194 in *Catalog of Hemingway Collection*, p. 27), Hemingway added what reads like a summary. In this undated passage Jake blames Cohn for what happened, says that he is writing his story just as it occurred, and sees that because it does not conform to the standards of other novels, many readers will not find it credible. He goes on to declare that his "passion and longing" for Brett were so genuine that at times he thought they would tear him apart, but at other times when she was absent, he got along fine. Not only does this sound as though it were Hemingway expressing his "passion and longing" for Pauline, but so too do Jake's last statements in this manuscript material. In what

reads like the feelings Hemingway would later in the same year express during his and Pauline's separation before marriage, Jake admits to the agony he felt just after he left Brett: that the world was empty, that nothing any longer had its old shape, that life was hollow, something to get through. Compare the manuscript with Hemingway's letters to Pauline, 12 November 1926 and 3 December 1926, *Letters*, pp. 220–23 and 234–35.

6. See, e.g., E. M. Halliday, "Hemingway's Ambiguity: Symbolism and Irony," *American Literature* 28 (1956): 17, rpt. in Weeks's *Critical Essays*, pp. 66–67; and Wylder, *Hemingway's Heroes*, p. 78.

7. Alice Hunt Sokoloff, *Hadley: The First Mrs. Hemingway* (New York: Dodd, Mead & Co., 1973), pp. 5, 6–7, 11–14, 24–30.

8. My chapter on *A Moveable Feast* treats the issue of Hemingway's filial betrayal during the twenties.

9. Sanford, *At the Hemingways*, pp. 183, 188.

DEATH IN THE AFTERNOON

1. Fatal though it may be to my argument in the following few pages, I, well, take the bull by the horns here to admit that none of the existing records of Hemingway's reading or libraries has turned up a copy of Walton's *Compleat Angler*. I find it hard to believe, however, that he had not encountered it at one time or another. And the resemblances that I discuss seem to me to be too strong for them to be merely coincidental.

2. Izaak Walton, *The Compleat Angler* (New York: Collier Books, 1962), p. 28; I parenthesize subsequent page references from this edition in my text.

3. See, for example, Tucker Brooke's brief account in Albert C. Baugh, *A Literary History of England* (New York: Appleton-Century-Crofts, 1948), pp. 609–12.

4. "The Dangerous Summer," *Life*, 19 September 1960, p. 87. Comparable statements appear in *Afternoon*, but Hemingway here adopts a perspective I can better return to in this chapter's last section.

5. See, for example, Robert M. Coates's review, "Bullfighters," *New Yorker*, October 1932, pp. 61–63; rpt. in *Ernest Hemingway: The Critical Reception*, edited, with an introduction, by Robert O. Stephens (n.p.: Burt Franklin & Co., 1977), pp. 115–16 (hereafter cited as *Critical Reception*).

6. Baker, *Life Story*, p. 242.

7. For Eastman's original review see "Bull in the Afternoon," *New Republic*, 7 June 1933, rpt. in Stephens, *Critical Reception*, pp. 130–32. I quote from Eastman's expanded essay in his *Art and the Life of Action*, rpt. in McCaffery, *The Man and His Work*, p. 62.

8. I use *voyeurism* advisedly. The sense of eavesdropping on sexual intimacies would be confirmed by a psychoanalytic interpretation of the ritual of the bullfight. As I remark later, among other things the bullfight enacts the primal scene fantasy, externalizing a child's notion of sexual intercourse as violent.

9. In *At the Hemingways* Marcelline tries at times to make her father appear to be good-humored. But the dominant impression she conveys is Clarence Hemingway's sternness and authoritarianism; see, e.g., pp. 31, 39–40, 44–45. Indeed, none of the sibling accounts of the Hemingway family portrays Clarence as a man who allowed himself much pleasure. Not even in *"Sunny" Remembers* does one find a picture of the doctor displaying anything that resembles his older son's most prominent feature, a broad smile. Of the book's eighteen pictures of him, he scarcely betrays a perceptible smile; most often he is in profile, looking at someone else in the photograph.

10. For a comparable view see Tony Tanner, *The Reign of Wonder: Naivety and*

Reality in American Literature (Cambridge: At the University Press, 1965). The prose sketches in *In Our Time* "are exercises in the unhysterical treatment of horror, attempts to achieve maximum factual clarity when confronted by scenes which are most calculated to stimulate a writer to emotional rhetoric" (p. 250).

11. Sanford, *At the Hemingways*, p. 124.

12. See, e.g., Grebstein, *Hemingway's Craft*, p. 77; Hovey, *Inward Terrain*, p. 105–7; and Sheridan Baker, *An Introduction*, p. 87. Hemingway included the story in his next collection, *Winner Take Nothing*, minus the conversations between Author and Old Lady.

13. Waldhorn, in his *Reader's Guide*, sides with the surgeon who "already knows what the officer must learn, that holding tight is almost all a man can salvage" (p. 134).

14. Baker, *Artist*, p. 143.

15. Hovey, *Inward Terrain*, p. 110.

16. For a succinct account of the conversion thesis, see Keneth Kinnamon, "Hemingway, the *Corrida*, and Spain," *Texas Studies in Literature and Language* 1 (1959): 44–61, rpt. in Wagner, *Five Decades*, pp. 57–74. For an extreme version of the thesis, see Broer, *Hemingway's Spanish Tragedy*, who argues that Hemingway's "unwillingness to entertain any perspective other than that dictated by particularismo and pundonor [respectively, extreme anarchistic individualism and primitive aggressiveness] underlies the author's work from *Green Hills of Africa* until the end of his life" (pp. 113–14). For a repetitive and overly rhetorical version of the conversion thesis, see Jose Luis Castillo-Puche, *Hemingway in Spain: A Personal Reminiscence of Hemingway's Years in Spain by His Friend*, trans. Helen R. Lane (Garden City: Doubleday, 1974), pp. 213, 297 et passim.

17. Baker, *Artist*, p. 154–61.

18. For a similar interpretation, see John Reardon, "Hemingway's Esthetic and Ethical Sportsmen," *University Review* 34 (1967): 13–23; rpt. in Wagner, *Five Decades*, pp. 131–44.

19. The obvious source for my discussion here is James Joyce's *A Portrait of the Artist as a Young Man*. Hemingway's friendship with the Irishman and high regard for his work seem sufficient to me to indicate that he knows—and that at some level of consciousness may be responding to—the working definitions of Saint Thomas Aquinas, so ably discussed by Stephen Dedalus; page references in my text are to the paperback Compass edition (New York: Viking Press, 1956).

20. Students of Kenneth Burke will recognize the debt my discussion of Hemingway's esthetic owes to "Beauty and the Sublime" in Burke's revised and abridged edition of *The Philosophy of Literary Form* (New York: Vintage, 1957). I quote him at length to avoid editorial distortion and to indicate how extensively his theorizing applies to Hemingway's practice:

. . . The whole subject of "beauty" became obscured in much aesthetic theory of the nineteenth century because it tended to start from notions of *decoration* rather than from notions of the *sublime*. There are many possible ingredients behind this motivation, among them being the fact that aesthetic theorizing was largely done *by* people in comfortable situations *for* people in comfortable situations. But there is a subtler factor operating here; poetry *is* produced for purposes of comfort, as part of the *consolatio philosophiae*. It is undertaken as *equipment for living*, as a ritualistic way of arming us to confront perplexities and risks. It would *protect* us.

Let us remind ourselves, however, that implicit in the idea of protection there is the idea of something to be *protected against*. Hence, to analyze the element of *comfort* in beauty, without false emphasis, we must be less monistic, more "dialectical," in that we include also, as an important aspect of the recipe, the element of *discomfort* (actual or threatened) for which the poetry is "medicine," therapeutic or prophylactic. And I submit that if we retraced the course of aesthetic speculation, until we came to its earlier mode, we should get a much more accurate description of what is going on in poetry. I refer to the time when the discussion explicitly pivoted about the distinction between the *ridiculous* and the *sublime.*

As soon as we approach the subject in these terms, we have in the very terms themselves a constant reminder that the *threat* is the basis of beauty. Some vastness of magnitude, power, or distance, disproportionate to ourselves, is "sublime." We recognize it with awe. We find it dangerous in its fascination. And we equip ourselves to confront it by piety, by stylistic medicine, and by structural assertion (form, a public matter that symbolically enrolls us with allies who will share the burdens with us). The ridiculous, on the contrary, equips us by impiety, as we refuse to allow the threat its authority; we rebel, and courageously play pranks when "acts of God" themselves are oppressing us. . . . Should we not begin . . . treating all other manifestations of symbolic action as *attenuated variants* of pious awe (the sublime) and impious rebellion (the ridiculous)?
. . . By starting with "the sublime and the ridiculous," rather than with "beauty," you place yourself forthwith into the realm of the *act,* whereas "beauty" turns out to be too *inert* in its connotations, leading us rather to overstress the *scene* in which the act takes place. Confronting the poetic act in terms of "beauty," we are disposed to commit one or another of two heretical overemphases: either we seek to locate beauty in the object, as scene, or by dialectical overcompensation we seek to locate it in the subject, as agent. Confronting the poetic act in terms of the sublime and the ridiculous, we are disposed to think of the issue *in terms of a situation and a strategy for confronting or encompassing that situation,* a scene and an act, with each possessing its own genius, but the two fields interwoven. [Pp. 51–52, 54]

Burke strikes me as employing some sophistry here. Responding to the sublime or the ridiculous we evaluate an agent performing an act within a scene; hence we evaluate not simply a "situation-confronting strategy" but the agent performing it as well, since it is he or she who interweaves those two fields. In effect Burke's esthetic theory, fond as it is of disembodied symbolic acts, seems partly an attempt to disguise the reentry of morality and ethics into the domain of esthetics. But his definition of the function of art as "a ritualistic way of arming us to confront perplexities and risks" assigns to art an ethical and didactic purpose that agrees well with Hemingway's work. Moreover, his three emphases—upon threat as the basis of beauty (a typical Burkean transmogrification of Freud's notion of art as wish-fulfillment), upon the act an agent performs in a scene rather than upon the scene or subject itself, and upon the obligation to accord judgments of sublime, ridiculous, or "attenuated variants" of those two—all three emphases remove art and the study of beauty from being a disinterested activity on the part of both creator and spectator. They insist upon the beauty of action, which applies cogently to the art of the matador.

21. Hemingway's study of the bullfight is consistent with his lifelong interest in athletics. But I would emphasize that his interest has been mistakenly viewed as an outgrowth of largely competitive and aggressive appetites. Those appetites exist in him, as they do in us, to be sure. But not to the exclusion of esthetic appetites as well. Indeed, inasmuch as no sport lacks some degree of esthetic movement—of linear grace, tactile fluency, physical rhythm, perceived vitality, muscular discipline, and improvisation—a good share of Hemingway's "outdoorsman's" interests seem dictated by a desire to see beauty and so to experience those emotions accruable to esthetic apprehension. Even more, Hemingway deserves some belated recognition as a pioneer in the esthetics of athletics. His efforts have been taken up more recently by educators and estheticians. See, for example, H. T. A. Whiting and D. W. Masterson, eds., *Readings in the Aesthetics of Sport* (London:

Henry Kimpton, 1974), especially R. Carlisle, "Physical Education and Aesthetics," pp. 21–32; H. Keller, "Sport and Art—The Concept of Mastery," pp. 89–98; and R. K. Elliiot, "Aesthetics and Sport," pp. 107–16.

GREEN HILLS OF AFRICA

1. Edmund Wilson, "Hemingway: Gauge of Morale," *The Wound and the Bow* (New York: Oxford University Press, 1947); rpt. in McCaffery, *The Man and His Work*, p. 221 (hereafter cited as "Gauge of Morale").

2. In "Notes on Dangerous Game: The Third Tanganyika Letter," *By-Line*, pp. 167–71, Hemingway assigns only the lion and the leopard the status of "dangerous game."

3. Wilson, "Gauge of Morale," p. 222.

4. See *By-Line*, pp. 162–66.

5. See ibid., pp. 403–16.

6. "Imperiled Flanks," part 3 of *African Journal, Sports Illustrated*, 10 January 1972, p. 29.

7. Hovey, *Inward Terrain*, p. 116.

8. Respectively, Young, *Reconsideration*, p. 97; Wilson, "Gauge of Morale," p. 220; Grebstein, *Hemingway's Craft*, p. 38; Waldhorn, *Reader's Guide*, p. 138; Hovey, *Inward Terrain*, p. 117; and Wilson, "Gauge of Morale," p. 220.

9. Respectively, Young, *Reconsideration*, p. 97; Hovey, *Inward Terrain*, p. 112; Waldhorn, *Reader's Guide*, p. 137; and Malcolm Cowley, "A Portrait of Mister Papa," *Life*, 10 January 1949, rpt. in McCaffery, *The Man and His Work*, p. 43.

10. Hovey, *Inward Terrain*, p. 110.

11. I refer here to Watts, *Hemingway and the Arts*, and to Raymond S. Nelson, *Hemingway: Expressionist Artist* (Ames: Iowa State University Press, 1979) (hereafter cited as *Expressionist Artist*). Watts does not ignore the esthetic of hunting, for she discusses Hemingway's "analogy between hunting kudu and visiting the Prado" (pp. 208–12). But it is puzzling why she fails to address the larger issue of how Hemingway's works respond to or challenge esthetic theories. Philip Young's foreword to the British edition of *By-Line* (London: Collins, 1968) also remarks the esthetics of hunting (pp. 23–24).

12. For an interesting philosophical consideration of hunting, see José Ortega y Gasset, *Meditations on Hunting*, trans. Howard B. Wescott (New York: Scribner's, 1972).

13. "Miss Mary's Lion," part 1, *African Journal, Sports Illustrated*, 20 December 1971, p. 4. The manuscripts of *African Journal* are still inaccessible, and I do not discuss this work at length elsewhere in my text. So perhaps this is the place to note that however piecemeal or patched *Journal* may be, its unifying principle is not *Green Hills'* esthetic one. Its unifying principle instead revolves around Hemingway's preoccupation with responsibilities, duties, obligations, pledges, and service. It, not *Green Hills*, deserves Philip Young's objection to Hemingway's "grinding need for self-justification" (*Reconsideration*, p. 97).

14. Hovey, *Inward Terrain*, p. 117; Waldhorn, *Reader's Guide*, arrives at a similar conclusion, p. 139.

15. "Miss Mary's Lion," p. 13.

16. Ibid.

17. Ortega y Gasset, *Meditations on Hunting*, p. 106.

18. Baker, *Artist*, cites Hemingway's description of the dead rhino as an example of ugliness (pp. 66–67).

19. Ortega y Gasset: "Suddenly, on the spine of a low ridge the stag appears to the hunter; he sees him cut across the sky with the elegant grace of a constellation,

launched there by the springs of his slender extremities. The leap of roe deer or stag—and even more of certain antelope—is perhaps the most beautiful event that occurs in Nature" (*Meditations on Hunting*, p. 91).

20. Rovit, *Hemingway*, p. 71; italics added. Hovey, *Inward Terrain*, also refers to Hemingway's "slaughter," p. 118, as does Grebstein, *Hemingway's Craft*, p. 38.

21. Grebstein, *Hemingway's Craft*, p. 39.

22. Leo Gurko, *Ernest Hemingway and the Pursuit of Heroism* (New York: Thomas Y. Crowell Co., 1968), p. 214; italics added.

23. Joyce, *Portrait*, p. 213.

AFTERWORD TO THE ESTHETIC PHASE

1. Hovey, *Inward Terrain*, p. 117; for similar conclusions see Young, *Reconsideration*, p. 97, and Waldhorn, *Reader's Guide*, p. 139.

2. Carlos Baker (*Artist*, pp. 165–74) and Sheridan Baker (*An Introduction*, pp. 90–96) are among the few who read *Green Hills* favorably, the latter even calling it "Hemingway's most mature book" (p. 90).

3. Ortega y Gasset, *Meditations on Hunting*, pp. 106, 110–11.

4. Respectively, Grebstein, *Hemingway's Craft*, p. 39; Carlos Baker, *Artist*, pp. 169–71; and Lewis, *Hemingway on Love*, pp. 68–75.

5. Waldhorn, *Reader's Guide*, p. 138.

6. Peterson, in *Direct or Oblique*, disapproves of the catalogue on the grounds that it is "meaningful primarily to himself of all the other things that he might have said about Spain but didn't. This kind of catalogue . . . seems to me illegitimate writing, a private indulgence in nostalgia" (p. 145).

7. Sanford, *At the Hemingway's*, p. 26.

8. In the third section of his discussion of *Afternoon*, Carlos Baker (*Artist*, pp. 154–61) argues the basic pragmatism of the Hemingway hero. Yet if, as he contends, the matador offers the model of the hero, then the trait the matador shares with the Spanish people in general—impracticality—is a trait that ipso facto denies pragmatism. To define the Hemingway hero as pragmatist notes only muscle and ignores the strong sinew of idealism and principles that I find in even his least heroic protagonists. After all, even the matador does not believe, as a pragmatist should, that the end justifies the means. Were he to do so, the bullfight would lack all semblance of art. Neither can one validly declare, though Baker tries to, that the matador and the Hemingway hero are only empiricists, "perfectly practical Benthamites," utilitarians. To argue this ignores the compound motives behind their actions. Worse, it fails to see that anyone who puts his life on the line for a symbolic act shows little practical judgment and deserves a more accurate label.

9. Rovit, *Hemingway*, p. 71; Hovey, *Inward Terrain*, pp. 118–19.

10. Hemingway objects to Waldo Frank, *Virgin Spain: Scenes from the Spiritual Drama of a Great People* (New York: Boni and Liveright, 1926), for interpreting the bullfight as "a searching symbol of the sexual act. The bull is male; the exquisite torero, stirring and unstirred, with hidden ecstasy controlling the plunges of the bull, is female" (p. 235). But the bullfight, like any richly symbolic action, condenses different levels of meaning and significance. So it is also valid to interpret it as does Steven R. Phillips "Hemingway and the Bullfight: The Archetypes of Tragedy" (*Arizona Quarterly* 29 [1973]: 37–56), as archetypally enacting the Dionysian myth and, thus, the religious, ritual slaying of the god. And Peterson, *Direct and Oblique*, correctly contends that the bullfight is also "a systematic, ordered, regressive ceremony" in which "one's irrational or animal-like impulses are symbolically destroyed and one is symbolically cleansed" (p. 38). For an excellent summary of the folkloric origins and meanings of the bullfight as marriage

ritual, see John McCormick and Mario Sevilla Mascareñas, *The Complete Aficionado* (Cleveland: World Publishing Co., 1967), pp. 12–26.

11. Rovit, *Hemingway*, pp. 70–71; Hovey, *Inward Terrain*, p. 118. A full psychoanalytic reading of the bullfight would also see in it the primal scene, the child's imagined version of parents' brutal violence during sexual intercourse.

12. Baker, *Artist*, pp. 154–55; John Reardon, "Hemingway's Esthetic and Ethical Sportsmen," pp. 131–44; and Philip Young, foreword to *By-Line*, pp. 23–24.

13. Rovit, *Hemingway*, p. 71.

14. Sanford, *At the Hemingway's*, p. 82.

TO HAVE AND HAVE NOT

1. See, for example, W. M. Frohock, "Violence and Discipline," *Southwest Review* nos. 1 & 2 (1947), rpt. in McCaffery, *The Man and His Work*, p. 256.

2. Baker, *Artist*, pp. 203–5.

3. For a different reading of this novel as tragedy, see Wirt Williams, *The Tragic Art*, pp. 107–22.

4. William James Ryan, "Uses of Irony in *To Have and Have Not*," *Modern Fiction Studies* 14 (1968): 330.

5. Arthur Miller, "Tragedy and the Common Man," *New York Times*, 27 February 1949, sec. 2, p. 1. Though Miller's thoughts follow Hemingway's novel by over a decade, they articulate ideas common to depression-era writers, ideas familiar to Hemingway.

6. Hovey, *Inward Terrain*, p. 134; Philip Young, "Focus on *To Have and Have Not*: To Have Not: Tough Luck," in *Tough Guy Writers of the Thirties*, ed. David Madden (Carbondale: Southern Illinois University Press, 1968), p. 49.

7. Robert Ornstein, *The Moral Vision of Jacobean Tragedy* (Madison: University of Wisconsin Press, 1960), p. 23.

8. My following discussion draws upon Gerald F. Else's brilliant translation and commentary, *Aristotle's Poetics: The Argument* (Cambridge: Harvard University Press, 1963); parenthetical numbers in the text are page references to this edition. For a fine, brief discussion of Else's major points about tragedy, especially "catharsis," see Lois M. Welch, "Catharsis, Structural Purification, and Else's Aristotle," *Bucknell Review* 19 (1971): 31–50. So far none of the records of Hemingway's libraries or reading show that he even knew Aristotle's work, but, as Reynolds demonstrates, Hemingway was a compulsive reader of literary criticism and was well versed in the classics (*Hemingway's Reading*, pp. 23, 25, 26, 30, 31).

9. *Aristotle's Politics and Poetics*, trans. Benjamin Jowett and Thomas Twinning (New York: Viking Press, 1957), p. 246; I drop Else here only because Jowett's more traditional translation conveys the meaning Hemingway would probably have used—if he used Aristotle at all.

10. For perhaps the best discussion of tragedy and its illegitimate pretenders, see Robert B. Heilman, *Tragedy and Melodrama: Versions of Experience* (Seattle: University of Washington Press, 1968), pp. 3–31.

11. See, for example, Lewis, *Hemingway on Love*, p. 121, and Donaldson, *By Force of Will*, p. 67.

12. Heilman, *Tragedy and Melodrama*, pp. 227–51.

13. Hovey, *Inward Terrain*, p. 135; Lewis, *Hemingway on Love*, 117.

14. For a view of Harry as victim, see Baker, *Artist*, p. 213.

15. Donaldson, *By Force of Will*, p. 110, also notes this ambiguity.

16. My discussion of this conventional formula uses William Flint Thrall, Addison Hibbard, and C. Hugh Holman, *A Handbook to Literature*, rev. ed. (New York:

Odyssey Press, 1960), pp. 156–58. Oddly, Robin H. Farquhar, in "Dramatic Structure in the Novels of Ernest Hemingway," *Modern Fiction Studies* 14 (1968): 271–82, overlooks this novel for ones whose use of dramatic structure is much more arguable and considerably more opaque than this one.

17. See, however, Hemingway's letter to Lillian Ross, 28 July 1948, in which he asks her to tell Brendan Gill of the worth of *To Have and Have Not*. He likens it to a jerry-built, quickly fortified military position that is flawed but defensible. He goes on to say that the novel is considerably better than most people regard it. And he admits that when he wrote it he was "all fucked up," "threw away about 100,000 words" that were superior to much of what he kept. He concludes by calling it "the most cut book in the world" (*Letters*, pp. 648–49).

18. Baker, *Artist*, p. 339.

FOR WHOM THE BELL TOLLS

1. "Concentrated action": Baker, *Artist*, p. 247, and Frederic I. Carpenter, "Hemingway Achieves the Fifth Dimension," *PMLA* 69 (1954), rpt. in *Hemingway and His Critics: An International Anthology*, ed. Carlos Baker (New York: Hill and Wang, 1961), pp. 196–200; "diffuse digressions": Frohock, "Violence and Discipline," pp. 259–60; "political orientation": Mark Schorer, "The Background of a Style," *Kenyon Review* 2 (1941), rpt. in Baker, *Critiques*, pp. 88–89; "contradictory politics": D. S. Savage, "Ernest Hemingway," in his *The Withered Branch: Six Studies in the Modern Novel* (London: Eyre and Spottiswoode, 1950), pp. 38–40; "stylistic range": Joseph Warren Beach, "Style in *For Whom the Bell Tolls*," in his *American Fiction, 1920–1940* (New York: Macmillan, 1941), rpt. in Baker, *Critiques*, pp. 82–86; "strained and verbose language": Nemi D'Agostino, "The Later Hemingway," *The Sewanee Review*, 47 (1960), rpt. in Weeks, *Critical Essays*, p. 156; "in-depth characterization": Sheridan Baker, *An Introduction*, pp. 111–13; "stereotyped puppets": Alfred Kazin, "Hemingway: Synopsis of a Career," in his *On Native Grounds* (New York: Harcourt, Brace and World, 1942), rpt. in McCaffery, *The Man and His Work*, p. 181 (hereafter cited as "Synopsis of a Career"); "positive theme": William T. Moynihan, "The Martyrdom of Robert Jordan," *College English* 21 (1959): 127–32; "forced conception": Stanley Cooperman, "Hemingway's Blue-Eyed Boy: Robert Jordan and 'Purging Ecstasy,' " *Criticism* 8 (1966): 78–96, and Young, *Reconsideration*, p. 106; "tragedy": Benson, *Self-Defense*, pp. 153–54, and Waldhorn, *Reader's Guide*, 169; "melodrama": Thornton H. Parsons, "Hemingway's Tyrannous Plot," *University of Kansas City Review* 27 (1961): 262–64. Wylder, *Hemingway's Heroes*, touts the novel to be "as close to aesthetic perfection as Hemingway could make it" (p. 164).

2. See Edward Fenimore, "English and Spanish in *For Whom the Bell Tolls*," *ELH* 10 (1943), rpt. in McCaffery, *The Man and His Work*, pp. 195–96; Baker, *Artist*, pp. 245–50; Kazin, "Synopsis of a Career," p. 181; D'Agostino, "The Later Hemingway," p. 156; and Stewart Sanderson, *Hemingway* (London: Oliver and Boyd, 1961), p. 93.

3. See, for example, Lionel Trilling, "An American in Spain," in *The Partisan Reader*, ed. William Phillips and Philip Rahv (New York: Dial Press, 1946), rpt. in Baker, *Critiques*, p. 78; and Hovey, *Inward Terrain*, who designates it a "gaudy tour de force . . . made tolerable by Hemingway's romanticizing the subject as a curiosity of gypsy lore" (p. 167).

4. In a letter to Max Perkins dated 26 August 1940, Hemingway vigorously objected to the suggestion that he cut this material, insisting about the smell-of-death material, for example, that it was necessary to the various effects he was after. He even compares such cuts to pulling a bass or an oboe from a symphony orchestra (*Letters*, 513).

5. To measure the epic inflation this passage experienced, compare its 47-word predecessor in *Death in the Afternoon*, p. 44.

6. See, for example, Frohock, "Violence and Discipline," pp. 259–60. Readers would do well to heed C. S. Lewis's observation in *A Preface to Paradise Lost* (London: Oxford University Press, 1942): "The misunderstanding of the species (epic narrative) I have learned from the errors of critics, including myself, who sometimes regard as faults in *Paradise Lost* those very properties which the poet laboured hardest to attain and which, rightly enjoyed, are essential to its specific delightfulness" (p. 2).

7. Else, *Aristotle's Poetics*, p. 569; subsequent citations from this edition are included in the text.

8. See Arturo Barea, "Not Spain but Hemingway," trans. Ilsa Barea, *Horizon* 3 (1941), rpt. in Baker, *Critics*, pp. 208–9; Parsons, "Hemingway's Tyrannous Plot," p. 263; and Young, *Reconsideration*, pp. 108–9.

9. For a scholarly discussion of the kinds of epic see Else's commentary, pp. 525–33 and 595–600.

10. Reynolds, *Hemingway's Reading*, pp. 63, 65, 100, 119, 198.

11. Martha Gellhorn remembers that at the time Hemingway was composing the novel in Cuba he was also reading "The History of the Peninsular Wars," (MG to GB, 7 March 1976). I assume that she has confused *Peninsular* for *Persian*, that Herodotus's nine-volume history was the work Hemingway was reading, for he includes the episode "The Pass at Thermopylae" in his 1,100-page anthology of war stories, *Men at War: The Best War Stories of All Times* (New York: Crown Publishers, 1942). Hemingway also includes in this epic-sized volume "Horatius at the Bridge" from Livy's *The History of Rome* (Robert Jordan alludes to the heroes of both works on p. 164) and "The March to the Sea" from Xenophon's *Anabasis*. This last abounds in epic struggles to cross mountain passes and rivers, those two geographic features essential to the heroism of Leonidas, Horatius, and now Robert Jordan.

12. My handbook sources are Thrall, *A Handbook to Literature*, pp. 174–76; and M. H. Abrams, *A Glossary of Literary Terms* (New York: Holt, Rinehart and Co., 1957), pp. 29–31. I rely also upon C. S. Lewis's distinctions between primary and secondary epics in his *A Preface to Paradise Lost*, pp. 13–51.

13. See Werner Jaeger, *Paideia: The Ideals of Greek Culture*, trans. Gilbert Highet (New York: Oxford University Press, 1945), vol. 1, esp. the chapters entitled "The Culture and Education of the Homeric Nobility" (pp. 15–34) and "Homer the Educator" (pp. 35–56).

14. See Hemingway's letter to Maxwell Perkins, 21 April 1940, *Letters*, pp. 504–5.

15. Thrall, *A Handbook to Literature*, p. 175.

16. Reynolds, *Hemingway's Reading*, item 300, p. 93.

17. See Keneth Kinnamon, "Hemingway, the *Corrida*, and Spain," for a comparable conclusion on Hemingway's use of type characters: "Hemingway had to sacrifice a minor point of psychological propriety in order to gain the more important objective of national scope. The microcosm of the guerrilla band is intended to represent the macrocosm of the whole Spanish people" (p. 60).

18. Thrall, *A Handbook to Literature*, p. 175.

19. The power of the supernatural might also be imbedded in the novel's language, as Robert O. Stephens argues in "Language Magic and Reality in *For Whom the Bell Tolls*," *Criticism* 14 (1972): 151–64, rpt. in Wagner, *Five Decades*, pp. 266–79.

20. Baker, *Artist*, p. 248, reads the Homeric parallels differently.

21. For a different view of the novel's structure, see Baker, *Artist*, pp. 245–47, and Grebstein, *Hemingway's Craft*, pp. 42–51. I commend the thoroughness of

Grebstein's analysis but do not share his conclusion about all the antitheses, counterpoint, and patterns of alternation: "the result is anything but monotonous or mechanical" (p. 47).

22. The exception to Hemingway's use of the civil war metaphor is the relationship between Jordan and Maria, little conflict or tension visible in it. Although congruent with epic conventions, it is incongruent with the novel's metaphor.

23. George Plimpton, *Writers at Work: The Paris Review Interviews, Second Series*, introduction by Van Wyck Brooks (New York: Viking Press, 1965), p. 220.

AFTERWORD TO THE ARISTOTELIAN PHASE

1. Lloyd ("Pappy") R. Arnold, in *High on the Wild with Hemingway* (Caldwell, Id.: Caxton Printers, 1968), recalls Hemingway commenting on his father's suicide: "But, he said that the basis of his father's dilemmas was domination, ' . . . by my mother, she had to rule everything, have it all her own way, and she was a bitch! . . . True, it was a cowardly thing for my father to do, but then, if you don't live behind the eyes you can't expect to see all of the view. I know that part of his view, and I suppose he was mixing it up some . . . and you do such a thing only when you are tortured beyond endurance, like in a war, from an incurable disease, or when you hasten a drowning because you can't swim all of the sea' " (p. 79; Arnold's punctuation).

2. Hemingway's antagonism toward capitalism may have been aimed at his uncle George Hemingway for failing to help his brother Clarence during the latter's period of financial troubles, which contributed to his suicide. See Hemingway's letter to his mother, 11 March 1929, *Letters*, p. 296.

3. The brilliant dramatic monologue "After the Storm," in which Harry's prototype is first given voice, supports this identification. The anonymous narrator is depicted as a barroom brawler and an amoral opportunist, someone who sees only loot, not human suffering, in the sunken ocean liner he happens upon. But his failure to penetrate the liner's porthole and to strip the jewels from the drowned woman in the stateroom suggests either his impotence or his unwillingness to gratify erotic impulses. Either way, his primary wish, to get paternal approval, seems evident in his motives for telling his story. One motive is to reveal that he is not an erotic rival. Another is to demonstrate his concern for a father figure. The last third of the story, that is, documents his attempt to reconstruct for his listener precisely what must have occurred and how the captain of the sunken liner must have felt when surprised by the quicksand. This act of imagination, compassion, and empathy reveals his feeling for a father figure, one who died a victim of the treacherous waters whose hidden quicksand erotically horrifies Hemingway's unconscious as the vortex in "The Descent into the Maelstrom" does Poe's and the shivering sands in *The Moonstone* does Wilkie Collins's.

4. Several letters Hemingway wrote during this period vouch for his self-contempt and his contempt for Pauline. He wrote to her mother 26 January 1936 confessing that he had been "gloomy" and had "had the real old melancholia" (*Letters*, pp. 435–36). A year later, on 9 February 1937, along the right margin of a letter to "The Pfeiffer Family" he wrote a note that seems to protest too much: "I'm very grateful to you both for providing Pauline who's made me happier than I've ever been" (*Letters*, p. 458). Two months before this letter Hemingway had already met his next wife. See also EH to Archibald MacLeish, 5 May 1943, *Letters*, pp. 545–46.

5. For the suicide motif see Robert E. Fleming, "Hemingway's Treatment of Suicide: 'Fathers and Sons' and *For Whom the Bell Tolls*," *Arizona Quarterly* 33 (1977): 121–32.

6. For a different reading of Jordan's killings, see Walter J. Slatoff, "The Great Sin in *For Whom the Bell Tolls*," *Journal of Narrative Technique* 7 (1977): 142–48.

7. David J. Gordon, "The Son and the Father: Responses to Conflict in Hem-

ingway's Fiction," in his *Literary Art and the Unconscious*, remarks that "the private nature of the battle Jordan is fighting" is due to his father's suicide, but concludes that it has no "formal relation to the narrative" (p. 188).

8. Hovey, *Inward Terrain*, regards Anselmo and Pablo as the novel's only "two contrasting father figures" (p. 163).

9. Richard Drinnon, "In the American Heartland: Hemingway and Death," discusses the homoerotic aspect of military society in Hemingway (pp. 12–18) and Jordan's disingenuous discussion of marriage with Maria (p. 15).

10. As my discussion here implies, the unconscious implications of *For Whom the Bell Tolls* also address Hemingway's ambivalence toward women. His several marriages show his need for heterosexual relationships, and his early and middle work values women enough to tie his plots to love stories. But the excessive brutality he writes into Maria's background suggests a deep-seated hostility toward women. After all, Hemingway's dramatization of Maria's character would be unchanged if she had only been raped. But to that disgrace he adds the horror of having her watch her parents' execution and the mortification of being sexually disfigured, as the shearing of her hair indicates. These details argue Hemingway's sadistic pleasure in vilifying Maria and, through her, the female sex. Jordan's rejection of Maria at the novel's end unequivocally demonstrates this to me; for that gesture reveals Hemingway's fundamental feeling that allegiance to women is ultimately an unworthy or ignoble commitment for a man. Likewise, Hemingway's ambivalence surfaces in his portrait of Pilar. He respects her strength and assertiveness inasmuch as they enable her to assume leadership of the band when Pablo defaults. Yet those very qualities figured large in the contours of the woman Hemingway presumably hated, his domineering mother. (For an interesting discussion of Pilar's resemblance to a second woman who generated strongly mixed feelings in Hemingway, Gertrude Stein, see Nelson, *Expressionist Artist*, pp. 38–40.) Despite their manifest differences, Mrs. Hemingway's alliance to a man whose professional status belied his private weakness seems duplicated in Pilar's alliances with Pablo and Finito, the latter a man whose professional status as courageous matador belies his private fear of bulls, even when presented with the mounted head of one as a tribute. Finally, though the novel might reflect Hemingway's love for his blond-haired third wife, projected as she seems to be in the tawny-haired Maria, the reverse seems more likely. For Martha Gellhorn, to whom the novel is dedicated, little resembles the adoring "rabbit," Maria. Indeed, the novel defines the kind of woman to whom Hemingway thinks he could be devoted and true—a subservient female who, despite " 'a great soreness and much pain' " (341), will nevertheless suffer coitus with him. A woman with backbone who pursued her own career, Martha might well regard Hemingway's portrayal of Maria as a slap in the face. I am not surprised at her declaration that she dislikes the book. But according to her own account, if there is some malice toward her in the novel, Hemingway had reason for putting it there: she was not an approving audience to the early version of the novel; and so, feeling abused and angry, he found hunting and fishing friends to read his material to (MG to GB, 7 March 1976).

ACROSS THE RIVER AND INTO THE TREES

1. Baker, *Life Story*, pp. 463–73.

2. Respectively, Benson, *Self-Defense*, pp. 52–53; Young, *Reconsideration*, pp. 117–18; D'Agostino, "The Later Hemingway," p. 158; and Hovey, *Inward Terrain*, pp. 177–78.

3. Harvey Breit, "Talk with Mr. Hemingway," *New York Times Book Review*, 17 September 1950, p. 14.

4. I own that this idea must seem farfetched. And that is exactly how Mary Hemingway saw it, as a sufficiently outlandish example of the kind of queries we

English professors bother her with to single it out for ridicule in *How It Was:* "The professors are invariably writing dissertations or articles for scholarly reviews on such ambiguous or abstruse topics as . . . that *Across the River and into the Trees* is an 'imitation' of the *Divine Comedy*. Did Ernest discuss Aristotle's *Poetics*, this scholar asked recently, and was he reading Dante and discussing him with me or others while he was writing the Venice book?" (p. 532). She did answer my inquiry, thought my "imitation" idea purely charlatanical, and emphasized that Hemingway took no time to read—and certainly not to discuss—Dante, either with his wife or friends. Indeed, the idea of discussing any book he was in the process of writing was completely alien to him. In their seventeen years together, he never once discussed his work with her, she maintains (MH to GB, 4 August 1975). There is this, however, in a letter Hemingway wrote to John Dos Passos on 17 September 1949: "Since trip to Italy have been studying the life of Dante. Seems to be one of the worst jerks that ever lived, but how well he could write! This may be a lesson to us all" (*Letters*, p. 677).

5. Perhaps I should accede to what Carlos Baker says, writing of resemblances between Hemingway's works and "the European masters," "that Hemingway's doctrine of 'imitation' is of a special kind. What he imitates is nature, the world around him, expansed before his eyes. Dante, like his renaissance audience, is dead. . . . What [Hemingway] seeks to imitate is not the texture, it is the stature of the great books he reads and the great pictures he admires" (*Artist*, p. 186). But Baker's statement fails to define Hemingway's special kind of imitation; the statement applies equally to a host of writers who could also be said to imitate nature, Alexander Pope among them. And Baker fails to specify what Hemingway does to imitate the stature of great books; indeed, one can emulate the stature of something else but not imitate its stature. Moreover, what makes Baker's own book so valuable is his analysis of Hemingway's artistic experimentation and literary sophistication. His critical approach might almost be called generic, so alert is he to the traditional genres, modes, literary devices, and allusions that surface so often in Hemingway's works that they are the means by which Baker discerns Hemingway's experimental virtues. Of *Across the River*, for example Baker remarks that its "mood is Dantesque" and that "it occupied a different genre within the broad range of possibilities which fiction may legitimately invoke" (*Artist*, p. xviii).

6. Lillian Ross, "How Do You Like It Now, Gentlemen?" *New Yorker*, 13 May 1950, rpt. in Weeks, *Critical Essays*, p. 23.

7. The novel's allusions to *Othello* might make us think that if Hemingway is consciously competing with a dead man, it is Shakespeare, not Dante. But those allusions have so little to do with the novel's plot or Cantwell's preoccupations that I see them—as I do the novel's frame tale of duck-hunting—as decoys. Hemingway would doubtlessly scoff at my reading, having rejected Philip Young's comparable notion that "the basic symbols in 'The Snows of Kilimanjaro' were derived from Flaubert and Dante," as Baker records in *Life Story*, p. 509. But to take in good faith Hemingway's rejections of specific interpretations would be critical naivety. It would ignore his defensiveness, his acknowledgment that undiscerned things may lurk in his fiction, his unwillingness to discuss his writing lest it crack the structure of the fragile part of writing, and his long-standing anxiety that " 'you'll lose it if you talk about it' " (*Sun Rises*, p. 245). For a different conclusion of Hemingway's rival, see Nicholas Gerogiannis, "Hemingway's Poetry: Angry Notes of an Ambivalent Overman," *College Literature* 7 (1980): 248–62, who finds evidence that *Across the River* was indebted to Gabrielle D'Annunzio's novels *Notturno* and *The Flame*.

8. Peter Lisca, "The Structure of Hemingway's *Across the River and into the Trees*," *Modern Fiction Studies* 12 (1966), discusses this feature: "the novel is really a first person narration of events in the past . . . but disguised as third person narration through the device of using the shooter as a *persona* through

whom the Colonel thinks about himself. The result is that we know the Colonel *only as he knows himself*, but with the authority and the effects which accrue to the interior monologue by virtue of its disguise as omniscient third person narration" (p. 236).

9. For all references to, and quotations from, the *Divine Comedy*, I use John Ciardi's three-volume verse translation (New York: New American Library, 1954, 1961, 1972).

10. Patrick Hemingway, "My Papa, Papa," *Playboy* 15 (1968): 264; the quoted description of language is from John Ciardi, "Translator's Note," *The Inferno*, p. ix.

11. Baker, *Artist*, p. 285; for a more sustained discussion of Renata's confessional role, see Horst Oppel, "Hemingway's *Across the River and into the Trees*," *Die Neueren Sprachen* 11 (1952), trans. Joseph M. Bernstein, in Baker, *Critics*, pp. 220–23.

12. Georg Lukács, *The Historical Novel*, trans. Hannah and Stanley Mitchel (London: Merlin Press, 1962), p. 284.

13. Hemingway includes this episode in *Men at War*, pp. 531–39.

14. See, e.g., Lisca, "The Structure," p. 235.

15. This comparison is also noted by Lisca, "The Structure," p. 250, and Lewis, *Hemingway on Love*, pp. 182.

16. Baker, *Artist*, pp. 268–74, also attends to Cantwell's divided nature, with different conclusions.

AFTERWORD TO THE IMITATIVE PHASE

1. Gwynn and Blotner, *Faulkner in the University*, pp. 149, 143. For Hemingway's response see Baker, *Life Story*, p. 461, and Hemingway's letter to Faulkner, 23 July 1947, *Letters*, pp. 623–24.

2. For a detailed account of the ups and downs of Hemingway's reputation, see John Raeburn's "Hemingway in the Twenties: 'The Artists's Reward,' " *Rocky Mountain Review of Language and Literature* 29 (1975): 118–46, and "*Death in the Afternoon* and the Legendary Hemingway," *Fitzgerald/Hemingay Annual 1976*, pp. 243–57. For selected book reviews of Hemingway's works, see Stephens, *Critical Reception*.

3. Sanford, *At the Hemingway's*, pp. 218–19. See also Hemingway's letters to his mother, 5 February 1927, and to his father, 14 September 1927, *Letters*, pp. 243–44, 257–60.

4. Harold Bloom explores this idea, albeit esoterically, in *The Anxiety of Influence*.

5. John Berger, *The Success and Failure of Picasso* (Baltimore: Penguin Books, 1965), pp. 180–86. I am grateful to my colleague James Todd for bringing this book to my attention.

6. Lillian Ross, "How Do You Like It Now, Gentlemen?" p. 23. For a variant of Hemingway's specific adversaries, see his letter to Charles Scribner, Sr., 6 and 7 September 1949, *Letters*, p. 673.

7. Baker, *Life Story*, pp. 476–77.

8. Having asserted this earlier, I should acknowledge that there is some critical dispute over precisely what Renata's "disappointment" for Cantwell is. Lewis, *Hemingway on Love*, p. 186, argues that she is pregnant, a conclusion that Wylder, *Hemingway's Heroes*, concurs with, pp. 188–93. Not only do I find more persuasive Lisca's argument in "The Structure," p. 236, that she is menstruating, but I do not understand how Renata's pregnancy would be a disappointment to a man who has no children, no way to keep his memory alive. Cantwell pities his " 'poor Daugh-

ter' " (110) simply because she will experience only a clitoral orgasm achieved through the manipulations of "his ruined hand" (153).

9. Baker, *Life Story*, p. 471.

10. Sanford, *At the Hemingway's*, pp. 224–32.

11. Baker, *Life Story*, p. 475, 487, remarks on the composite identity of Cantwell. Though Hemingway dedicated this novel to Mary Hemingway, his letters to Lanham indicate his deep respect for this professional soldier as well as his wish to be deserving of Lanham's regard; see, e.g., his letters of 15 April and 11 September 1950, *Letters*, pp. 686–88, 714–16.

12. Baker, *Life Story*, p. 468.

13. Baker reports that when Hemingway was composing *Across the River* he got his gorge up against his mother. Hearing of her intention to grant an interview to *McCall's* magazine, he warned her that if she granted it "he would cut her off without a penny." In the same context Baker reports, "Sometime in the Depression, when Ernest had ordered her to sell the worthless Florida real estate, she had warned him never to threaten her: his father had tried it once when they were first married, and he had lived to regret it" (*Life Story*, p. 474). Now that his mother was seventy-seven, he had little fear of reprisal. See his letters to Charles Scribner, Sr., 27 August 1949, and to his mother, 17 September 1949, *Letters*, pp. 670, 675–76.

14. Baker, *Life Story*, p. 455.

15. Gregory Hemingway, *Papa*, p. 1.

16. MH to GB, 4 August 1975.

THE OLD MAN AND THE SEA

1. Ernest Hemingway, "An American Storyteller," *Time*, 13 December 1954, p. 72.

2. See Katharine T. Jobes, ed., *Twentieth Century Interpretations of "The Old Man and the Sea": A Collection of Critical Essays* (Englewood Cliffs, N.J.: Prentice-Hall, 1968); for more recent discussions of the novella's Christian, mythic elements, see John Bowen Hamilton, "Hemingway and the Christian Paradox," *Renascence* 24 (1972): 141–54, and Sam S. Baskett, "Toward a 'Fifth Dimension' in *The Old Man and the Sea*," *Centenniel Review* 19 (1975): 269–86.

3. For a different reading of Santiago's wishes, see Baker, *Artist*, pp. 306–7, and Benson, *Self-Defense*, p. 174.

4. Rovit, *Hemingway*, sees Santiago in mythic terms that echo the brother's keeper role, saying that Santiago "has been a champion of mankind for men and not for himself. He has brought back from his isolation a fragmented gift offering to his fellows, an imperfect symbol to suggest where he has been and what he has found there" (p. 89). For a different emphasis upon the fraternal motif see Lewis, *Hemingway on Love*, pp. 203–6, 211–13.

5. I agree with Hovey, *Inward Terrain*, pp. 201–3, who contends that among Hemingway's motives for writing *Old Man* is his wish for reconciliation with his own father. Having reached the age at which his long-internalized father presumably poses no real threat to his own psyche, and harboring guilt for parricidal wishes in daydreams and in earlier works, Hemingway may here be making fictional amends. A sure way to do this is to create a father image refulgent with benevolence, courage, and harmlessness. This possible intention is buttressed by seeing Hemingway's wish for reconciliation projected in Manolin's worshipful attitude toward Santiago. Further, because the marlin's "power and his beauty" complement Santiago's qualities, the old man and the huge marlin form a double image of an idealized father whom this novella applauds. Nevertheless, from a slightly altered perspective Santiago and the marlin are the ancient antagonists, son and father, of the Oedipal struggle. If we rightly interpret killing bulls and

shooting large animals as displaced enactments of parricidal wishes, then the logic of identifying oversized creatures with father images must apply here too.

6. Compare Rovit, *Hemingway*, p. 92.

7. See Charles K. Hofling, M.D., "Hemingway's *The Old Man and the Sea* and the Male Reader," *American Imago* 20 (1963): 161–73, for an insightful discussion of some of the reasons readers become emotionally involved with Santiago. And see, too, Hemingway's pleasure in readers' praise of the novel, EH to Wallace Meyer, 26 September 1952, *Letters*, p. 783.

8. Baker, *Life Story*, pp. 460, 473.

9. Ibid., p. 489.

10. Baker, *Artist*, pp. 379–82.

11. For a well-researched and cautious conjecture that the novella was written in the mid-thirties, see Darrell Mansell, "When Did Hemingway Write *The Old Man and the Sea?*" *Fitzgerald/Hemingway Annual 1975*, pp. 311–24.

12. EH to Charles Scribner, Sr., 20 July 1951, *Letters*, p. 732.

13. Baker, *Life Story*, p. 506. See also Waldhorn, *Reader's Guide*, p. 255; and Hemingway's letters to Philip Percival, 4 September 1955, *Letters*, pp. 845–46; to Charles Scribner, Jr., 25 February 1952, p. 756; and to Archibald MacLeish, 15 October 1958, p. 886. This last letter's reference to "Gigi" is one of the few letters in which Carlos Baker uses ellipses: "Occasional brief deletions have been made in order not to hurt the feelings of living persons" (p. xxv).

14. Wylder, *Hemingway's Heroes*, pp. 219–21; see also Leonard Lutwack, *Heroic Fiction: The Epic Tradition and American Novels of the Twentieth Century* (Carbondale: Southern Illinois University Press, 1971), p. 87, and Benson, *Self-Defense*, p. 178: "Santiago catches his fish to prove, in part, that he is a more worthy father-mother than the boy's real parents." Unlike me, neither Wylder, Lutwack, nor Jackson questions Santiago for such motives. Though Wylder calls them "sinfully human," he also insists upon their saintliness inasmuch as they perform the Christ-like function of delivering "Manolin from the authority of his parents," of " 'setting a man at variance against his father,' " says Wylder, quoting from Matthew 10:35. What Wylder is unwilling to question is why Santiago's authority is preferable to Manolin's parents'. A nobler motive would be to free Manolin from the authority of all father figures, to encourage the boy's independence and, thereby, his maturation.

15. For a different view of this conflict, see William J. Handy, "A New Dimension for a Hero: Santiago of *The Old Man and the Sea*," in *Six Contemporary Novels: Six Introductory Essays in Modern Fiction*, ed. William O. S. Sutherland, Jr. (Austin: University of Texas Press, 1962), pp. 63–64. I emphasize "ordered" to remark that it is one of the few additions Hemingway made to his typescript of the novel, inserting the words "at their orders" in the novella's third sentence, " . . . and the boy had gone at their [his parents'] orders in another boat . . . " See item 190 in the Hemingway Collection. This addition emphasizes, I think, Santiago's conflict with Manolin's parents and with Manolin's obedience.

16. MH to GB, 21 November 1975.

17. Arnaldo and Matilde Rascovsky, "On the Genesis of Acting Out and Psychopathic Behavior in Sophocles' *Oedipus*: Notes on Filicide," *International Journal of Psychoanalysis* 49 (1968): 390–94.

18. Hofling, "Hemingway's *The Old Man and the Sea* and the Male Reader," acknowledges that Santiago "is in conflict about the dependent aspects of" his and Manolin's relationship. But surprisingly he regards it as a conflict of "only moderate intensity" and accepts at face value "the essentially unambivalent nature of the Old Man's emotions and behavior toward Manolin. The fisherman shows a sustained kindness to the boy, a graciousness even, which *could not exist* in the presence of strong, negative feelings" (p. 165; italics added).

ISLANDS IN THE STREAM

1. Carlos Baker, *Artist*, pp. 379–84, 389, 397, tells that Hemingway wrote a nearly 1,000-page draft of the "Bimini" section between 1946 and April 1947, although he may have begun it as early as 1945. He returned to the section during the summer of 1951 and began revising it, cutting by three-fifths a 484-page portion of the original manuscript. But it remained a relatively amorphous manuscript until Mary Hemingway and Charles Scribner, Jr., worked on it during the winter of 1969–70. Drafted in the early weeks of December 1950, the "Cuba" section was completed, Hemingway declared, on Christmas Eve. He apparently never returned to it. Mary Hemingway made only a "few block-deletions" in it. The "At Sea" section, written during the spring months of 1951, required only "copy-editing." My study of the *Islands* manuscripts shows that Mary Hemingway and Charles Scribner, Jr., resolved, for better or for worse, four problems. One was the narrative point of view. On the revised manuscript/typescript that Hemingway worked over between 1 May and 6 August 1951, he questions whether to leave the section as a first-person narrative told by George Thomas, a painter, or to change it to a limited third-person narrative, told through George's perspective (*Catalog of Hemingway Collection*, p. 15, item 103). A second problem was whether to keep what Hemingway had drafted as four chapters of book 2, Roger and Helena (i.e., Audrey), lovers, driving from Miami to Louisiana (*Catalog of Hemingway Collection*, p. 14, item 98, sections 14–18, pp. 680–907 in holograph; or p. 15, item 102, 180-page uncorrected typescript). The third problem was whether to change Roger Hancock's or George Thomas's name to Thomas Hudson. The significance of this problem cannot be underestimated, for along with it came the fourth problem of whether to keep the three sons Roger's, as in the original and revised manuscripts, or to make them George Thomas's.

2. Watts, *Hemingway and the Arts*, p. 189.

3. Baker, *Artist*, p. 392, and Nahal, *Narrative Pattern*, p. 216.

4. Joseph Campbell, *The Hero with a Thousand Faces* (1949, rpt. Cleveland: World Publishing Co., 1956), p. 352.

5. Had Mary Hemingway and Charles Scribner, Jr., left Roger Hancock (Davis) father to the three boys and then assigned him the name of Thomas Hudson, as the corrected typescript shows Hemingway did in places, then Hudson's aggressiveness and brooding remorse in "Cuba" and "At Sea" would be consistent with his character as portrayed in "Bimini."

6. Respectively, John W. Aldridge, "Hemingway between Triumph and Disaster," *Saturday Review* 10 October 1970, p. 25, and Richard Lehan, *A Dangerous Crossing: French Literary Existentialism and the Modern American Novel* (Carbondale: Southern Illinois University Press, 1973), p. 54.

7. Baker, *Artist*, pp. 405–7.

8. See Otto Rank, "Examples of the Double in Literature," in his *The Double: A Psychoanalytic Study*, trans. Harry Tucker, Jr. (Chapel Hill: University of North Carolina Press, 1971), pp. 8–33.

9. Baker, *Artist*, p. 394, notes the parallels between Roger and Hemingway in the thirties.

10. See Freud's "Mourning and Melancholia" (1917) in *Standard Edition*, 14: 237–58.

11. See his letters to Charles Scribner, 20 July and 5 October 1951; to Patrick Hemingway, 16 September 1950; and to Wallace Meyer, 4 and 7 March 1952; *Letters*, pp. 730–32, 738, 734, 757.

12. See, for example, the collection of reviews on the novel in Stephens, *Critical Reception*, pp. 439–76.

13. Baker, *Life Story*, p. 460.

14. MH to GB, 21 November 1975.

15. Baker, *Life Story*, p. 443.

16. Ibid., pp. 433, 442–43, 448.

17. Ibid., pp. 456–57; see Hemingway's letter to Gen. Charles T. Lanham, 25 August 1946, *Letters*, pp. 609–10.

18. *The Fourteenth Chronicle: Letters and Diaries of John Dos Passos*, edited, with a biographical narrative, by Townsend Ludington (Boston: Gambit, 1973), documents Dos Passos's fondness for Patrick Hemingway in letters, pp. 483–86, and for Patrick Murphy, pp. 423, 472.

19. See Calvin Tomkins, *Living Well Is the Best Revenge* (New York: Viking, 1971).

20. Baker, *Life Story*, p. 271; see Hemingway's letter to Gerald and Sara Murphy, 19 March 1935, *Letters*, p. 412.

21. Ludington, *Fourteenth Chronicle*, pp. 475–76, 479, 483, 486. In *Life Story*, p. 271, and *Letters*, p. 412, Baker apparently confuses Patrick, who died of tuberculosis, with Boath, who died either of mastoiditis, according to Ludington, *Fourteenth Chronicle*, or of spinal meningitis, according to Tomkins, *Living Well*, p. 125, and Andrew Turnbull, *The Letters of F. Scott Fitzgerald* (1963, rpt. New York: Dell, 1965), p. 425.

22. Hemingway's filicidal wishes would have focused upon Gregory. His refractoriness included, he owns, experimentation with drugs and taking sides with his mother against Hemingway (*Papa*, pp. 6–8). His attitude toward *Old Man* as "sentimental slop" would not mollify his father's wishes (Baker, *Life Story*, p. 506).

23. See Calvin S. Hall, *A Primer of Freudian Psychology* (New York: World Publishing Co., 1954, rpt. New American Library), pp. 60–69; and Fenichel, *Psychoanalytic Theory of Neurosis*, p. 187.

THE DANGEROUS SUMMER

1. Hotchner, *Papa Hemingway*, pp. 237, 239; I parenthesize in my text subsequent page references to this book. Baker, *Life Story*, says the finished manuscript was 120,000 words (p. 552).

2. Castillo-Puche, *Hemingway in Spain*, comments upon Hemingway's distraught tinkering (pp. 318–22, 325); I parenthesize in my text subsequent page references to this book. Among the more conspicuous unravelings are the references to seeing Antonio at Cordoba—an episode never directly addressed in the text—and the vagueness in the Valencia bullfights in the second installment; with no clear transition Hemingway switches from a standard *corrida* with its three matadors to the first genuine *mano a mano*, Ordóñez and Dominguín each fighting three bulls.

3. Mary Hemingway declares that because the published chapters are so abridged, any reading of *The Dangerous Summer* is completely irrelevant. Even more, there can be, she maintains, no justification for believing that the work is an important part of Hemingway's canon (MH to GB, 14 February 1976). Now that the manuscripts, typescripts, notes, and fragments for *Summer* are a part of the Kennedy Library's Hemingway Collection, students and scholars may be able to determine for themselves whether the text is important to Hemingway's canon. See *Catalog of Hemingway Collection.* "Recent Accessions," 5 January 1982, Items 354, a-g, n.p., Vol. I.

4. *The Dangerous Summer, Life*, 5 September 1960, p. 86; I parenthesize in my text subsequent references to the three installments: part 1, "The Dangerous Summer," pp. 77–109; part 2, "The Pride of the Devil," 12 September 1960, pp. 60–82; part 3, "An Appointment with Disaster," 19 September 1960, pp. 74–96.

5. See also Shay Oag, *In the Presence of Death: Antonio Ordóñez* (New York: Coward-McCann, 1969), p. 172: "The overall treatment of the fights [Hemingway] saw and the conclusions he drew are not only portentous and melodramatized, but in some cases unjust and inaccurate too. Given the fact that he was understandably impassioned by Ordóñez and for years had been aware of the quality of his art, there was surely no need to work up the rivalry of *Los Dos* into some kind of bloodthirsty *Duel in the Sun*."

6. For the Spanish reaction see, for example, Castillo-Puche, *Hemingway in Spain*, pp. 244–47. In noting these discrepancies I admit that there is a question of Hotchner's and Castillo-Puche's reliability. But the two authors' antipathy for each other is some guarantee of their fidelity to many of the facts of the summers of 1959 and 1960. And when in doubt, I have consulted Oag's book. Castillo-Puche made no attempt to hide his contempt for Hotchner (e.g., pp. 82, 196), causing Hotchner to sue the Spaniard's American publisher for libel, a suit that won Hotchner $125,000, even after the decision was appealed. For his part, Hotchner does not acknowledge that Castillo-Puche even existed, much less that he was part of the quadrilla that danced attention around "Ernesto."

7. Although he is not known for distinguished literary criticism, John O'Hara came to much the same conclusion in a September 1960 letter to William Maxwell, his editor at the *New Yorker*: "There was always great art in Hemingway, often when he was at his mumbling worst. But in the Life pieces we see our ranking artist concerned with a disgusting spectacle, adopting a son-hero and wishing him dead in conflict with a former son-hero, Dominguin, whom he also wishes dead. He wants to see them die, to be there when they die, and I got the feeling that he particularly wanted Dominguin to die because Dominguin had not been as easy to adopt as Ordonez. Hemingway is *afraid* to lose Dominguin in life, and rather than lose him in life he wishes him dead. The competition between the two bullfighters, as presented by Hemingway, actually gets us away from the bull ring and could just as well have been a fight with knives between the two son-heroes. It is a terrible thing to get old that way, as Hemingway has done; to feel so strongly about two young men that you want them to kill each other, to play the one you like less against the one you like more—Ordonez against Dominguin" (in Matthew J. Bruccoli, *The O'Hara Concern: A Biography of John O'Hara* [New York: Random House, 1975], p. 270).

8. Lloyd R. Arnold, *High on the Wild*, p. 28.

9. Baker, *Life Story*, p. 549.

10. Ibid., p. 532.

11. Hemingway's bias against Dominguín is corroborated by Oag, *Presence of Death*, p. 173, and by Peter Viertel, "Luis Miguel Dominguín," *Gentlemen's Quarterly* 34 (April 1965): 128, 133.

12. Hotchner, of course, was no more present at Manolete's goring than Hemingway had been at Joselito's, Granero's, or Varelito's fatal gorings, even though *Death in the Afternoon* implies that he was. For a more detailed account of the Manolete-Dominguín rivalry, see Viertel, "Dominguín," pp. 126, 128.

13. Baker, *Life Story*, pp. 72–73.

14. See Hemingway's letter to Patrick Hemingway, 5 August 1959: "Being around Antonio is like being with you or Bum except for having to sweat him out all the time" (*Letters*, p. 895).

A MOVEABLE FEAST

1. Mary Hemingway, "The Making of a Book: A Chronicle and a Memoir," *New York Times Book Review*, 10 May 1964, p. 27.

2. Baker, *Artist*, pp. 375–76 n.

3. For the history of Hemingway's composition of *Feast*, see Baker, *Artist*, pp. 351–54, and, more recently, Jacqueline Tavernier-Courbin, "The Mystery of the Ritz Hotel Papers," *College Literature* 7 (1980): 289–303. Both scholars remark that the alleged chronology of the book's composition is riddled with contradictions. And there is proof, of course, that some of the material had been composed long before 1957, most notably the Ford Madox Ford sketch. It had formed part of the two chapters that Hemingway cut from *The Sun Also Rises*—following F. Scott Fitzgerald's advice—as reported in Philip Young and Charles W. Mann, "Fitzgerald's *Sun Also Rises*: Notes and Comments," *Fitzgerald/Hemingway Annual 1970*, pp. 1–9.

4. See, for example, Arthur Mizener, *The Far Side of Paradise: A Biography of F. Scott Fitzgerald* (New York: Vintage Books, 1960), pp. 212–15.

5. Baker, *Artist*, p. 367.

6. The best account of the grudges is Joost, *Ernest Hemingway and the Little Magazines*; but also see Baker, *Artist*, pp. 358–69; Robert O. Stephens, *Hemingway's Nonfiction: The Public Voice* (Chapel Hill: University of North Carolina Press, 1968), pp. 113–14, 124–25; and George Wickes, "Sketches of the Author's Life in Paris in the Twenties," in *Hemingway in Our Time*, ed. Richard Astro and Jackson J. Benson (Corvallis: Oregon State University Press, 1974), pp. 28–38. Robie Macauley, "A Moveable Myth," *Encounter* 23 (1964): 56–58, succinctly examines the flaws in Hemingway's portrait of Ford.

7. See, for example, Edmund Wilson's review of *Islands in the Stream*, "An Effort at Self-Revelation," *New Yorker*, 2 January 1971, in which he comments that Hemingway "allows himself little scope for malignity" in the novel (p. 60).

8. Hemingway's contempt for Fitzgerald's irresponsible ways would have been plainer had the published version of this epigraph included the sentence that Hemingway's finished typescript had left in: "He [Fitzgerald] ever needed some one as a conscience and he needed professionals or normally educated people to make his writing legible and not illiterate." See Jacqueline Tavernier-Courbin, "The Manuscripts of *A Moveable Feast*," *Hemingway notes* 4 (1981): 12.

9. Hemingway's draft of an unpublished section on Ford harshly condemns him for his lies and for his offensive odors (item 180, Hemingway Collection, pp. 1, 3).

10. Hemingway's compulsion to be responsible is further verified by the trip he made to Paris in September 1959 to ensure the correctness of the Paris streets he refers to. Even Mary Hemingway was infected, making a trip to Paris in October 1963 to double-check her accuracy. See Baker, *Artist*, pp. 353 n, 358 n; Valerie Danby-Smith, "Reminiscence of Hemingway," *Saturday Review*, 9 May 1964, pp. 30–31, 57; and Mary Hemingway, *How It Was*, p. 502.

11. Item 188 in *Catalog of Hemingway Collection*, p. 26, is the typescript of Hemingway's "finished" version of *Feast*, a version that differs significantly from the published text. Though many of the changes made by Mary Hemingway and L. H. Brague, with whom she worked on *Feast*, were perhaps necessary, the decision to alter Hemingway's sequence of the early chapters was neither necessary nor wise. Hemingway has the chapter "Une Génération Perdue" follow "The End of an Avocation" and precede "Hunger Was a Good Discipline." Although the published sequence provides continuity by keeping together the first two chapters on Stein, his sequence better emphasizes the contrast between Stein and Sylvia Beach, the bad and good mothers of *Feast*. The second chapter, "Miss Stein Instructs," balances Gertrude's dogmatic condescension against Sylvia's trusting assistance in Hemingway's intended third chapter, "Shakespeare and Company." Similarly if "Génération" had been left to come just before "Hunger," Hemingway's intended point would have again been italicized, for Stein includes him among the lost generation that has "no respect for anything." But Sylvia, a concerned "mother" in "Hunger," is confident of his ability: " 'But, Hemingway, don't

worry about what [your stories] bring now. The point is that you can write them. . . . They will sell' " (71). In addition, though a minor point, early in the "Génération" chapter Hemingway mentions that he could get books "from Sylvia Beach's library or find [them] along the quais" (26). This might well puzzle a reader the first time through *Feast*, since it is not until the next two chapters that Hemingway acquaints us with both Sylvia and the bookstalls along the quais. For several of the changes in Hemingway's *Feast* manuscripts, see Jacqueline Tavernier-Courbin, "The Manuscripts of *A Moveable Feast*." For the significant changes see my article, "Are We Going to Hemingway's *Feast?*" in *American Literature* 54 (1982): 528–44.

12. Hemingway's full account of his behavior after returning to Paris—to find that Hadley had indeed lost everything—is in the Hemingway Collection materials for *Islands in the Stream*. See pages 883–907 of item 98, the manuscript version of book 2 of "Bimini," and pages 34–43 of items 102 and 103, the typescript of same, *Catalog of Hemingway Collection*, pp. 14–15.

13. Hemingway's reference to Hadley's *"work* at the piano" verbally slights her talent as a pianist. He also acknowledges no gratitude for the $8,000 left her when her maternal uncle died. That money propitiously expedited their first trip to Europe and enabled him to practice his craft without the immediate threat of poverty (Sokoloff, *Hadley*, p. 40).

14. Hemingway's only rival would be Joyce, the only other responsible family man in the memoirs. But Joyce, Hemingway notes, can afford to dine habitually at Michaud's, an "expensive restaurant for us" (56). And the one exchange Hemingway has with Joyce occurs after a chance encounter on the boulevard Saint-Germain. Hemingway insinuates that Joyce was returning from a self-indulgent afternoon at the matinee by himself (212).

15. Baker, *Artist*, p. 353. This holograph is not among the Hemingway Collection's items for *Feast*. And Charles Scribner, Jr., who has seen it, declares that he does not know where it might be.

16. Baker, *Life Story*, p. 532.

17. See also Hemingway's letter to Philip Percival, 25 May 1956, *Letters*, p. 860.

18. Compare Grace Hemingway's letter chastizing her son's supposed misconduct shortly after he turned twenty-one (Baker, *Life Story*, p. 72).

19. EH to Mrs. Madelaine H. ("Sunny") Mainland, ca. 15 August 1949, *Letters*, p. 663.

20 Hovey, *Inward Terrain*, p. 217, also identifies Gertrude Stein as a surrogate mother.

21. Sanford, *At the Hemingways*, p. 49.

22. Ibid., pp. 59–60; see also pp. 5, 18.

23. Quoted in Charles Norman, *Ezra Pound* (New York: Macmillan, 1960), p. 275; other excerpts from "Homage" are on pp. 269, 278.

24. Sanford, *At the Hemingways*, p. 30.

25. Norman, *Pound*, p. 248; Sanford *At the Hemingways*, pp. 23–39, 224.

26. Sanford, *At the Hemingways*, p. 123; Norman, *Pound*, pp. 280–82.

27. See Hemingway's letters dated 4 April, 10 and 31 August 1943, *Letters*,pp. 544–45, 548, 549–50.

28. Eustace Mullins, *This Difficult Individual, Ezra Pound* (New York: Fleet Publishing Co., 1961), records both Hemingway's gift of money to Pound (p. 19) and his use of the Nobel Prize to announce that 1954 was "a good year to release poets" (p. 341). Michael Reck, *Ezra Pound: A Close-Up* (New York: McGraw-Hill, 1967), confirms this latter fact and notes that Pound framed in plastic the $1,500 check Hemingway sent him after receiving the Nobel Prize (p. 84). Baker, *Life Story*, notes that Hemingway had sent an earlier check for $1,000 to Pound during

the week of his own fifty-seventh birthday (p. 534). Hemingway's brief tribute to Pound is in the sixteen-page pamphlet *Ezra Pound at Seventy*, by Hemingway, E. E. Cummings, and others (Norfolk, Conn.: New Directions, 1955); excerpts are included in Jack LaZebnick's "The Case of Ezra Pound," *New Republic*, 1 April 1957, p. 17. See also Hemingway's letters to Archibald MacLeish and Robert Frost, 28 June 1957, *Letters*, pp. 876–80; and to Pound, 26 June 1958, *Letters*, p. 883. For a brief account of Hemingway's artistic relationship to Pound, see Harold M. Hurwitz, "Hemingway's Tutor, Ezra Pound," *Modern Fiction Studies* 17 (1971–72): 469–82; and E. R. Hagemann, " 'Dear Folks. . . . Dear Ezra': Hemingway's Early Years and Correspondence, 1917–1924," *College Literature* 7 (1980): 202–12.

29. Sanford, *At the Hemingways*, p. 227.

30. Ibid., p. 129.

31. Ibid., pp. 223–32.

32. Ibid., p. 229, italics added.

33. Ibid., p. 228.

EPILOGUE

1. EH to Bernard Berenson, 24 January 1953, *Letters*, p. 801.

2. Ibid., 2 February 1954, pp. 828–29.

3. EH to Charles Scribner, Jr., 25 February 1952, *Letters*, p. 755.

4. EH to Wallace Meyer, 21 February 1952, *Letters*, pp. 750–51.

5. From *Letters*, respectively, to Howell Jenkins, 8 January 1922, p. 61; to Sylvia Beach, ca. 15 January 1925, p. 146; to John Dos Passos, 9 February 1929, p. 295; to Henry Strater, 14 October 1932, p. 369; to Charles Scribner, 24 February 1940, p. 503; to Evan Shipman, 25 August 1942, p. 539; to Archibald MacLeish, 5 May 1943, p. 546; to Col. Charles Trueman "Buck" Lanham, 2 and 14 April 1945, pp. 579, 586; to Gen. E. E. Dorman-O'Gowan, 2 May 1950, p. 691; to Mrs. Charles (Vera) Scribner, 18 February 1952, p. 749; to Dorothy Connable, 17 February 1953, p. 806; to Bernard Berenson, 15 September 1953, p. 825; and to Adriana Ivancich, 9 May 1954, p. 831.

6. Reynolds Price, "For Ernest Hemingway," in his *Things Themselves: Essays and Scenes* (New York: Atheneum, 1972), p. 203.

Index

Beneath the entry "Hemingway, Ernest" I have grouped five major subentries: BOOKS BY, FICTIONAL CHARACTERS OF, MISCELLANEOUS WRITINGS OF, PSYCHOLOGICAL ISSUES IN THE WORKS OF, and SHORT FICTION BY. See Author's Note (p. xi) for short titles of Hemingway's works.